There's No Place Like H⬤me

A YEAR IN TRANSITION FROM WORKING TO STAY-AT-HOME MOM

JANE BEDARD

◆ FriesenPress

Suite 300 - 990 Fort St
Victoria, BC, V8V 3K2
Canada

www.friesenpress.com

Author's photo by Michelle Quance

ISBN
978-1-5255-2880-4 (Hardcover)
978-1-5255-2881-1 (Paperback)
978-1-5255-2882-8 (eBook)

1. Biography & Autobiography, Women

Distributed to the trade by The Ingram Book Company

Table of Contents

Prologue

Some people express feeling lost. Me? I'm not lost, but I have misplaced myself. Not unlike leaving my car keys on top of the toilet or misplacing five pounds during my most recent diet, only to find them a few weeks later in the cookie aisle, next to the Puffs, right where I left them. They were there the whole time—it was just a question of looking a little harder.

This is the year of looking a little harder, and today, September 3, 2013, is the first day of the rest of that year. Lots of parents celebrate this day—the one where kids go back to school and a blanket of sanity flutters down to rest on a frantic home like soft snow quietly covering the landscape. Quiet. Writing this down makes me somewhat emotional given that I've been romantically yearning for the opportunity to get started on "This Year" for a long time.

Typically, I'd be rushing out the door, taking my kids to their school, then sprinting off to my school to teach all those eager little chipmunks the ins and outs of the French language. Or perhaps I should say, all *lez eenz and owts ov de Fwrensh langage* (When you say it in a French accent, it sounds so much more exotic.) I enjoy my work and think I do a pretty good job; in fact, the nicest compliment I ever received was from a very athletic boy who told me that French was his second favourite subject after gym. As long as I'm up against gym in a boy's world, I'll take a silver medal any day of the week.

For one whole year, I am taking a leave of absence from work to return to my other job, as the CEO of Bedard Inc. It is an opportunity to integrate, fulltime, back into family life and to examine life as it was and as it is. Despite all the consistent change and growth, does our family still embrace the same vision and values with which we started so many years ago? How can I use this year to help create the best version of us? If I am to be the foundation of this structure we call a family, making sure I am of sound construction is key to our success.

My goals are three-fold: First: I need to re-dedicate myself to myself. I look forward to reacquainting myself with me and figuring out what the hell happened over these forty-seven years that moulded me into the person I am today.

Second: I'd like to relocate that part of me that has been neglectful in the roles of wife, mother, sister, daughter, and friend. It seems that working me has sent all of the other me's into the shadows and vice-versa. When I'm at work, I'm thinking about home, and when I'm at home, I'm thinking about work. I have been living the conflicted life of so many parents who can't seem to juggle it all and feel they are failing everyone, not least themselves.

The last goal is to put this journey down in writing. For years, I have carried around notebooks in which I write thoughts, ideas, expressions, jokes, quotes, stories, advertisements, book excerpts, therapy sessions, and even (morbidly) eulogies. All of these notebooks represent a secret desire that someday I could be brave enough to let someone see my passion, and perhaps see me, as a writer.

I'm in a bit of a panic though, and I feel like I need to get these words down on paper quickly because I'm running out of them—words, that is. When I was pregnant, I used to think that my placenta absorbed my vocabulary to nourish the growing baby inside me. The more babies I had, the fewer sentences I could string together. But the baby stage ended, and the pre-menopausal phase began, and those words continue to siphon out of my brain and swirl into the toilet of age-related maladies, to be flushed away for all time. It's not sweet anymore that my husband finishes my sentences. It's necessary.

There's also this character called Self-Doubt hanging around. This hefty fellah rides piggy-back on my shoulders wherever I go, eating carbs and gaining weight, ready to curse and spit up half-chewed éclairs on me as I ponder decisions, create goals, or open my mouth to speak.

Let's not forget the financial ramifications of taking a year off. Of course, the bank has not offered up any gift, grant money, or sponsorships to offset the loss in revenue for this year, but I believe that, if you open yourself up to the universe, the universe will respond in a grateful, thanks-for-opening-yourself-up-to-me kind of way. Homelessness could also be a consequence, in this waterfront Toronto neighbourhood called the Beaches, which has recently transitioned from a Ford Fiesta to a Mercedes Sedan kind of town, but acknowledging that would not be using the power of positive thinking, and I am all about the power of positive thinking. I didn't learn this from any self-help book, but from my older sister, Anne, who believes in the Power of Positive Parking. She can drive to the front of a busy mall, even on Christmas Eve, will a spot to open up, and it usually does. So, based on this sound financial logic, I think everything will be okay, despite the loss of my entire salary for a year.

Besides answering the questions of who I am, how I got here, and where I'm going, I am looking forward to pushing the reset button on family life and rededicating myself to getting to know its members again, and to appreciate living in the moment instead of lingering in the jet stream of a consciousness that just passed by.

The kids complain that they need new shoes. "I just bought you new shoes!" I respond agitatedly.

"That was months ago. They have holes, and they're too small."

What happened between size two and size three and a half? What did I miss? I think we need to reflect on those same questions from a family perspective: Who are we? How did we get here? And where are we going?

When I talk about such goals with my working friends, I am met with raised-eyebrow suspicions: "Did you win the lottery?" And then there's the question at which every stay-at-home mom cringes: "What will you do with yourself all day?"

I often hear envy creep into their voices. Those who are in a far better position than us financially tell us we're lucky to be able to do this. The truth is, we can't afford to do this, but we also decided that we can't afford not to do it, because (and this will become my mantra for the year) if not now, when? My kids are young now, whether that's convenient or not, so let's commit; we've got one shot at this parenting thing, so let's do it the best we can and not look back.

What some of my working friends don't see is that this decision will require sacrifice and commitment and will open the gates to adventure and growth. This is part of the journey. We're used to going to book clubs and reading about women who are attempting to do the same thing. Some of their stories are weighty, many having faced hardships that are beyond our scope of imagination as they flee oppression, violence, or debilitating grief, and some are people with a different kind of baggage, lighter and less worn but still too big for carry-on.

Regardless of the relative heaviness of their situations, we all sit with them at the baggage claim, cheering them on and waiting to see how it all turns out.

I wonder how my story will turn out!

Fall Term
SEPTEMBER TO
DECEMBER

1.

Joining SAHM's Club

I am more than giddy. I am insanely, ecstatically, uncontrol-lably, annoyingly, pull-me-down –before-I-hit-the-ceiling-fan happy. I am a teacher, and it is the first day of school, except ... I'm not going. Instead, I am playing hooky for an entire year (also known as a leave of absence), so I am walking—nay, skip-ping—my kids to school and then ... going home.

YIPEEEE!

The daytime underworld of the Stay-at-Home-Mom (SAHM) is something I had to get my head around again. I had worked for six years, stayed home for six years, during which time I had three sons, worked for six more years, and was now facing a second, voluntary tour of duty at home, this time with all three boys at school.

There is an unspoken bond that links parents together, and when I don't race from the playground back to my car, or just slow the car down near the school so the kids can jump and roll out, the circle of sisterhood (still almost exclusively women) slowly begins to open up and accept me as one of their own. No ceremony. No hazing. No membership fee. These SAHMs are going to be my people for the next year, and I look forward to meeting them. For example, after dropping off the kids, my first stop is the drugstore, where I meet a mom with a stroller. She is squirming in her post-maternity jeans and looks at me from the line and growls, "Goddamn hemorrhoids."

Now that I am in "the club," I feel invited to respond and pass on an unconventional, homeopathic remedy, which seems to rattle her slightly: "What you want to do is cut up small pieces of garlic and use one each night as a suppository for three nights. Works every time."

She looks at me nervously, like I'd just looked that up in my Wiccan spell book. In what other context can you tell a complete stranger to stick a piece of garlic up her ass and think it would be helpful? It seems disgusting, but so is being a mom sometimes. And, as my brother (a chiropractor and healer) says, "Never underestimate the power of garlic. Not even a hemorrhoid will want to hang around if garlic is in the house (or in the anal cavity, as the case may be).

The next day, the woman in front of me at the coffee shop collects the most massive cup of coffee I have ever seen, the size of a tennis-ball can: an oversized, supersized cuppa java. We nod politely to each other, exchanging sympathetic looks as I glance at the double stroller in front of her, occupied by a single traveller. She looks weary, a look with which any parent empathizes.

"I wish they would all sleep through the night once," she says, perhaps to me.

"How many do you have?" I ask, always ready to collect the Exasperation Medal for having three compared to the average Canadian family with 1.6 kids.

"Eight," she replies.

Gulp.

"Wow, eight!" is all I can muster, as I take the mommy medal from around my neck and hand it over.

"You?" she asks.

"Only three." I don't think I've ever said 'only' three.

"Three is hard. I had trouble with three. After that, it gets easier."

Or you've lost so much sleep that you think eight kids are easy because you're delusional or catatonic, or hopefully smoking something so fricken awesome that it makes you forget you have eight kids. We chat briefly, and she reveals her survival technique: Don't sweat the small stuff.

And then she is gone. She'd had her quick fix of connecting with another person who wasn't asking for food or school supplies and away she went. I watch her in awe as she slowly shuffles down the street. My new sister. Don't sweat the small stuff? No kidding.

2.

How Sweat It Is

I've read that Clint Eastwood, in his prime, could do 1000 push-ups in a row and that even today, in his eighties, he still works out *at least* once a day. If an octogenarian Dirty Harry can work out eight days a week, I think I can add an extra sit-up here and there.

Over the past six years, during my most recent return to work, my reasonable standard of fitness had regressed from a variety of somewhat challenging fitness options, to a quick stop at the gym, to a casual bike ride, to a short walk to the bakery. As part of this journey, I officially name Dirty Harry as my inner fitness coach, so that I have him to curse when he harasses me into doing five more burpees.

Keeping a gym membership was a question mark for this year, given the expense, but it was deemed a necessary one because if I'm not physically active, I'm a complete bitch, which might explain my mood for these past six years. When my husband subtly suggests that I go for a walk or a bike ride, I know I'm on the precipice of an irrational act and should take my irate serotonin out for some air (although sometimes he catches it too late and everyone pays).

Setting fitness goals evolves quickly. I think about setting measurable goals of something like 500 sit-ups and 100 push-ups a day, inspired by Clint, but setting unrealistic goals is a great way to set myself up for failure, so I revise downward quickly. My new goals are to improve strength, endurance, flexibility, and discipline, with the bonus of losing a few pounds and inches. These are wonderfully vague and the coward's way to start, charting my improvement using a precise measuring tool known as: just a feeling of how I'm doing. How can I help but succeed? It's similar to my kids' first term report card, where there are boxes for the teachers to check, which offer only huge generalities like progressing very well, progressing well, or progressing with difficulty.

Perhaps this strategy is a bit of a cop-out, but until I experiment more with what the older version of me is capable of doing, this is the way to go. Funny, in the olden days, I was running the stair climber on level ten and Getting Physical with Olivia Newton-John, preparing my body for sporting events and dating. Now I'm chasing kids on level four at a gentle Michael Bublé pace, much of my motivation coming from not gaining enough weight to have to buy new clothes.

I met a woman in the gym once and confided to her that I was dissatisfied with my workout. She told me that the best workout is always "the one you just did." I learned quickly how true this was after I cancelled several gym visits for a variety of emergencies, like the life-or-death cat-food-buying incident or the desperate odd-sock-sorting dilemma. You just can't plan for these things.

My gym offers a wide variety of classes, and since I haven't tried most of them, I think it best to try as many of them as I can, so I can discover which suits my goals best. After checking the schedule of classes, I arrive at the gym and enter the large, dimly lit, generously mirrored room, enthusiastically ready to jump into my new fitness regime. The chosen inaugural class is something I'd done years ago. It was a simple weight-training class where I could start with light weights and equally light expectations, despite sneers from Clint and—What was that? Did Clint call me a pussy? Back off, cowboy! A cinnamon roll can easily replace you, so drop the attitude!

The instructor for this class is Lisa, a fun and fit leader whom I know will deliver a challenging but entertaining class. The room is nearly at capacity, filled with sculpted bodies and a uniform of black Lululemon clothing. I am a bit confused; there is not a muffin top in sight. The equipment they are assembling isn't what I remember using, but I recall that Lisa likes to mix things up. I follow along, grabbing what is left of the dumb-bells, weight bars, mats, and steps, along with my son's sippy cup, filled with Gatorade, from my plastic, shopping/gym bag.

My confusion escalates when a large man enters the room and strides to the front with a microphone strapped to his head. He is not Lisa. He is a large, black, intense-looking man in black track pants and a black tank top. He stands at the front of the room, looks us up and down, and reminds me of a young Louis Gossett Jr. when he played Gunnery Sergeant Emil Foley in An Officer and a Gentleman. I cringe as I see myself taking on the role of Richard Gere's Mayo-naise.

I turn to the chiselled woman beside me and ask hopefully, "Is this the Puffin Weight Class?"

"Oh no, sweetie," she says with humour and empathy. "You must have an old schedule. This is Boot Camp. That's James. Get ready to sweat!"

Boot Camp. Of course. Looks like I will have to earn my stripes quickly. Clint squints his approval.

After confirming that my classmate will roll me to the side of the gym if I pass out, I resign myself to the upcoming torture and wait for the music to begin. After the first two minutes, I already know which parts of me will be in agony the next day. There are up to 850 muscles in the human body. There is one muscle called the orbicularis oculi, which is in charge of closing the eyelid. That's the one that will not hurt.

In a haze, I hear James yelling, "To da left! To da right! Eight more! Now eight more! Now eight more! Now EIGHT MORE!"

When he walks by me, checking my form during squats, I half-expect him to say, "Get your lazy ass lower to the ground before I roundhouse kick you in the head until your brains bleed out your ears!" James gives me an almost imperceptible nod and goes on his way.

The music is familiar but plays at high speed, like a 33-record playing at 45 (for those of you who remember or are discovering vinyl). And with that pace and volume, you can't help but be motivated to keep up. Being the competitor that I am, I do keep up, not wanting to show that my thighs are shaking and my shoulder throbbing and my neck stiffening (mostly from turning to see how much time is left on the clock).

After an hour of crawling under imaginary barbed wire, and lunging lengths of the gym, not to mention countless push-ups and sit-ups, the class ends. I barely lift my equipment back to its place. James approaches to ask how I'm doing. I think I should say, "Thank you, sir. May I have another?" Instead, I barely whimper, "I'm okay."

He quickly lights up with a beautiful smile (this is my reward!) then remembers his persona and says gruffly,

"Good job. You coming back?"

In my best Schwarzenegger, I say, "I'll be back," which comes out more like Miss Piggy than Arnie. It doesn't have the same kind of strength of conviction either, but I hope he understands my intention.

Despite the physical demoralization of boot camp, I feel surprisingly upbeat. For a few years, I have relied on my own lame efforts at pretending to keep fit, but what I really need is to be pushed and beaten into submission. This initial outing garners a "progressing with difficulty" grade. Clint stands by the exit, as I hobble out of the gym, but refuses to open the door for me. Bastard.

3.

Home Run

According to Stats Canada, in 1976, nine in ten non-working mothers in a single-earner family were stay-at-home parents. In 2014, 6.6 in 10 of non-working mothers were stay-at-home moms. For a variety of reasons, moms went back to work and shared in the financial contributions to the family, but not all fathers felt it necessary to share in the ongoing needs at home and women maintained those duties as well, eventually becoming overworked and overstressed. Psychologist Shari Thurer wisely wrote: "Motherhood versus personal ambition represents the heart of the feminine dilemma."

Many of the women I meet in the yard had felt that pull and decided they would rather not leave their children in the care of someone else. If they were going to take on the role of a SAHM, they were going to do it with the same drive that pushed them to succeed in their former workplaces.

As I encounter more of these SAHMs, it becomes clear that they take their jobs very seriously, and why wouldn't they? Considering their accomplished backgrounds in careers such as publishing, marketing, banking, accounting, advertising, human resources, and legal, social, and medical work (to name a few in my schoolyard), they had worked hard to get where they were and weren't about to settle for cruising through this next phase of their lives nonchalantly. They pay attention to their kids' lives and volunteer in classrooms, on field trips, and on school committees. They know what their kids are eating and who their friends are. They chauffeur their kids to games, practices, lessons, and clubs. Most of the women I meet are not on maternity leave but have made a conscious decision to change careers for a period of time. (I should also note that the Beach community in Toronto, in which I live, has a relatively healthy social status, where many parents can afford to stay at home by choice and not because of any financial directive.)

But do you know who is sitting in the back seat of their cars, farting with their kids on their way to soccer or ballet? Other kids whose parents are at work. As I infiltrate deeper into SAHM territory, I realize how fundamentally important these moms are to the fabric of our community. Without volunteers in schools, field trips would not run, and special, in-class programming would end (which wouldn't matter because funding for many of these events would not exist). I had no idea how important these women were to the enhancement of my children's experience at school.

If parents weren't at home, many kids would not have the opportunity to participate in programming beyond school. How do you get your daughter to hockey practice an hour away, at 5:00, if you're working nine-to-five? What happens when playing in a league has come to include weekend tournaments that begin Friday morning (on a school day) and end Sunday night in a town that requires a hotel stay? If you don't have a flexible job or don't want to hand over your vacation days to get your kids to these events, these moms are your saviours.

These moms were my saviours for years, and I am so grateful to them. How many times, in a panic, have I asked someone to pick up my kids or to drive them to practice? In desperation, I was asking people I barely knew for help until I couldn't do it anymore. I was the universal receiver, and it didn't feel right. My kids couldn't keep up with the schedule because there was no schedule. All they knew was that Mommy was wound up tight, so don't mess with her. Don't tell her she's late again. Don't mention that she's wearing two different shoes. But DO tell her, gently, that she's tucked her skirt into her pantyhose. Again.

Now I am present, and I drive the van filled with gassy kids, and I can offer to help out in a pinch, and I can bring the (homemade) muffins to the game. Not once do I consider this to be an "us versus them, working mom versus non-working mom" competition, which I know creates tension and resentment in many schoolyards. I am not smug in my newfound ability to participate more fully in the daily lives of my children. In fact, I am grateful for the opportunity and am particularly empathetic to working moms, and do my best to proactively alleviate stress where I know they would feel it—where I know I felt it. It is a much more comfortable role and having the capacity to give back feels good. And now that I've joined the playground club, I wear the daytime uniform exclusive to this group, consisting of yoga pants and flip-flops, which makes it nearly impossible to put on two different shoes or show off my underwear through my pantyhose.

4.

Omelette à la Mouche

Full Disclosure: I am a Starbucks Junkie, a member of Starbucks Nation, a bona fide, Starbucks, star-struck groupie, who will go miles out of her way to sip from that white, non-recyclable chalice filled with the fragrant fountain mixture, which originates in the River of Bergamot, and I just can't give it up—not for all the tea in China.

I frequent there often and use it as my office when I need a change of scenery. If I added up the money I've spent there over the years, I would likely find that I should own shares of the company. It's also a place I can play the starving artist role and not worry about my appearance while I work. I don't consider myself to be a high-maintenance kind of person. My make-up, if the occasion deems it necessary (and it rarely does), takes about forty-five seconds—a minute and a half if I have to meet the Prime Minister at an evening gala, which almost never happens. Okay, so that's actually never happened. But given my financial commitment to the caffeinated world of lattes and Frappuccinos, I have high expectations of the service when I'm there.

I remember travelling in Thailand, staying on an isolated island in a little beach hut, with just a backpack and a boyfriend. At breakfast, the waiter for the beach shack brought me an omelette with an extra-large, extra-black fly baked right in among the mushrooms. I understood there would be cultural differences and lower standards of culinary presentation in this far-removed part of Thailand when I saw the Chinese toilet (also known as "that hole in the ground"), but nonetheless, I had to send the fly back. I couldn't even use the joke, "Waiter, what's a fly doing in my omelette since his English was poor and the crispy fly obviously wasn't doing anything, let alone the backstroke. Since there was no chance the waiter hadn't seen the insect in the first place, I didn't like my chances of getting a fresh omelette plus complimentary guava juice to quell my PTFS (Post Traumatic Fly Syndrome).

When the waiter returned with my new breakfast, the only thing new about it was that, in the place where the fly had met its fiery demise, there was a hole cut out of it, a little larger than the size of an extra-large, extra-black fly. The waiter had gone to the trouble of cutting the beast out of my food, so there was no way I could send it back again, and yes, I ate it. See? Low maintenance.

That was a long time ago, and while my culinary and sanitary expectations have elevated slightly, I'm still pretty easy to please, except when I order my tea at Starbucks: a tall, no fat, no foam, kids' temperature Earl Grey tea latte (also known as a London Fog), if you're wondering. But ... I pay a lot for a cup of tea, so I want it the way I want it. The key is in the vanilla syrup, and when they forget to add it, which happens too often, the drink isn't worth watering my already lifeless plants. It's like ordering a rum and Coke, but without the rum. Where's the fun in that?

The last time they forgot, I approached the barista at my local Bucks, who looked flustered, like he had just wandered in off the street and been handed an apron, and said, "Excuse me, but I think you forgot to put vanilla in my drink."

"You want more vanilla?" he said.

"No, I want some vanilla. You can't have more of something if you don't have any to begin with."

He took my drink and added one pump of vanilla.

"How many pumps of vanilla did you add?" I asked with slight irritation.

"One."

"How many are supposed to be in it?"

"Three."

"Then would you please put two more pumps in?"

"You want two more?"

"I want what's supposed to be in it."

"Okay, but this will be very sweet for you."

Not surprisingly, I never saw that barista again.

It's a luxurious purchase, beyond my current pay grade, and most definitely a hassle when I have to go out of my way to get it, but holding that cup in my hand makes me feel warm, and cool, and urban, and it's an addiction that will be hard to give up once my unemployed butt can't afford to dole out that kind of green. I'm wondering if there is a Starbucks rehab facility somewhere out there. Luckily, I have a small stack of gift cards from my working days, which should feed my addiction for a little while. After that, I may have to start dipping into my children's Educational Savings Plan, selling off clothes, or driving for Uber. Whatever it takes to get my fix.

5.

Boys and Their Balls

"Just this once!" I plead with my three boys. "I've been watching action movies all summer! Now you have to sit through one romantic comedy with me. It will be good for you—not one person dies."

"Will there be kissing?"

"Absolutely."

"Then no beeping way. I'm not watching this beeping movie."

Eight-year-old Cole has figured out that, while he is not allowed to swear, he is entitled to "beep" out his own curse words as they do on TV.

"If I can sit through the Avengers three times and Spiderman twice, not to mention all of the Bonds and Bournes, then you can do this for me."

Reluctantly, my three boys all sit down, arms folded, and brace themselves for their torture.

After five minutes, they lose it. Popcorn flies towards the TV, with insults hurled at the screen and at me.

"How can you watch this beeping movie? It beeping sucks."

"Don't say 'sucks.'"

"Then it beeping beeps."

I don't even know what the name of the film was; it was so fleeting. This is life with boys. And as much as I adore them, occasionally I get bruised from bumping into the meteors of testosterone floating around the room. My first teaching job was at an all-boys school, where I read books and attended seminars about boys, and I get that they're different. I understand that they have hormonal surges throughout the day that make them do or say things they usually wouldn't do or say. And while my own boys are generally lovely, they certainly ain't girls. As I watch them, I wonder how much of the city's power they could fuel if only their energy could be harnessed.

I have always been very active and am still one of the few moms who play tag and football with my kids and their friends. More and more, however, I am being targeted as the slow kid who is picked last for teams and is chased in a game of tag when "it" is too tired to try for anyone else and needs an easy prey. I'll play that part just to provide a good role model for the other kids, but it pisses me off that I'm losing my edge.

I have to laugh when I speak with friends who have girls who like to bake and knit and read. They want to play sports too, but they also like to power down for a while. My eldest, Satchel, is 15 and has more cerebral moments in his day than his two younger brothers. He likes to read and work on the computer, but his affection for my husband and me now comes in the form of a pent-up, hormonally fuelled, surprise tackle. When I arrive home and know he's already there, I have to sneak around like Inspector Clouseau, waiting for Kato to jump out of the fridge or down from the chandelier. He's getting so strong now, however, that my husband takes the brunt of his affection. The other day I was inadvertently blocking his well-worn path between the dining room and the refrigerator. He came up from behind, picked me up, deposited me a few feet away, and continued on toward the frozen pizza.

According to Star Trek, at warp one, the U.S.S. Enterprise is travelling at the speed of light. At warp two, it is moving at ten times the speed of light. I think my boys run somewhere between the two. Or they're asleep. Take today for instance: This morning, Tanner, my 10-year-old, had cross-country practice before school, rugby after school, and soccer in the evening. And somewhere in between all of this, he will complain that I didn't play tennis with him. He will play tag at recess and lunch and go until he can't stand up anymore, not because he wants to but because he needs to.

Of course, this is not representative of every day, and while they are busy, my boys are not over-programmed. If they were, they would be too tired to do homework or to focus in school, or to ask for more physical activity; however, if I were working, they would not be doing nearly enough, which adds to the stress at home. There's nothing more exhausting than hyper kids with no outlet. Being too tired or too busy to take them to a park or a practice or to play with their dad or me is not an option.

How many times have I been hit in the back of the head by a football in the living room? How many times have I walked in the door and dropped my bags of groceries in order to catch a tennis ball careening toward me? This morning, I went to put on my shoes only to be surprised by a golf ball tucked into each one. My house smells like dirty socks. There is nothing decorative or breakable anywhere, not even artwork on the walls. And the balls! There are always too many balls around, but it all keeps me sharp, and despite the bumps and bruises along the way, I can't imagine it being any other way.

6.

Adventures with ME!

I am plotting to assemble my "people." The word plotting seems very contrived, but I'd like to sell the gals in the playground on the idea that, just because we're stay-at-home moms, it doesn't mean we have to stay at home; perhaps there can be adventure close to home?

Many of these women are just finding time to themselves again after years of spending their days with very young children. At some point, after they've made breakfasts, lunches, and volunteered at school, they discover snippets of time and begin to jog or do a yoga class. Some are even contemplating going back to work again. But once you've been away from formal employment for a while, even the thought of looking for a paying position becomes daunting. Staring at a resume showing a huge gap in time is disheartening. Skills are out of date, confidence is shot, attention span limited, and everyone wants that job with occasional shift work from ten to two, September to June. If I could find that niche where smart, efficient, hard-working people were required between ten and two, weekdays, during the school year, I would have an army of eager workers signed up in a heartbeat. Don't get me wrong, as a teacher, I'm lucky to have the work schedule that I do, but if I could just find that niche...

With my own "one year off" always in the back of my brain, I am mindful not to waste a moment of it. I am irritatingly happy with my newfound lack of structure. But I'm wary of falling into routines that would sabotage the year. It would be so easy to be complacent and follow the flock to the gym or the jogging path or the grocery store day after day. Some of the long-term SAHMs don't feel my sense of urgency, because there is no clock ticking with its annoying rooster alarm, ready to crow at the end of their independence. I seek adventure while I have the opportunity, and I want to invite others to come along for the ride. So, I am starting a club, for lack of a better word (as "club" connotes a sense of membership and exclusivity and that's not my intent). It's called ME (My Expeditions), and everyone is invited. The vision is to find accessible, affordable adventures in our own city, where we can enjoy an event and each other's company once a month.

I start by emailing a mysterious invitation to a group of moms whom I have recently met or whom I know from before my working days, hoping that those who are willing to take a leap and show up to this intriguing event will also want to find other new and fun things to do. I title the invite, Beyond the Book Club and include the following message:

We've been reading about and cheering for all of the heroines at our book clubs. Isn't it time to become the main character in our own story? Please join me on a quest. It starts on September 26th and ends in about 50 years. Drop by my house for tea and scones and a short presentation on what adventures await. No sales. No membership. Just an opportunity to hang out with other beautiful, creative, curious, and spirited women like you. Hope to see you there!

Some women reply immediately. Yes! Sounds intriguing! (Spirited.) Others are slower to respond and are non-committal (Cautious but with potential). And others don't react at all (suspicious, uninterested, or just too busy). One woman, who came out to adventures later, confided that she initially thought I was trying to sell something other than adventure. But I am happy with the way things are going and am excited that some people are asking if they can bring a friend. I work on a slideshow presentation on adventures that we can explore in our own city.

On the day of the meeting, I clean the whole main floor with my power vacuum (floors, tabletops, microwave, etc.), defrost my homemade, copycat, Starbucks pumpkin scones, and buy a large teapot. I rehearse my presentation, beginning with why we need to do this. At the last minute, I come up with the three criteria for being part of this group. Just by showing up, the girls have already met them:

1. They have an interest in intrigue and adventure. It's time to get out of routines and spice things up a little. We also have to think about the limitations of our experiences. We can't necessarily eat, pray, and love our way around the world or go on a bender to Vegas, but we can become tourists in our own neighbourhood and our own city.

2. They have to be willing to take a little time for themselves. I think that a lot of moms feel guilty about taking time out when there is always a full laundry basket, an empty fridge, a calendar that requires updating, or a dog that needs walking. Everyone is very busy, but what is unique about our stay-at-home time is that we have some flexibility. The point of this group is not to burden ourselves with the need to find babysitters or a carpool for another evening out, but to do these jaunts during the day. It has to be accessible, affordable, and convenient.

3. They have to be women. This was the only exclusion. We are at a time in our lives where many of us are approaching or are already experiencing menopause. And that doesn't have to be a bad thing. While it comes with hot flashes and mood swings, according to Christiane Northrup (in her book, The Wisdom of Menopause) "This is also the most creative time in a woman's life. It is a time of shedding off the old skin and the emergence of a shiny, new, creative, independent, empowered person." Perhaps that creativity reveals itself only in the variety of ways one can think of to occasionally kill one's husband, but it's there. This seems like the perfect time for exploration, creation, and rejuvenation. And this outlet may save our poor punching-bag husbands from a few bites and bruises.

As a part of the presentation, I want to talk about why this is important to me and what inspired me to start this group. The first slide on the screen is a picture of my mother and my little sister, Clare. These two women are so important that they deserve their own pages, and so I must defer their stories for later chapters.

I divide my presentation into five categories: health and fitness, intellectual curiosities, entertainment, local sightseeing, and charity work. When you start to examine what's available nearby, you can gain a whole new appreciation for what your city has to offer. The slideshow displays pictures of beer tours, musicals, soup kitchens, horseback riding, fundraising, Ted Talks, and various alternative fitness classes. It ends with a cycling wine tour of wine country, a couple of hours away— something we could do with a little more planning. The second last slide shows what we could do with a lot of planning and commitment: a cycling wine tour in Tuscany. Think big, right? The final slide reads:

The End.
And the beginning.

The room is electric with energy and enthusiasm, and I use that momentum to introduce the first adventure: Japanese Hot Pilates, which is unlike hot yoga in that the rock floor is heated, not the room. There is a half-hour of rock bathing, allowing the silica rock to flush out toxins from the body, followed by a gentle hour of Pilates. Yummy.

The group is sold. A date is organized, future dates are agreed upon, and we're off. I hear discussions of potential expeditions and see contact information being exchanged. I hope the energy lasts beyond the plate of pumpkin scones. The gals go home, and I send out the yoga info, along with dates for them to add future adventures. Like a book club, one or more persons can sign up to choose and run an event for each month. I've never organized anything like this before, but it feels so necessary that I've got a confidence I never had before. Fingers crossed.

7.

Communication Breakdown

Writing allows me to embrace the introverted side of me. If I'm upset, I go to my journal instead of dealing head-on with disagreements. I avoid conflict like a person with arachnophobia might scream and sprint from a gigantic spider lowering itself down from the ceiling onto her bed in a recurring dream (I'm still trying to work through that one). Perhaps it's because I come from a family of reluctant communicators.

I've thought about this a lot lately since I've finally gained the time to do so. After all, a large part of this journey I'm on is trying to discover who I am as a person (and mother, and wife, and so on). At least in part, that means figuring out why I am that person. Where did I come from? What variables shaped the person I am today? Although I tend to overlook it, there is absolutely no denying that my parents played a large part in nurturing and moulding me from an adorable, blank-slate infant into a Starbucks-swilling, pantyhose-exposing mother of three, with delusions of writing grandeur and the attention and disapproval of Clint Eastwood—although, put in those terms, they likely would deny it.

Or maybe they wouldn't. Who can say? The Russian culture, the one in which my father grew up, wasn't an affectionate or communicative one. When parents spoke to their children, it was often in harsh tones with direct imperatives. With the arrival of WWII, people became even more stoic and secretive. This is how my father was raised, in an environment where actions often spoke louder than words. No one complained about life, because if you were still alive, you were considered to be doing quite well. No one discussed feelings, because it was easier to hide the atrocities you witnessed and how you felt about them deep in the back of your brain. It was all just too much to take in, especially for a child.

And my father, Victor, saw it all. He was six-years-old when the war broke out, and like many who were a part of that battle, his experiences are too bizarre and heartbreaking to be believed. The older he gets, though, the more these stories surface, and he reveals what it was like for him to grow up in such gruesome conflict. When I begin to put his journey down on paper, it makes me embarrassingly aware that he endured unthinkable conditions, while I strut around complaining about how tragic it is that the barista forgot to put vanilla in my non-fat, no-foam, Earl Grey tea latte.

My Grandfather, Michael, was born in the Ukraine but was educated as an engineer in Russia and developed a vast knowledge of the transportation systems used throughout the country. Therefore, when the Nazis captured him, he was considered to be quite useful. Under the threat of death to his family, he was forced to assist the enemy. For two years, between 1942 and 1944, my father, his brother, Tony, his parents, and his grandmother lived on the front lines in two railway cars, so that my grandfather could help guide the Nazis through the rail systems. My grandmother was even allowed to keep a goat and a couple of chickens in the cars—unheard of luxuries for their circumstance.

But when the direction of the war started to turn, the Nazis had to retreat, and Grandfather's skill set was no longer necessary. They were relocated to a hard-labour camp in Austria, where he became part of a group of prisoners, most of them Jewish, used to dig out anti-tank trenches to slow down the approaching enemy. Grandmother was sent to work in the munitions factory, where she lost part of her thumb to a faulty bullet. My father watched, each morning, as near-skeletal men boarded trucks for the day's work. It was not lost on him that those trucks returned at the end of each day carrying fewer men than at the beginning, yet he somehow managed to detach himself from the horrors of those realities. Witnessing death was a daily occurrence; seeing lifeless bodies in tall piles was an everyday view, and he became impervious to the sight and smell of them.

Air raids during this time were commonplace. British and American spitfires would fly by, shooting at anything and everything, forcing those on the ground into bomb craters (large holes in the ground left by previous bombs) to avoid the spraying shrapnel. The Spitfires were followed by bombers, which dropped phosphorous bombs that are now banned by the Geneva Convention. My father remembers one of those days when he heard the air raid sirens, which sent his family running from their building toward a bomb crater. They noticed immediately that my father was not with them and turned back. They dove to the ground, pressed against the shelter they had deserted, and waited out the storm of ammunition. When all became quiet, they crept back into the building and found him trapped under a fallen armoire, staring at an undetonated bomb, which must have made its way through a window and lay just a few feet from him. Despite his youth, my father was familiar with all kinds of weaponry and braced himself for the explosion and the burning fire, which would swallow them all up. The family froze, watched, and waited for the bomb to wake up, but for some reason, it never did. Tragically, another bomb did explode, right in the bomb crater where they were supposed to have been, killing close to fifty people.

Someone or something seemed to be watching over them, but beyond this inexplicable "good luck," their survival also involved no small amount of quick thinking and some eerily intuitive decisions. As the war ended, a train filled with Jewish prisoners was to transport them to another facility, and Grandfather was going to accompany them on the trip because of his experience with the tracks. Grandmother had a terrible feeling. "Stay," she said. "Don't get on that train." He heeded her warning and discovered later that those prisoners were ordered off the train and into a field, where they were executed by machine-gun fire.

The war eventually ended, and the prisoners were rounded up by the Moroccans and handed over to the Americans, but the adventures continued. Rescued prisoners were moved by the Americans to Displacement Camps (previously Nazi-soldier barracks) until it could be decided what should be done with them. There were lists created of all of the assembled people and in which rooms they resided. When the Russian army arrived, they demanded access to those lists, so that they could retrieve any surviving Russian citizens and deport them back home, where they would be charged with treason. During the war, Russian soldiers were notoriously always told, "Save the last bullet for yourself." So, it was presumed that, if you had survived the war despite being captured, it was because you had betrayed your country.

The Americans could do nothing but watch as Russians took back their people, only to inflict more terror upon them. When soldiers came to my father's family's room to take them back to their home country, my grandmother, thinking quickly, feigned a heart attack and swooned, grabbing at her chest. Soldiers relented but stood guard outside the door to see if she would survive. Luckily, theirs was a room with a window and an eavestrough. Mother, father, and two brothers quietly slid two-stories down the drain pipe to escape. They left behind my father's grandmother, who was too frail to attempt the escape.

Unfortunately, there is no happy ending here. The family was captured again by the Russians and placed back under watch. In a bold move, my grandfather somehow obtained a bottle of liquor and offered it to the guards outside his room. According to plan, they overindulged and eventually passed out, allowing the family another opportunity to escape. Off they went again, on foot, soon to be chased by soldiers who had discovered their absence. They ran through farmers' fields and came upon a barn, where they dove into a haystack and lay motionless, praying their trackers would do a quick check and move on. All four of them lay among the sharp, itchy straw, listening to their pursuers enter and search the barn. They held their collective breath as bayonets began piercing through the haystack, stabbing centimetres from their bodies. For a 10 and 14-year-old to remain calm enough not to scream or move during this hunt is unbelievable. That no one was hurt or found is a miracle.

Eventually, it was the Americans who found them and sympathetically rewrote their documents, identifying them as residents of Tarnopol, a small town in the Ukraine. They were finally outside Russian jurisdiction but continued to live in the American displacement camps, where my father and

Tony would get into mischief with the toys of the day: weapons abandoned by fleeing Nazis. They played Russian Roulette with revolvers. They tinkered with undetonated grenades, taking turns removing the inner-cartridge without touching the outer casing. They experimented with anti-aircraft guns— Tony once accidentally firing one off too close to Victor, throwing him ten feet and giving him temporary hearing loss. They had to hide these daily adventures from their mother like they were wartime versions of Tom Sawyer and Huck Finn.

Even though they were gone, the Nazis continued to cause chaos and fatalities. Before fleeing their barracks, they hid bombs there, set on timers, so that they would detonate at random interludes and locations as rescued prisoners settled into the rooms. Once, my father and his family found an old movie projector in one of the towers of the U-shaped building in which they were assigned. They were watching a film when my grandfather excused himself to use the washroom, which was located in the tower at the other end of the "U." While he was there, one of these bombs exploded in the middle of the building, collapsing it and killing or injuring everyone who wasn't in the towers, which remained standing. My grandfather, unaware of the depth of destruction, walked out of the washroom and fell four stories. Legend has it that (likely in a state of shock) he stood up from the rubble and walked away, uninjured, in search of his family, who were also miraculously unharmed.

They moved to Belgium, where they lived for six years before immigrating to Canada, arriving with thousands of others at Pier 21 in Halifax, Nova Scotia. It all reads like a Hollywood screenplay, and I think it should be. It certainly has the makings of an exciting book. (Hmm. Perhaps my next project has chosen me?)

So, with this as the background for my father's upbringing, how does he communicate in today's world? Almost every decision his parents made had one concern in mind: What do we need to do to survive? In today's world, we fret over having to choose between a forty-inch or a fifty-inch television, or this SUV versus that minivan. I can guarantee my dad's parents never read a book on parenting; they were too busy trying to stay alive.

Nowadays, parenting seems to require constant communication, checking in, knowing when to interfere or back off. So, how does someone like my dad relate to his teenagers with no frame of reference upon which to draw? It's not that he didn't care. He cared deeply. He just couldn't always verbalize it. Here are two of the best examples I can think of:

1. Many years ago, my dad felt certain my older sister, who was in high school at the time, was having sex with her boyfriend. My dad called her into his bedroom, had her sit on the bed in front of him, and said (simply but sternly), "Just stop it."

"Stop what?" asked my sister, feigning ignorance.

"You know what I mean. Stop it."

And with that, he walked out. That was the big "birds and bees" talk, and I suppose my sister was supposed to pass that golden, coming-of-age nugget on to the rest of us because that's as close as any of us would ever get to the topic of (shhh) sex.

2. I had changed schools in the fall of my third year of university in the United States. Back then I was headstrong and independent, and my father was busy running a successful company, so we did our best bonding four times a year: twice on the way to the airport and twice on the way back. Here's how one of my favourite springtime conversations went:

Dad (awkwardly): So ... what's the exact name of the school you go to?

Me (exasperated): Coastal Carolina University.

Dad (slightly embarrassed): Oh. Someone asked me the other day, and I realized I didn't know.

Me (speechless):

And perhaps the reason why I choose to write.

Now, however, as I look back at the growth of our family, I believe the person who has undergone the most change is my father. While he used to be counted on for some offensive remark or backhanded compliment, he has metamorphosed. Dad's views on politics, immigration, race, unions, wars, athlete's paychecks, and women used to rival that of Archie Bunker. These days, he's just become too old to expend that kind of energy on things that he's finally accepted (or at least accepted that he can't change). Dad's second wife, Vicky, whom he married seventeen years ago, is a strong, educated, patient, kind, and independent woman, who has tempered his bad habits and shrunk his appetite for inappropriateness. She has motivated him to him to eat well and exercise daily and has reunited him with his love of singing by encouraging him to join a local choir. I genuinely believe that it is thanks to her that he is still around to know his grandchildren.

My dad had very little formal education, but he was street smart. No one messed with him, particularly not the stray cat he finally caught, who had been spraying all over our back deck, creating a most uninviting stench. If our neighbours had been looking out from their second-floor window that one fateful morning, they would have seen a black cat flying over our garage roof, a clean spiral as if launched from a seasoned quarterback.

Another time, a homeless man had been quietly squatting under our back deck for who knows how long, setting up a small refuge as his nighttime home. He was, no doubt, startled when Dad surprised him early one day with a good-morning-you-have-60-seconds-to-move-out-of-here butcher knife hovering inches from his face.

Once, while driving, he witnessed the driver of the car in front of him throwing a soda can out the window and onto the street. Dad got out of his car, picked up the can, followed the driver several kilometres to the next traffic light, knocked on the guy's window, threw the can back in, and said to the startled man, "I think you dropped this. "

My dad and I have been like two rivers, meeting and separating, crisscrossing throughout our lives. We have recently become quite close again, even though he might say (tongue in cheek) that he only wants us to visit him so that he can spend time with his grandkids. Through the writing and researching of this book, I have a greater appreciation for where he's come from and what he's been through. He has seen war and peace, famine and excess. He has worked hard for everything he has, starting a small business from scratch, and he has shown unwavering loyalty to and protectiveness of his family, friends, and close business associates. Like Archie Bunker, beyond the occasional off-colour joke and opinionated commentary, there is a tenderness and humanness about him that exposes him as a kind, gentle and (yes) tolerant man. More and more, I look to him as a survivor, an idealist, an adventurer, a romantic, and a believer in hope, and if I can learn from his example and attempt to be more like him, then I will be a better person for it.

8.

Hair Today. Gone Tomorrow.

In the spirit of austerity, I give up those lovely pampering luxuries I would usually have bestowed upon myself in preparation for going back to school at the end of the summer. Instead, I give myself a pedicure, which looks fine from a distance; however, a kindergarten kid could easily berate me for colouring outside the lines and leaving clumps of Perfect Pink scattered across my toes. This would easily earn me another check in the "progressing with difficulty" report card box, but it would have to do.

Next, instead of my usual cut, style, and highlights, I buy the boxed version of hair colour, which makes me a little sad because I love, love, love my hairdresser and love what I feel like when I walk out of her salon. We have been a couple for over twenty years because she is a miracle worker. In the old days, I could just walk into her salon and say, "Give me whatever Meg Ryan has." Later, when I started to question Meg's judgment, particularly where Russell Crowe and Botox were concerned, I would say, "Do whatever you think," and she would get to work. No discussion. No picture. Just go.

Once I walked into her salon and boldly announced, "I want bangs."

Her quick reply was, "No, you don't."

I know that if I told her I was trying to save money, she would offer to give me a discount, as she has done before depending on my employment status, but I'd rather not be her pro-bono work this time. I will miss her desperately, but it's only for one year, and I've given up any attempt at looking professional, which is the message my toenails are screaming.

My boys are oblivious to the maintenance women require to look the way they do. That I come home every now and then with painted toes or highlighted hair is of no concern to them. Sometimes they notice a haircut, and sometimes they just look curiously to figure out what's different, and then walk away, preferring to turn on Sponge Bob than figure out the Mommy Puzzle.

The only time they've looked twice was when we were all overrun with lice for three months. Every night, we'd use the nit comb on each other, launder our sheets, vacuum our upholstery, and bag our stuffies with no success. Finally, one weekend, the boys all got their heads shorn and resembled a tiny company of soldiers. The following Monday, I also had my hair shaved to within an inch of my head. My boys walked past me in the playground, looking for their mother (the one with the long, blonde locks). While this was a liberating feeling, having no tangles or elastics, or even a brush to maneuver, it was also a really bad look for me. Unfortunately, I don't have the cheekbones, or the beautiful skin, or the anything else that would make me worthy of asking my hairdresser to "Give me the Halle Berry" and think I could get away with it.

Now, without my hairdresser, and so as not to send my boys into shock when they meet and perhaps marry someone who requires more than thirty seconds of daily beauty maintenance, I thought I would initiate them by allowing them to participate in one aspect of women's beauty. I open my box of drugstore highlights, put on the magical cap, and ask my eldest son and my husband to take turns using the crochet needle to hook and pull clumps of my shoulder-length hair through the holes in the cap. I can get them to do this by seating myself a few feet in front of the TV while the baseball game plays, so they can tug at my scalp and not miss a play. This is tedious work, it hurts me, and neither can understand why it has to be done.

Next, Tanner uses the paintbrush to brush on the peroxide, and Cole complains about the "beeping" smell. End result? As you would expect, it doesn't work, and I still have three-inch roots, except my hair now has the texture of straw and crunches when I pull it back into a ponytail. And my boys think I'm vain and ridiculous, but at least they've had a small peek into the lengths some women will take to change what they were born with. My kids naively believe that wanting to alter our looks is unnecessary and superficial. Hello, of course it is, but they don't understand that this unnecessary work has made 40 the new 30, or in my case (after my unfortunate peroxide encounter), 47 the new 58.

9.

Life is a Highway
(that Ends in a Lake)

The confirmations for Japanese Hot Pilates start to come in, so perhaps now would be a good time to introduce one of the inspirations for the adventure club: my mother. She was a free spirit who loved travel and adventure. She grew up in a small town near Surry, England, with three younger brothers. Like my father, she was young when the war broke out, and her father went away to fight. With four young mouths to feed, her mother taught her to be very practical with her money. When she married my father, he would hand over his paycheck to her at the end of each week, and somehow, she would stretch those dollars so thin they were translucent.

Settling in Toronto, she used my father's conservative paycheck to feed and clothe four children, pay for tennis lessons, take us on family budget vacations, and somehow buy real estate on the side. I wish I had her gift for frugality. Her one mistake was putting all of her own wish-list eggs in my dad's retirement basket. She had big plans for once he retired, far-away plans, which would take them around the globe. Ownership of a bed and breakfast awaited their return, where she would host interesting people and chat them up for hours on end. She loved to talk to people and listen to their stories, and they loved to tell them to her.

I'll never forget the time she dialled long-distance to England for her regular Sunday call to her mother; this was in the day when you had to actually ask the operator to connect you to the person at the other end of the line, like at the end of Pink Floyd's, Young Lust. After a good ten minutes of chitchat, she hung up, and we asked how Grandma was doing.

"I don't know. She wasn't home," she replied in her English accent.

"Then, who were you talking to?"

"Oh, that was the operator. What a nice bloke. Plans on working at the telephones until he can get into business school. I daresay he'll do well. Clever lad."

My mother never wanted to inconvenience anyone or cause them any discomfort. This meant she also carried the gene that steered her clear of uncomfortable situations—a family trait. When I started menstruating for the first time and whispered the news to her, she responded with, "Do you know what to do?"

"I think so."

"Do you have the right equipment?"

Equipment? Hmmm, would I find feminine hygiene in sporting goods or work safety?

"I think so."

"Okay then."

And that was the extent of the welcome to womanhood party, which was not unlike the aforementioned birth-control talk my sister received from my father.

So, my mom was planning and saving and saving and planning. She stoically plodded along, dreaming about the future. My parents went on short cruises and island stays on occasion, but those trips would only whet her appetite. Travel brochures were filling up her drawers, but my dad was not ready—not ready to not work yet. I understand it can be a scary thing to give up something you've been doing for forty years with no notion of what's on the other side and no certainty of financial stability for the long haul. Mom had plenty of notions of the other side, and perhaps that's what frightened Dad the most, so he delayed retirement.

What eventually frightened Mom the most was the malignant melanoma scare she'd had at the age of 43. During the months of harsh treatments, she went to church and prayed, prayed for ten years of good health so that my sister Clare, her youngest, would have at least eighteen years behind her and be able to make her own decisions as an adult. Mom didn't want to leave a child behind. This turned out to be a tragic miscalculation because ten years later, to the month, after a series of seemingly unrelated symptoms appeared, cancer was found throughout her body, and she was diagnosed as incurable. This was October of 1991. I was 25 and engaged to be married, and my older brother and sister were already married, and so only Clare was at home and still in school. By the time Mom found out, she was too sick to tick anything off of her bucket list.

So, the obvious question to me is this: Why ask for only ten years? What about twenty or thirty or forty years? What is the magic number when you might be considered too greedy to deserve some kind of divine intervention?

In February, just five months after her diagnosis, I watched my mother stop breathing in her hospital bed.

Minutes earlier, I confessed to her heavily medicated, failing body that a friend and I had sunk my Honda Prelude (the one she'd loaned me money to buy during university) in a lake, during a terrible storm. It was an honest mistake, as most sunk-my-car-in-a-lake stories are. It was monsoon season in South Carolina, and the rains had swelled the lake water in a golf-course community up and over the road so that in the pitch black of night, we couldn't see that the road actually turned and paralleled the shoreline. The underwater road went left; we went straight. I had been afraid to tell her for the past three years, even though I had the car dredged, dried out, and running well again. I was always paranoid to open the hood in front of her (in case she caught glimpses of the seaweed that popped out every now and then). I don't know why, but as she lay there on her deathbed I just had to tell her. I thought I saw her brow furrow with the confession because (of course) she would have had no clue what I was talking about. Then I told her I loved her, and she surprised me by squeezing my hand.

Moments later, our family gathered around her. A reverend had been called in to say a prayer for her departing soul. We waited in silence for several minutes. Then my brother, Peter, who has a strong, spiritual connection, told her it was okay for her to go. He looked at us all and said, "Sometimes they need to hear that it's okay to go … that we'll all be okay." And then she took her last breath. She was gone. We were motherless. It was the first of many holes to open up in my heart. It was a vacancy that could never be filled—a place where all those things I would want to tell her in the future would end up, echoing and bouncing around in that aching void.

It is partly in her honour that I encourage others to get up and do something for themselves that's exciting or unique, something to look forward to, even if it's once a month, even if it's down the street. It's fun to have grandiose ideas about what we'll do down the road, but why watch the clock until then? What are we waiting for?

P.S.

While my poor little car was in the shop, drying out, I had no way to get to school for my evening poetry class, so I decided to write a poem about my little engine that eventually could:

The problem with my car
Is that it doesn't float;
The mechanic told me so
After I'd used it as a boat.
The road just turned to water;
The wheels began to grope.
The bubbles starting rising;
I had no periscope.
Cold cascades came rushing in,
Thick with sludge and slurp;
This lake was hungry for my car.
I'm sure I heard it burp.
I took the nearest exit,
In no mood for a dip,
I assure you that this captain
Did not go down with her ship.
The mechanic, he is happy;
He has made a friend for life.
I visit him so often,
I am like a second wife.
And now my car is running,
But with a complex quite insane.
She hesitates to budge an inch
When it begins to rain.

10.

The Cat Came Back

Now that I've been home for a month, I can't help but notice the two balls of fur, which occasionally go to the trouble of opening one eye when I enter one of their many sleeping environments. I'd like to be more patient with our unappreciative cats, but let's be honest, aren't all cats unappreciative by nature? They stroll across the table where I'm typing and look at me, annoyed that my hands are impeding their ability to lie across the warmth of their keyboard. Sometimes they wait for a break in the action to commandeer the keys; other times they casually saunter over and slowly and discretely nudge my fingers away with a tacit attitude as if to say, Is there a problem here?

I never wanted pets. Animal-rights activists will want to skin me alive, but I have enough dependents whose needs are not being met; why would I want two more? The sales pitch my husband gave me was this: They are kittens, which will be delivered on Christmas morning, wearing bells and bows! And they are free!

The free, bell-and-bow-wearing kittens arrived on Christmas morning, right on schedule. The kids thought the kittens were cute and visiting us for Christmas day, but when they awoke the following morning and the cats were still there, well ... the honeymoon was over. The cats had already been off to the laundry room to mark some territory and make us aware of how unlucky they felt at having been ripped from the farm where they were born and sent to the zoo in which we live. They sprayed their wretched scent on the clothes in the hamper, peed in the dryer, and left tufts of white hair on everything we owned.

Their names are Ace and Maple, and five years after adopting them, I still wonder why I let my husband wear me down and allow them into our home. Sure, they're cute and a lot of fun to watch when I slip them catnip or scare them into flight by jumping out at them from around a corner, but they come with their share of problems.

Last year, on December 30, I noticed a bright blue piece of Christmas ribbon following Ace around the room. It looked like it was tangled on his back leg, but on closer inspection, I found that the ribbon was actually protruding from his butt. Perhaps with a gentle tug, the ribbon would slide right out? A gentle tug sent the cat's appendages splaying out in four directions like I had yanked all the strings on a marionette at the same time. He righted himself and went screeching under the couch. This was the beginning of an adventure neither of us would enjoy.

If you Google "string coming out of my cat's butt," you will be presented with over 5,780000 results. Apparently, there are more than a few other cats out there as dumb as ours. The Google consensus was that, if he began to hide or vomit, he should be taken to a vet. The next morning, right on cue, I was met with cat barf on the carpet, and the cat was nowhere to be seen. Once we located him behind the dryer, off we went to the nearest emergency animal hospital, as our regular vet was closed on New Year's Eve.

Some pet owners have The Number, which is the amount they would be willing to spend on their animal to preserve its good health. Some owners have no limit to what they would pay to save their furry family member. Our number was $500.

The vet's assistant coddled Ace, comforted me, and then took our poor cat to the back room for some tests. Blood work and an I.V. for dehydration came to a total of $1200. Excuse me? Didn't I just write $500 was my limit? I do not remember any fee consultation. Somehow, I agreed to an x-ray, to see how far up his intestines the string went, for $200. The assistant assured me that, if it didn't go too far up, it might just make its way out by itself. Not surprisingly, the x-ray was inconclusive, but they could sedative the cat and use forceps to reach in and pull the string out. If the ribbon wasn't tangled around anything, it would come out easily, and that would be it, for just $300 more. That didn't work, and we were no further ahead, except I was out $1700 and couldn't find my way off of that crazy train.

We live in a very pet-friendly neighbourhood, where animals are treated very much like people. We often walk past a large advertisement on the side of a bus shelter. On it is a picture of a dog with the caption, "Shouldn't he have the same health care as you?" I want to ninja my way over there one night and vandalize this sign in black Sharpie with: NO. THIS IS A DOG. I know I'm offending some pet owners, but as the owner of children, there is nothing I wouldn't do to keep my kids healthy, but I can't, in good conscience, make these same sacrifices for a pet, even if I have grown attached to the little shit.

The vet's assistant thus far had been lovely and empathetic. She moved between the invisible vet and my holding cell, each time leaving me there for up to twenty minutes, enough to keep me suffering over the future of my cat and my bank account.

She knew how to pull at the heartstrings, and at just the right time, moved in for the kill.

Surgery. No other option. Open him up and follow the string to its end for a mere $3500! That's $3500 more than the $1700 we've already racked up and $4700 more than our limit. The number snapped me out of my guilty haze. I told her I couldn't do it. I was upset. My kids and husband were now waiting at home so that we could leave to spend New Year's Eve with out-of-town friends. The vet's assistant gave me a slightly disapproving look and left me again for a prolonged time (probably to get her nails done for a New Year's Eve party), then returned to offer me an assistance program that I could purchase—a loan, which would allow me to pay the debt off over three years. I could pay $5200 today or $5200 plus interest over three years. I told her again, I couldn't do it.

She quickly did a full one-eighty and was no longer my BFF. She didn't comfort me but aggressively fed into my guilt. All I wanted her to say was that the only other solution would be to put the cat down. I was actually ready to do that. I just couldn't bring myself to say it. Just give me the option, and I'll take it. I was in tears. The assistant subtly shook her head in disgust that I wouldn't succumb to whatever it would take to save Ace and left me in the room for another twenty minutes to anguish over the decision.

When she returned, she told me flatly that the vet thought (I still had yet to see the vet—he sent his henchman in to do his dirty work) that the cat was too young to be put down. Either I pony up $5200 or leave the cat with them to have surgery and be put up for adoption to find a suitable home. I was shocked at the manipulation and emotional blackmail. "How much does it cost to adopt a pet?" I asked.

"$60," said the servant of the devil.

"So, I can have my cat back for $5200 or anyone else can have him for $60?"

Her silence confirmed as much.

I didn't know what to do. I wanted to run to the back and take Ace away from this place, but I was so upset that I wasn't thinking straight. How far could this go? I played my last card, calling her bluff. "He's yours."

She barely raised an eyebrow and left me in the room again, returning ten minutes later, giving me enough time to reconsider.

"You'll have to sign some paperwork," she said with disdain.

I signed it all, smudging the ink with my tears, but I couldn't see any other way. After a minute or two, she asked me to leave the room, and I went out to reception, sobbing and waiting for Peter and the kids to pick me up. I couldn't explain what had happened over the phone, so they had no idea. Eventually, the assistant told me to leave the office because I was upsetting the other clients. They should be upset, and they should see my state as a warning that this was a dangerous place. They were about to be taken for a long and expensive ride.

Peter was shocked at the story but agreed it was the only option. We talked about having a friend go in and adopt Ace in a few days, but we weren't sure of their adoption process. For all we knew, he would be given to friends of the vet or office staff. Several hours later, the vet called, and Peter answered my cell phone. He wanted us to know that our cat had had surgery and that it was successful. "As far as we're concerned, he's your cat now," said Peter flatly.

A few hours later, as we somberly ate dinner with our friends, the vet called again to let us know that Ace was awake and doing well. Our New Year's was drained of all its fun and we went to bed early. The next morning, the vet called again to inform us that Ace had had a restful night and was in good spirits. They were relentless. Figuring out how to explain to the kids that the cat would be fine but would not be coming home didn't help us ring the New Year in jubilantly.

Our New Year's host, who is a lawyer, offered to send a letter to the vet, threatening a lawsuit for emotional blackmail and inhumane treatment. His offer was that the vet hand over Ace for the cost of the adoption fee. He sent an email, and we dropped off a hard copy in the vet's mailbox the next day.

That evening the vet phoned and offered to cover half the cost of the surgery. Peter accepted, just to put an end to the ordeal. To our surprise, the vet called again the next morning, perplexed, as he had only just read the email and hadn't opened his snail mail. He was shocked and angry at our accusations. We had no sympathy for him. We picked up Ace, paid $2600, and closed the door for good on that relationship. As far as we're concerned, Ace has used up the cat healthcare fund. If Maple gets sick, he is out of luck—there is no more money left in the kitty.

11.

A Brief Pause for Menopause.

Not a day goes by when I don't think, Wow, if I were at work today, this would have been very complicated. Between drop-offs and pick-ups, practices, homework, appointments, food-related chores, and laundry (notice there is no mention of cleaning, which is becoming a problem), as well as trying to keep up with my writing, I need all the time I can get. But one of the perks is that I can also take a break every now and then and say yes to other less practical things, like going to the taping of a talk show.

My sister, Anne, has extra tickets to a popular talk show taped in Toronto, so I ask my friend Nella to join us. While it's fun, and we have special participatory jobs given to us by the audience host, whom Anne knows, what is most interesting is the guest, Suzanne Sommers. At 67, Suzanne still looks very much like Chrissie Snow from Three's Company (although her '70s wear is replaced by a skin-tight, leopard-print dress, showing off those voluptuous curves for which she was so famous). She certainly isn't playing the role of the dumb blonde anymore. With twenty-five books under her belt (that's authored, not read), she has become a passionate researcher of and reporter on health issues. She challenges conventional medicine and looks for safer, healthier alternatives to harsh treatments and everyday maintenance for women.

As the universe continues to unfold in front of me, Suzanne happens to be touring to promote her new book on pre-meno-pause, and we are all given a free copy. Had I not been there, I probably would have bought it myself because she talks about mood swings, sex drive, sleep patterns, and yes, forgetfulness. I find myself being one of those irritating audience members the camera focuses on who is always nodding her head, "Yeah girl, I hear you, and I know exactly what you're talking about. You came here today to talk to me, and we are totally on the same page!"

The show actually takes almost four hours to tape, with no offering of food or water for the audience. We all learn a few things about hormones and hormone-replacement therapy, Anne gets to test drive some eyeshadow on camera, and we leave with the goal of researching alternative menopausal treatments and whatever diet (or plastic surgeon) will help us to wedge ourselves into a skin-tight, leopard-print dress.

It's hard to empathize with menopausal women until you experience it yourself. My first symptoms came just this year, with irregular periods, not elongated ones, but joyfully closer together with accompanying issues of rage. These feelings were sometimes so obviously out of my control that it was frustrating and hard on my relationships. Sometimes, I could only weep, and if I was alone, growl or scream. When I brought it up with my doctor, she took out her business card, wrote something out on the back, and handed it to me ... like it was a clue to the secret treasure chest of happiness. "Keep this in your wallet," she said. "When you feel out of control, try to remember to read it."

It read: This is not me. My husband is a good man.

Now, with a few months of pre-menopause under my ever-expanding belt, I am trying really hard to listen to my body and be aware of the direction in which my mood is heading. If I feel like I am becoming irrational or just overly sensitive, I do my best to remove myself from a potentially volatile situation, like the war that erupts between Peter and me over organic versus regular milk. Organic costs triple what regular milk does, but it makes me feel better about what goes into the kids' bodies. This is one of those wars that he has no idea is occurring, but to me is a fierce battle. I don't know if he has given any simplified explanation to the boys for my quick exits to another room, or out for a walk without asking if anyone would like to join me, just because I sneezed one of those mood-altering sneezes. When these swings occur, I'm not sure if it's just their boy nature not to notice, but my guys don't ask any questions. If there are no waffles in the freezer, then there might be cause for concern, but for now, they can keep their innocence. After all, one day they'll have encounters with their own partners' alter egos. Oh, yes (evil laugh) ... they'll have their chance.

12.

In Defense of Bacon

Why science has not genetically modified chickens to be born breaded and ready for deep-frying is a mystery. Most kids (okay, my kids) these days will only salivate when they approach food from a box. Actually, that's not entirely true. While they do concede that fast food is often toxic and tasteless, the ten-cent toy inside the kiddie meal is irresistible and worth every carcinogenic calorie that they must ingest to get it. To avoid slowly poisoning my children, I made the concession that, occasionally, we would go through the drive-thru and order just the toy, not the food. Eventually, the fun of the toy, with a life expectancy of seven minutes, lost its appeal and I could focus on coaching them into making better food choices.

This brings me back to the chickens. I have purchased the books by the celebrities about picky eaters and how to hide the cauliflower in the macaroni, and the carrots in the spaghetti sauce, but the kids know. They can't pinpoint exactly what's different about the food, but it's different enough to make them turn up their noses. Some hard-ass parents still insist that kids should not be allowed to leave the table until they finish their food. I say that's fine if you want to hold out and clean up the vomit that your son left because he was forced to eat the broccoli that his chicken nugget-lined belly rejected. When I was a kid, I got in trouble because the dog barfed up the Brussels sprouts I'd been feeding her under the table, which has shaped my own (sometimes soupy) parenting behaviour.

I enjoy eating fabulous food and will try just about anything, but I like to cook like my cats like to swim. I'll try new recipes, then undoubtedly fail because I've misread a measurement, or a cooking time, or chosen a poor substitution for an ingredient I'm lacking; then I frantically try to save it with no instinctive cooking sense, trash the whole experiment, and make a Hail Mary call to the Thai joint up the street.

It may have something to do with my mother and her practical plats du jour. Cooking for a family of six, being on a meagre allowance, and just simply being born British made her meals ... let's say ... predictable. The menu was reasonably straightforward: macaroni and cheese pie on Monday, meatloaf on Tuesday, spaghetti on Wednesday, and so on. In her defence, she rarely hosted dinner parties, but on holidays, like Christmas or Easter, no one could cook up a roast leg of lamb with mint jelly, vegetables, roast potatoes, Yorkshire pudding, and gravy like Mom. To this day, it is my favourite meal, even though I haven't had it for years. I certainly haven't attempted to make it because Satchel has been a vegetarian for three years now—a decision he came home with one day after much time spent quietly pondering the ethics of meat-eating. And so, for lack of a better expression, at just 10-years old, he went off meat, cold turkey.

Where the ethical voice in him came from at such a young age, I can't say, but he's stuck to his guns (in a figurative, non-violent, gun-toting kind of way). As he is usually also the voice of reason in our household, Peter and I also gave it a shot (again, figuratively speaking). We were mostly vegetarian, falling off the wagon for the occasional piece of bacon—and please don't judge; it's bacon after all! After a year, my taste buds, utterly bored with beans and tofu, sniffed out a meaty buffet, and I threw in the towel. Peter, however, has maintained his diet for two years now, which earns him and Satchel my respect for sticking to it and my occasional resentment for having to accommodate their preferences in my cooking fiascos.

13.

Life's Rich Plan

Peter and I have always believed in the Ready, Fire, Aim approach to budgeting, which has (for the most part) served us pretty well (or so we have ourselves believing). It's a few days into October, however, and we've just gone over our first month of finances since the beginning of Project Me. Things look slightly grim. I am not surprised. Of course, we probably could have more money stashed away for retirement. We certainly could have more money to put down on a mortgage. And we definitely could pass more often on some of the non-essential items that we thoughtlessly buy. No more impulse magazine purchases at the checkout, no more clothes, no more drugstore spending sprees, when I would typically wander around, picking up scented candles, funny greeting cards, and just-in-case gifts. I once even bought a set of stereo speakers at the drugstore. But I always go back to my specialty tea as the symbolic culprit for all of our woes. If I could just wean off of Starbucks, everything would be fine, and we would be billionaires by now.

Here is the level of detail regarding our budget as we planned for my year off: spend less, save more. And now I have a huge knot in my stomach as I try to comprehend not only meeting our monthly bills but also factoring in the unknowns, like car repairs, kids' programming, and health costs. For our trip in March Break, I have scratched out Jamaica and replaced it with outdoor adventures in the backyard—if the snow has melted. I might even sink as low as re-introducing the dreaded kids-at-home projects. The thought of doing arts and crafts or baking with my boys feels like March Break suicide.

I have been there before: At home with young kids on a rainy day with nothing to do and ready to throw a brick at the television if I had to listen to Caillou's squeaky, whiny, little baby voice one more time. As a quick aside, regarding Caillou, it is my conspiracy theory that it was he who drove moms to take Prozac or St. John's Wort. Most thought it was their own kids and postpartum hormones that were driving their anxiety or depression, but it was him, invading their subconscious like some invisible, mind-altering gas. Does Caillou not know what a bad example he sets for kids who emulate his stubborn, selfish, manipulative behaviour? Wow, did I write that out loud? Think I've been holding that in for way too long. Feeling better.

Back to money and lack of it. We have been here before, wondering which fairy godmother was going to swoop in and "show us the money!" My husband doesn't get flustered, and most of the time, I am just as laid back. I have always made impulsive decisions, creating a vague plan to justify the choice, following this logical reasoning: That seems like fun. It used to drive my mother crazy, and at times she even seemed to resent my "seize the day" attitude. She would ask, "How do you do it? How do you always land on your feet?"

I'm sure she really wanted me to succeed, but I think she wanted me to experience some level of disappointment so that I could learn some lessons and become more responsible and practical, the same way she did. But it appears I didn't learn a thing.

I have a black and white picture of her when she was young, standing in an English field, on a tall fencepost, balancing precariously on one foot as if she were a marble cherub atop a fountain in Italy, reaching up playfully toward some giant toy the sky. This is the mother I want to remember: the free spirit, unaware that she could fall off that post, not the one on the ground, who learned how to be practical, always looking down in case one of her dreams actually fluttered down, landed on her doorstep, and she accidentally stepped on it.

I have friends who admire our risk-tolerant natures, and I have other friends who shake their heads, concerned for the irresponsible, sometimes emotionally charged choices we make. But regardless of the approach any of us take, in the end, we all worry about the same things, whether our decisions are meticulously calculated or just loosy-goosey throws of a dart. Somehow, Peter and I always land on our feet. Call it luck, call it optimism, call it good karma, but really, it's all perspective. Truth is, sometimes we make plans that don't pan out, and we end up making our share of lemonade, but it's usually pretty tasty. Our kids have come to understand that we love to dream, and while not all of our dreams will come true (Machu Pichu is still on my radar), making plans, sacrifices, and sometimes detours are all part of life. As our good friend Jeff says (several times a day), "It's all part of life's rich plan."

Facing my economic anxiety today is far less frightening than thinking about what might happen tomorrow. It's also far more comforting to appreciate what I have right in front of me, which is pretty darned amazing. I have to learn to take the same perspective toward our current financial challenges that I do towards most everything else: Somehow it will all work out. How? I don't know. It just will.

Lao Tzu, an ancient Chinese philosopher and considered to be the founder of Taoism, said:

If you are depressed, you are living in the past.
If you are anxious, you are living in the future.
If you are at peace, you are living in the present.

I choose peace.

14.

The Rainbow Connection

Cole says, in his best Family Feud, game-show-host voice, "One hundred people surveyed. Top five answers for why I hate school are..." Our house is a combination game show/sitcom. At most dinners, there's always a game going on—our own versions of Match Game, Family Feud, or Unlimited Questions (our dumbed down version of Twenty Questions). There's also usually quotes from favourite sitcoms flying around at any given time ... not that there's anything wrong with that.

The kids come by it naturally. Peter, whose role can be inter-changeable between my husband and my fourth child, loves to play games and being so competitive, I jump in when I can. I should have known life would be like this when Peter proposed, which was the ultimate contest.

We had been dating for around six months when Peter came up with a challenge. He was trying to convert me to being a classic-rock chick from my pop-girl roots, which was a serious undertaking and worthy of a hefty reward. The rules of the game went like this: Peter could choose any rock song that was playing on the radio and designate a number of points to it, depending on the level of difficulty. As the only contestant, my goal was to name the artist/group performing. Starting at 100 points, if I answered correctly, the allotted points were deducted from my score, and if I was incorrect, those points were added. If I ever reached zero (and this illustrates Peter's Hari-Krishna-like persistence in converting me), he would ask me to marry him.

Let the game begin! I play hard. I like to win. So ... I studied. Fortunately, Peter's friends took me aside for private tutoring, introducing me to more obscure songs, like "Going up the Country" by Canned Heat, or songs without any lyrics, like "Jessica" by the Allman Brothers.

It was an epic tournament. Sometimes, I'd surprise him with an unexpected answer and other times he'd win out. My score wavered for the first few months. Then the accumulation of knowledge started tipping the scales in my favour. I had drunk in the lyrics of Bob Dylan, The Who, Joni Mitchell, Pink Floyd, The Stones, and The Band. My score descended into danger-ously low territory, while Peter's musical choices became more challenging ... and still I chipped away, hovering in the ten-point range. Every song was filled with photo-finish anxiety.

Then one day, in the car, "Operator" by Jim Croce started playing on the radio. I had seven points left. Peter felt sure this was something off the beaten path of standard rock and roll and offered up the whole bag of chips. "For seven points," said he, confidently.

Now, when I was growing up, my mother used to listen to a radio station that played music mothers liked to listen to, and one artist who showed up time and again was Jim Croce. Not too fast, not too slow, with a little boyish cheekiness thrown in for good measure. I knew many of his songs: "Bad, Bad Leroy Brown", "Time in a Bottle", "You Don't Mess Around with Jim", and of course, my favourite: "Operator".

Holy shit! This was it! As a competitor, I wanted to win. But as a 24-year-old, did I want to be engaged? My heart was beating, my brain spinning with the consequences of my answer.

"Win the game! Win the game!" said my ego.

"Be careful," said my brain.

"What about me?" questioned my heart.

The clock was ticking. Then, as coyly as the miller's daughter must have asked, "Is your name Rumpelstiltskin?" I asked, "Is it Jim Croce?"

Game, set, match ... me!

Peter didn't propose then and there, probably because he couldn't believe what had just transpired but within a month we were engaged. I guess we both won because that was twenty-two years ago. Thank-you, Mom and Jim Croce.

When Peter and I got married, less than a year after the proposal, neither of us wanted too much to do with the planning of the wedding. I am not one of those girls who kept a binder of wedding paraphernalia, with pretty much every detail planned well before I even met my groom. If it were only up to me, we would be on a beach, down the street from my house, in flip-flops, with some food trucks waiting to serve tasty tacos and pulled-pork sandwiches.

More importantly, however, was the overwhelming knowledge that my mother was gravely ill. I half-heartedly shopped for a wedding dress with my sisters, and we moved the wedding date up by seven months so that she could attend, but she never made it. Three months before the event, she passed away, and we considered postponing the wedding. We were all so numb, retreating in and out of grief to sporadically face the real world—the one without our mother. After a dark while, we concluded that perhaps a party was just what our family needed, and we put the plan back in motion.

Luckily (there's that word again), my mother-in-law, Anne, who had four sons and no opportunity to take on the auspicious role of mother-of-the-bride, very graciously, respectfully, and with my best wishes, did just that. She became a rock star of a wedding planner.

While my awesome mother-in-law handled the nitty-gritty details of the wedding, there was one thing about which Peter and I were concerned: the music. It was also our only skirmish (unless you count the minor stress that arose when the bride was ready to walk down the aisle, and the groom called to say that he was on the 16th hole but promised to be there on time). Had Peter not used his one wedding veto, we would have had Kermit the Frog sing our first song of the evening. In my opinion, "Rainbow Connection" from The Green Album was obviously perfect for us.

Paul Williams, one of the co-writers of the song, said that "...it's about being on a spiritual path, examining life and the meaning of life... It's a metaphor for the call to adventure, you know? That voice is something inside of us that says you can do anything. There's a great mysterious world out there, let's go see it."

Who wouldn't want to get married to a song with a message like that? Peter, that's who. "Harvest Moon" by Neil Young was to be "our song". (Ironically, we found out at the wedding that the DJ didn't have "Harvest Moon" in his repertoire, so we used Cat Stevens' "Father and Son", which wasn't nearly as meaningful as Kermit's ballad. I suppose it was all part of life's rich plan.

15.

Teach Your Children Well

Once again, the universe is answering me. Just as the pinch of our budget is tightening even more, I get an email from the parent of a student I used to teach. She has heard I am off for the year and wants to know if I can tutor her two kids. I am open for business. It would only be for a couple of hours a week, around dinner time, so I could still get my kids from school and to programs, and it wouldn't interfere with ME adventures. Her kids are eight and eleven, they are sweet, I enjoy working with them, and feel like I am contributing to the finances again, even if it is minimally.

This is so different than working with my own kids, who sometimes abuse me for my input. They ask for help, I try to give it to them, and then they get impatient with me because "That's not how my teacher does it."

So, I say, "Fine, see if you can get your teacher to help you. Good luck with that."

Their class sizes are huge, and several kids require a lot of the teacher's attention. Eventually, they ask me to come back and help again, and I hold firm until they beg out of frustration. It's not a fun cat-and-mouse game that we play some nights, and I wish it were easier to help them, but I think most parents find it hard to teach/coach their own kids. In their eyes, we know nothing and aren't any good at anything, despite the number of times we tell them otherwise. Cole and I had this conversation the other day:

Cole: Can you help me with my book report? It's taking too long.

Me: Sure.

Cole: I have to do a chapter summary for each chapter.

Me: Okay, let's see what you've got. Hmmm, your summaries are pretty long. You haven't left out much. Perhaps you could try including just a few of the important parts and leave all those small details out.

Cole: No, my teacher says we need to tell about each chapter. She'll think I didn't read it if I leave stuff out.

Me: I doubt she'll think that. Leaving stuff out is what a summary is. It makes the reader more intrigued and want to know more. Then they might want to read the same book.

Cole: My teacher will get mad at me. Forget it. I can do it.

* One hour, one chapter, and two "summary" pages later *
Cole (meekly): So, how do I know which stuff to leave out?

16.

Taking Care of Business

For the first time since I've been off work, I had to defend myself against the question every SAHM loathes: "So, what is it that you do all day?"

Yes, this comes from a suit-and-heels friend (of the office-cubical variety) with no kids and no pets, who is too busy riding the corporate wheel to appreciate how someone like me can fill a day when I don't actually work. I appreciate the job she does and the stress it carries, and I know that it is something I would never want to do. She takes care of business and then takes care of herself. But I don't think she has any idea what it must be like for people who have dependents depending on them. Now, I have one job (as the CEO of Bedard Inc.), a very complex and demanding position with amazing (emotional) benefits but, of course, located deep in the not-for-profit sector.

I couldn't work in her environment, with deadlines, and face time, and rude, pushy people ready to stab her in the back if she doesn't stay on her game. She leaves home early and comes home late, exhausted and ready for bed so she can start all over again the next day. I don't have to ask her what she does all day because I kind of know, so I suppose my question to her might be, What makes you want to do that all day? And if she were on her toes, she could counter with the same question, because ... sure, I have deadlines and deal with rude, pushy people, and I work late, sometimes all night if there is a stomach flu going around, and I am sometimes so exhausted I can't function, and then there are times when I go slightly mad by the monotony of my days, and the white background noise, which is the sizzling sound of my brain frying inside my head. She does it for money, pride, respect, fulfillment, exhilaration, and I do it for precisely the same reasons—except for the money, fulfillment, respect, and exhilaration (Sometimes it's hard to feel exhilarated or fulfilled when you think about what you've accomplished in a day and it adds up to three loads of laundry, five hot-dog lunch entrees, and twenty-five other things that you can't remember, but which were very necessary). At the end of the day, we should both take a deep breath and thank our lucky stars that we are fortunate enough to be able to choose what we do because not everyone does.

17.

Neighbourhood Dawgma

As I walk the neighbourhood, I am stunned by the number of dogs around and by the number of small dogs in particular. In fact, I have a theory about small dogs, which will offend everyone who owns a small dog, so if you have one, skip this part. It doesn't mean anything. It's just a theory, and it is based on only my own observations with no hard data to back it up. Okay, here it is:

The owners of small dogs fall into three categories and one sub-category:

1. Women (who could be part of a couple) who do not have kids (or whose kids have grown up) and have adopted a small dog to fill a void. A small dog gives them a living thing that they can nurture, worry about, talk to, dress up, groom, and cuddle. These dogs put them into a community of other dog owners with whom they can share doggie notes, concerns, and grooming adventures—not at all unlike moms in the school playground. It is a natural conversation starter with any stranger who also has a dog, which creates an immediate bond.

2. Moms, whose kids are a little older, around 6 years and older, who have become more self-sufficient. Their purpose to

be available for their kids is dwindling slightly, and they also feel a void. A dog forces them to get out and walk every day, and even though they all say that the dog is *for the kids*, because *the kids* have been asking for one for a long time, and *the kids* are finally able to help care for a dog but, *the kids* are actually often indifferent to the dog after the honeymoon puppy phase. Now that the kids' needs are fewer, the dog also becomes the new built-in excuse to refuse invitations because "I have to leave early to let the dog out." Or "I can't come because I can't leave the dog alone for that long." We call this group, "stay-at-home-dog-moms" or SAHDMs, which is a little tricky to pronounce.

3. Senior women, who have retired several years before, and have time on their hands and need the company and unconditional love an animal brings. Their husbands have passed on or have developed selective hearing, and the small dog fills the emptiness as it requires hours of attention daily. It doesn't talk back, or feign interest, or say it's going to pick up tomato juice on the way home and then forget.

4. Puppy Whipped. This is a fourth, unofficial sub-category, but it's what I call grown men on the street, walking or carrying a small dog. It just looks unnatural for a big, burly guy to be holding such a delicate, vulnerable creature unless he's on his way to a BBQ and the butcher shop is closed! My theory is that the size of the dog has a direct and inverse relationship to the amount the man was consulted regarding the kind of dog to purchase. The larger the dog, the more input he had over the decision. If a man has a tiny (teacup) dog, you can bet your kibble bowl he didn't see it coming because either he was reading the sports section during the dog-selection conversation or because he wears the panties in the family. This is not to say the dog doesn't grow on him or that he doesn't love it, but he is embarrassed to acknowledge that this tiny ball of fluff

and pink bows is a symbol of his masculinity and that he would much prefer to be showing off his Great Dane.

Why target a small dog and not just any dog? Small dogs are naturally better suited to smaller, city dwellings, but they are also needier. The kinds of dogs I'm talking about are small enough to throw thirty-five yards for a touchdown—smaller than a breadbox. They are generally higher maintenance because they can be brought just about everywhere, and they are brought just about everywhere. They are on laps, on planes, in restaurants, in purses, even in strollers and child-carriers these days. They need grooming and wear little costumes, along with expensive little hairdos with bows, which are symbols of the hold they have over their owners. A lot of things bother me about the little princesses but perhaps the most grating thing about them is the high-pitched barking. Stop the barking. It's not cute, or adorable, or most of all, infrequent.

Anne, my mother-in-law, has a penchant for Cavalier King Charles Spaniels, which is on the cusp of being a small dog. The first one she had flown in from Ireland, where (apparently) the best ones are made. They had an affair like no other. That dog was loved by her like Romeo loved Juliet or like Jenny loved Oliver in A Love Story, and when little Kearny passed away, it was just as tragic.

When she recovered from the loss, my mother-in-law adopted another CKCS, except this time from a local breeder to cut costs. As it turns out, you get what you pay for, because this dog was possessed— severely, psychologically affected. Sometimes she barked at and chased invisible things floating in the air, and other times, she stared off into space, catatonic, for extended periods of time. She was unpredictable and seemed highly anxious. There was talk of an exorcism, but eventually, the dog had to be given away, and my mother-in-law was at a loss again.

After she had recovered from that second grieving period, CKCS number three, Scooter, arrived on a direct flight from Ireland, where the best ones are made. Scooter was the saviour and came from the same high-end breeder from whence Kearney came, so we knew he'd be a keeper. But Scooter had a small flaw: He barked and jumped up on people when they arrived at the front door. Barking is barely tolerated by my mother-in-law, but jumping up is just plain unacceptable. A call was made to a trainer.

The trainer explained over the phone that her methods were direct and unorthodox, but effective and that she had time to see Scooter the next day. At the arranged time, the trainer rang the doorbell, and right on cue, Scooter barked and ran to the door, elated at the prospect of greeting a visitor. As the trainer entered, Scooter excitedly tried to leap up on her, at which point the trainer booted little unsuspecting Scooter clear into next year. He skidded across the hardwoods and into the back of the couch in the next room. Shock and awe. "That'll be 250 dollars please." Rest assured, it worked. Scooter still jumps up on anyone who comes to the door, but she never went near that trainer again.

18.

Feeling Hot, Hot, Hot

The inaugural field trip for ME takes off in late October and seems primed for a successful landing. We are eight ladies, sweating, stretching, and bathing in the rainforest heat of Japanese hot Pilates. We lay quietly on the hot rocks for the first half an hour, acclimatizing and tiptoeing out occasionally to refill our water bottles. By the time our instructor arrives, we are warm and supple and ready to fold our bodies into whatever shape is required.

We realize quickly that all the heat in Hades won't be enough to allow us to bend the way we want to. It is an excellent exercise in paying attention to our bodies as one muscle after another screams to be noticed during various stretches and poses. I like this more than the hot yoga I experienced before, mostly because the room is a small rectangle with numbered spaces around the walls. No one is directly in front of or behind anyone else. Each participant chooses one of the limited areas, which means there is no overcrowding. And most of all, no one has to look at the furry, Speedo-wearing, sweat-spraying participant two feet in front of her. It is also very gentle. No balancing on one-foot poses that only showcase my lack of balance, during which I would typically grab onto a neighbour for support, sending her falling over as the first in a line of sweaty Dominos.

At one point, our angel-voiced instructor says, "Don't push yourself in this pose. You have your whole life to learn it." That is a very accommodating timeline indeed, and I wish that more tasks could have that kind of leeway—like cleaning the grout around my windows. "I will clean that gunk out within my lifetime" sounds reasonable. By the end of the hour and a half, we are detoxified, stiff, and tired (but energized) by the experience. Another interesting observation is that, when we all exit the building, each of us pulls out our cell phones only to find no calls. We had made ourselves unavailable for almost two hours, and no one hunted us down; no one expected anything of us. We proved it was possible.

After a quick beverage, we are back home before noon with the whole afternoon to get back to routines. Mission accomplished. I think the success of this trip has motivated people to think about coordinating other outings. By the end of the day, the months of November and April have been adopted, with lots of talk bubbling about other endeavours. I know December will be a challenge, but perhaps an event that involves something Christmas-y might fly. I think that, with a little management and a little motivation, this can really work.

19.

Nostrils Up

know my little sister, Clare, would have liked yesterday's Pilates trip and the whole ME thing altogether, especially since (although my mother was one source of inspiration) the club was created with her in mind. She loved adventure more than anyone I know. She travelled, and lived abroad, and had many friends all over the world. She always regaled us with crazy stories from her time away, like a favourite, quirky, old uncle, who visits every now and then and tells tales you were never quite sure you believed but loved listening to anyway.

In 2006, Clare was 32 and eight-months pregnant when she found a lump in her breast. It turned out to be a very aggressive cancer, fuelled by the enormous amounts of estrogen produced during her pregnancy. In a heartbeat, joy turned to dread. Instead of bathing in her newborn's very existence, Clare spent most of that first year of motherhood in chemotherapy or recovering from surgery after having one breast, then the other, removed. Throughout all the hospital procedures, each time she was given a break in her appointment schedule, despite feeling sick, she and her wonderful husband, Adam, were off travelling again, making up for lost time and introducing their young son, Nathan, to the world.

Two years after her original diagnosis, Clare paid, out-of-pocket, for a private PET scan. Even though her doctor gave her a clean bill of health, she had a bad feeling in her gut, and she knew there was technology that provided more detailed imaging than the standard health care the province provided. Her premonition was correct. The cancer had spread to her liver, lungs, and bones. I will never forget that phone call from the hospital, picking up the receiver, and hearing uncontrollable sobbing. "I'm dying," was all she could say through her tears.

As a quick aside, not many people can say that their employer is one of their favourite people, but I feel blessed to be one of them. I had only just been hired to teach by Steve, the former headmaster at my current school, when I sent him an email regarding my sister's condition because I couldn't say the words out loud. He is one of the most empathetic people I know (and one of the funniest), so when I walked into his office shortly after sending the email, without saying a word, he hugged me, and then cried with me until we caught our breath and he offered his full support in whatever I needed. I use an expression of his often, in trying times, because it gives me hope and makes me smile to think of him: "Keep your nostrils up, Bedard. When you feel the water rising, nostrils up."

Clare's ability to bounce back from bad news and to keep her sense of humour was astounding. The day after her heartbreaking update, we found ourselves standing in line at Starbucks. When she heard the barista ask for her order, she turned to address him but was quickly cut-off because he was actually addressing the customer standing in front of Clare. Clare turned to me and said, with a shrug, "I guess I'm kind of in a hurry now."

And it was like that for the next four years. Through the treatments, the hope, the despair, and every emotion in between, she handled it all with grace, humour, and courage. She made it okay to talk about her disease and comforted those who struggled to understand why it had chosen her. She studied options and kept abreast of experimental treatments for which she might qualify, and when she sat with doctors, she was so knowledgeable it was difficult to tell who was the doctor and who was the patient. She became the poster child for young women with breast cancer, appearing in a documentary on the subject called, I Don't Have Time for This, and raising money and awareness for the disease, which is no longer considered an older woman's illness.

Like my mother, she prayed for four good years so that she would live to walk her son to school. And like my mother, her prayer was answered. She walked Nathan to school in September, four years after her condemning diagnosis, but by November, she was too weak to make the journey. She got her four years but fought hard to fill every single day.

She was admitted into the hospital on Christmas Eve. My sister Anne and I were with her in the hospital a few weeks later, camping out for the night, when her breathing became rapid. We called for a nurse, who told us that the end was near. We held her hands, watched, and waited. Then she suddenly opened her eyes wide, after having been sedated for days, which shook us. She was still fighting to stay alive, her body swollen from steroids and yellow from the jaundice brought on by a failing liver. I remembered what my brother had said at the end of my mother's life. Sometimes they need to hear it. I told her, "It's okay to go."

"We love you," said Anne.

Her eyes closed again, and a moment later, she stopped breathing. Our sister was gone. Our family was shrinking. My heart was missing another piece.

Nostrils up, Bedard.

20.

Which House is Our House?

Even though the community in which I grew up was just fifteen minutes from the heart of downtown Toronto, it was still small enough that I knew everyone on my street. I could walk just about anywhere I needed to go, and there was plenty of space in the parks, on the boardwalk, and on the bike paths.

The Beach (or The Beaches) is a waterfront community, complete with boardwalks, bike paths, parks, ravines, schools, beach volleyball, sailing, paddling, public swimming pools, an outdoor ice rink, a baseball diamond, and a main street filled with restaurants, bars, and boutiques. It's an awesome place and used to be one of the city's hidden gems. Not so anymore.

Even as I sit here writing, I hear the constant sounds of construction closing in around me. The whirring and screeching of the saws are slicing pieces of my sanity away. There are developments along the main street, as condos take the place of old homes and stores, and parking has become a nightmare. At dusk, the skyline is spattered with sleeping cranes, like a cemetery of leaning crosses, commemorating the death of an old building and the birth of a taller, more sparkly one. Our secret had been discovered.

My in-laws don't like to visit because they can't find parking anywhere, and I get it. The parking-enforcement officers are kept busy, lurking in alleys, and hiding in sewers, waiting for the forgetful or the risk-taker to leave a car unattended or un-paid for, even for a moment. I went into a pizza shop to pick up a pie the other day, was gone for no more than ninety seconds, and was greeted by a $30 ticket on my dash with no officer in sight. Even more frustrating is the fact that the tickets are now made of a material you can't even rip up out of frustration. You can throw it on the ground and jump up and down on it all day long, but that just makes it look dirty and you look insane.

Our neighbourhood is known to be pedestrian-friendly, but with the increased traffic and the road rage during rush hour, it's feeling more dangerous than inviting. It's not enough that there is now a streetlight and a crossing guard at the main inter-section by the school. Drivers are mowing down kids like pins in a bowling alley. They run yellow lights, drive up on the curb on corners, and cut off cyclists who bang on their windows and swear like the Italian Mafia. Our walk to school is an assault on us in so many ways.

When my sister Clare announced she was sick, we were at a point where we were having a hard time affording life in Toronto, and with the mounting danger on the streets, it seemed obvious that we should check out of the city. So, we bought a house we could afford near Clare, in a newish cookie-cutter development in the suburbs, complete with a variety of plazas and malls and big-box shopping. Plazas, and malls, and big box! Oh my! My kids were young enough that they couldn't recognize our house on our street because they all looked the same. On the way home from our daily outings, the younger two (who were not yet in school) and I would play a game called

Which House is Our House? We'd walk down our street, and the boys would point to each house, asking, "Is this our house?"

"No."

"Is this our house?"

"No."

"Is this our house?"

"No."

"Is this our house?"

"Yes! Hold on ... sorry, no."

One day, the kids and I went out to play in a local parkette and have a picnic. We were used to living by a big lake with large parks and towering trees that kept us cool, which seems ironic given that we're considered city folk, but this suburb was desert-hot, dry, and dead. We went from parkette to parkette in search of a tree big enough to give us enough shade in which to spread out our picnic blanket. In the end, we gave up, found our house, spread our blanket in our air-conditioned living room, and turned on the television.

That our boys didn't play hockey didn't help our chances of survival in the suburbs. Not playing hockey was a conversation ender, a relationship killer, a loser label. Add the fact that our eldest son did gymnastics, and you might as well tar and feather us on the spot. We immediately came to the conclusion that we had very little in common with most everyone.

While we lived in our cookie-cutter house for those eleven months, I was interviewed by the local television station as "The Person on the Street" no fewer than four times, because there were no other people on the street. Nobody walked anywhere. It was deserted except for those in the mall parking lots, searching for their cars.

Each time I was accosted by the same news journalist, asking my opinion on some current local issue: the winter weather, about which I was ruthless; the protected moraine area, about which I knew little; the summer aridity, about which I was ruthless. The clincher came when the news was doing a story on what appeared to be a mass exodus from city to suburb. The question was simple: "Why do you think people are swarming to the burbs?"

Well, I had ruthless opinions about this topic, no filter, and was quick to say, "Well, obviously, it's absolutely a financial decision."

The obvious subtext being, why would anyone live here if they could afford to live anywhere else? The next morning our real-estate agent called.

"I saw you on the news again last night. Are you moving?"

"Yes, I think so."

In fairness to the suburbs, they have a lot to offer, and people who choose to live there are lovely and happy. We know a lot of those people. They have bigger, more beautiful homes, lots of space, excellent facilities, and tons of programs for kids. This is definitely an "It's not you, it's me" kind of break-up. So, if you are a suburbanite, you can hate me for being a crazy, urban snob, or pity me for being incapable of adapting to affordable living.

Since Clare had been given a clean bill of health at the end of eleven months, we came crawling back to the city, bought a fixer-upper that we couldn't afford, and therefore couldn't afford to fix up. The floors were so crooked that the kids fell off their chairs regularly, visitors got vertigo, and all the toy cars, marbles, and crayons ended up at one side of the house. After five years of living there, we brought in a very experienced carpenter to give us an estimate on fixing the floors, without actually gutting the entire house. He was a tough, old, weathered Italian, who looked like he could build a whole house without the use of a tool. He walked up and down the halls and up and down the stairs. He measured and calculated in his head, and a few times he started to suggest something: "Maybe you could ... nah, that won't work." Finally, he came upon a solution. In his very thick, Italian accent, his advice to us was as follows: "I know what you should do. Run. Run very far and very fast."

And we did just that. Amazingly, the crooked house had appreciated over the years. We renovated what we could to make it more presentable, had an open house, and within three hours had an above-asking offer. The day the house closed, we watched some men in a truck pull up in front of our poor, little house and begin to gut it top to bottom. Cole was the most affected. It was the first house he could remember living in, which made him sentimental, even though we moved to a nicer rental, just a block away. "What the beep are they doing to our house? Why the beep can't we still live there?"

Nowadays, buying a home in our fair city is anything but fair. Tiny homes are selling for a million dollars, after which they are levelled, gutted, or have additions built. Our rental is a cozy house, and as serendipity would have it, is right up the street from my childhood home. It's only steps away from everything we need: Starbucks, the bakery, the school, the beach, the tennis courts, and the park. We even have a Ping-Pong table in the basement. It's almost perfect. With a family of five, one bathroom is awkward, especially when we arrive home from a long car ride and go swarming upstairs toward it like it's a Best Buy Black Friday opening. And we can't fit even a small trampoline in the backyard, much to Tanner's chagrin. We are finding that the city is closing in on us. Even though my goal this year is to reconnect with my community, I am feeling like my community is challenging my loyalty.

21.

Nature Calls

About ten years ago, I paid $9.99 for a CD to help me get to sleep, which had nothing on it but the sound of waves rolling on to the shore. I lay down one evening and switched it on for the first time. The introduction was soothing, offering the gentle, consistent lapping of water and whispering of wind. It was the white noise sound of therapy, quieting and detoxifying my brain. But then, just as I was drifting off, almost like some kind of bizarre joke, the wind picked up and the ripple of the water turned into a crashing cacophony of nature, as thunder and lightning slowly permeated the audio canvas, and a storm moved through my head. Any peace that had settled into my mind went sprinting out in search of a raincoat and boots. The next sound was the crack of that CD hitting the inside of the garbage can.

And now I sit in front of similar waves, except they are real. Somehow, last year, we bought a little cottage on a Lake Erie beach, less than two hours from Toronto. At the end of a dead-end road, surrounded by modest summer retreats, we come here to regroup and reconnect and be quiet, although at the moment I'm outside writing, wearing my hat and coat, laptop on my lap, to avoid the wrestling match that's going on inside.

It's only our second year here. We rent it out for all but two weeks of the summer, to help pay for it, and use it the rest of the time. It's one of the few winterized cottages on our road, so we spend time up here in the off-season, and it has become our sanctuary from the city. Lake Erie is the shallowest and warmest of the great lakes, with water temperatures often above 80°F during the summer. The kids play in the lake for hours without all the usual high-end toys. We have no motorized watercraft, and I'm not sure we would have them even if we could afford them. The previous owners left us a canoe and a kayak, rubber rafts, and floaty toys. We need only to throw a tennis ball or a Frisbee into the water with the boys, and they're good to go for hours.

As I look out from our back deck, stretching to my right is a kilometre of empty, open beach where we play football, rugby, and ultimate Frisbee, or just walk and breathe the fresh air. It's a very Kennedy-esque kind of scene, on a much smaller scale, with less alcohol and fewer Secret Service. To the left are cottages that have been passed down through generations, filled with friendly neighbours.

We are so incredibly fortunate and grateful to be able to call this place home (away from home). We've named it "R.S. Cape." Get it? Our Escape? The people from whom we bought it were lovely and took great care of the place. They lived here year-round, and so (unlike most seasonal cottages) everything was fixed and updated. And like in many cottage sales, the furniture was included, which was of good quality and comfortable. When the deal closed, we raced up to spend the first weekend, a long weekend, and brought some friends with us to explore.

On arrival, we found that the previous owners had left more than just the furniture. The beds were made for us. There were clean towels in a basket ready for the beach. There was a bottle of wine for Peter and me on the counter and Freezies for the kids in the freezer. Beautiful dishes, glasses, and cookware filled every cupboard. Rummaging through the place was like Christmas for me ... only better. In the basement were all kinds of gardening and building tools, which Peter would have to learn to use. His instrument of choice is a normally a roll of duct tape, but he was inspired by the buffet of wrenches, hammers, and screwdrivers, and looked keen to find something to fix, which caused the rest of us great concern.

Our two youngest love the freedom they're allowed when we're at R.S. Cape. They jump out of the car and race down to the beach, cartwheeling, ball-throwing, and tackling each other on the sand. I never thought we'd be cottage people. I always thought we wouldn't want to be tied down to one place and feel obligated to spend our vacation time there instead of travelling, but as long as we can keep renting it out, we can still voyage to other lands now and then.

Having said that, every time we pack up to head back to the city, I can see why people don't want to return from their cottage at the end of a week or a summer. The thought of it makes it hard to breathe, just imagining the pollution seeping into our lungs—not to mention the crowds, the traffic, the construction ... ugh. This is definitely not a case of absence makes the heart grow fonder, and again, it makes me question the merits of the city. On the other hand, the closest Starbucks to the cottage is one hour away. That's a long way to go for a cup of tea.

22.

Dancing to a Different Drummer

Scream is the name of the fitness class I've signed up for, and it makes Boot Camp look like circle time at the Mommy and Me Play Group. How many lunges, squats, rows, and push-ups can one do in an hour? For most, it's a lot more than I can. I've never stopped to rest so many times in one class. My muscles are screaming, thus the name of the class. My legs are not fully functioning when I leave the room, and I have to concentrate on picking one foot up off the floor then the other to simulate walking, as my muscles defy the synapses sent from my brain. The stairs to the locker seem unusually steep, and I move slowly, not knowing if, should I choose to shower, I would be able to get out again. Would someone eventually find me? Should I bring snacks?

The Zumba class I took last week didn't go so well either. Spending an hour confused, unsteady, and two steps behind the rest of the class wasn't the fun I imagined it would be. It reminded me of the tour of Alcatraz I took with Peter and his brother Michael, just after we were married. We had the audio tour, so all three of us put our headphones on and pushed the start button at the same time so that we could follow the tour together. A few minutes in, they began roving off in a different direction and observing things that my recorded guide was not asking me to observe. They were gawking at various parts of prisoner cells, rattling bars, nodding in unison, and enjoying their tour immensely, while I struggled to keep up, fast-forwarding, rewinding, pausing my tape, and waiting. I watched them, baffled, and wondered what they were hearing that I was not. It was so frustrating, and I was about to go back to the entrance to find out if I had somehow received the wrong tape when I saw them laughing hysterically and realized they were improvising their whole tour just to confuse me.

This is Zumba for me, except there is no apparent conspiracy. I really am just listening to a different tape in my head and dancing to a different drummer, who isn't very good apparently. Eventually, I discretely shuffled to the back of the room and danced spastically freestyle until the end of the class. Clint didn't even come inside for this one, he was so sure it would be a dud. I haven't been spending enough time on my fitness lately, so next week I'm planning a sneak attack on my body, a full-on ambush on my unsuspecting muscles.

"Good luck with that," whispers my body.

"Go ahead. Make my day," growls Clint.

23.

Get Off the Dough, Man!

Okay, so I am all over this school volunteering thing. I am lucky to be able to attend/help out with all the things going on at the kids' school. I'm doing so much shuttling of kids and even their parents to games and races that I may have to have my van painted school-bus yellow. Tanner and Cole are playing on the rugby and volleyball teams, and Tanner is running in the city finals of cross-country, all of which have commitments this week, not to mention regular soccer and tennis, and Satchel's commitments.

I often have a small army of kids coming over for lunch, and I have no problem asking for help on the reciprocal side. This is so different from last year, where I felt like the odd man out, stressed about how the kids were going to get here and there, and always disappointed at having to miss their events.

There is a group of women who are consistently involved in volunteering. They make the classrooms more manageable by helping out; they make field trips easier by supervising, and let's talk about fundraising! I think there must be money laundering or evidence of a Ponzi scheme buried deep in the back of the Parent/School Association filing cabinet.

My personal favourite is the cookie-dough fundraiser. This stuff is like crack—buckets of addictive, all-natural, nut-free dough that we're supposed to bake, but which often never sees the inside of the oven. I empty boxes of containers and help sort and distribute around five hundred of them for the school with my friend, Stella, who is one of the youngest participants in our ME adventures. Stella is happiest inside the hot-yoga studio and rarely misses a day. No wonder she's so calm and cool outside the studio.

Stella and I sort sugary dough that spans across the gym floor for parent pick-up, and at the end of the day, I take home the order for myself and for the teachers at my own school, who have come to depend on the dough for the holidays. I back the van up at my school gates with upwards of forty buckets of swirled butter and heaven and hand them out to my peers like some kind of slick dealer. Teachers casually walk up to the minivan, slip me some cash, and retreat into the shadows with their stash. "Be careful," I warn them. "It's a strong batch." But someone always goes too far, and after an indulgent weekend, comes back with all the markings of an addict who has fallen off the wagon: shaky hands, lack of focus, paranoia, tighter pants, chocolate chips stained across a sweatshirt that hasn't been changed in days, topped with a nest of raisins in their greasy hair. Inevitably, they call me a few days later trying to get another fix, but I'm out of product and can't be an enabler even if I wanted to be. Seek help. Call your sponsor. Get off the dough, man.

There is also the spring-flower fundraiser, where (last year) I bought four large trays of Impatiens, which lived up to their (almost) name. I watched them die quickly on the back porch when I couldn't find time to locate the garden beneath the weeds in my backyard, let alone plant something in it.

My last encounter with gardening ended in what is now referred to as The Extreme Gardening Incident. The weeds covering our entire front lawn had grown to between two and four feet, and we were (not surprisingly) the embarrassment of the street. The constant fertilization of the area was compliments of the generous parade of dogs, which passed by daily and left substantial contributions on our "lawn" and even on the concrete walkway. I've tried several sting operations but have yet to catch the offending parties.

So, I spent weeks digging up the entire yard, then lined it with a weed-proof tarp, planted an array of hearty, low-maintenance flowers and plants, covered it with soil, and added rocks collected from the beach to feign landscaping. I placed the last stone in my masterpiece and stood in the middle, admiring my efforts, and then jumped backward out of the grandeur to avoid stepping on the foliage, landing on a rogue rock and badly twisting my ankle. It was embarrassing to tell people that I had a cast on my leg from a gardening mishap and not a parachute landing gone awry.

I have decided that my thumbs will never be green, because (indeed) they are barely opposable, and so flowers were added to that group of dependents I avoid (like our cats) because they require even minimal amounts of attention for survival.

24.
Adult Toys and Charity Work

A November ME event has been planned, and invitations have been sent. This is a really cool idea from Stephanie, who, like Stella, is one of the hipper, younger members of the group. Here's how hip Stephanie is: A few months ago, she hosted a sex-toy party for some of the more openly declared avant-garde of the neighbourhood. This was like any other home product party, except instead of the Avon Lady displaying lipsticks and Christmas ornaments, we had Tracy passing around an array of colourful products with names like The Hot Rod Enhancer or The Ultimate Indulgence.

I showed up at the sex-toy party straight from working late, drank three or four glasses of wine on an empty stomach, and wound up offering what I thought was witty commentary on each mysterious item that was passed around the group. After the presentation, catalogues and order forms were passed around, and lewd, confessional conversations filled the rest of the night.

The morning after, I found a receipt on my bureau. What? Over $500 on sex toys? Yup, that was my Visa number and my signature proudly sprawled across the bottom of the page.

Later on, slumped under my desk at school at recess, clutching my receipt in one hand and a phone in the other, I sheepishly whispered to the woman from the sex-toy store, "I'm sorry..."

Because I am a good Canadian, I had to start the conversation off with, "I'm sorry", as in, "I'm sorry for driving so close in front of you that you had to rear-end me." Anyway...

"I'm sorry," I whisper, "but I was at a product party last night and got a little, uh, over-enthusiastic. I'm going to have to return the Plush Bendy and the Spiral Rabbit, but I'll keep the Seduction Soy Candle."

Peter, on hearing the story, said only, "Well, if you're going to overspend on something, I'd rather it be sex toys than shoes."

Back to Stephanie's invitation for her November ME event. She found a Habitat for Humanity, Half-Day-Build event, where instead of building homes for humans, we would prepare for a different kind of lodging, creating kits for a gingerbread-house building-and-decorating holiday fundraiser activity. What a great way to get into the Christmas spirit and to help out the community at the same time. In hindsight, perhaps I should have kept that Plush Bendy and offered it as a tree ornament to Stephanie to celebrate her dual role as dominatrix/Christmas Elf.

The only problem is that there are minimal spots—only seven during the school day when many of us are free. And seven have already signed up. I hadn't thought that there might be events where there would be more of us than could be accommodated. I hadn't considered, as I invited women (willy-nilly) to join our big adventure, that some might be disappointed at being turned down from an event, and possibly be deterred from participating in another event.

This isn't as easy as I thought it would be. I thought that by having a different person take on each month, I could sit back and watch this tree take root, but like any new enterprise, it takes nurturing and managing. I can only encourage these women, and instill confidence, by lettting them know how wonderful they are and how appreciative I am that they want to take a seat on this crazy ride and occasionally take a turn driving the bus.

25.

It's All About ME

Peter and I went to the memorial service for a fallen friend twice this month: once on the day of the service and once a week before because I got the date mixed up. One of my major weaknesses is my lack of attention to detail. I forget dates altogether or arrive way too early, but most often I'm late—late for surprise parties, work, appointments, and even childbirth.

It's not that I love the thrill of living on the edge of on-time, or that I don't respect timelines or other people's time. It's just that I hate waiting unnecessarily, so I figure out where I have to be and when, and work backward from there, always assuming that nothing will go wrong along the way—no traffic, accidents, construction, bad weather, bathroom stops, or flat tires. I can't even count how many flights I missed until I met Peter, who likes to arrive at the airport four to six hours in advance of takeoff.

Peter is, by now, so used to my screw-ups that he doesn't often get overly irritated or even surprised when I make a tactical error. When we arrived at our friend's "first" memorial service, we noticed there weren't a lot of cars in the parking lot. More and more often, Peter doesn't even bother to park the car when we show up at an event. He just drives me to the front door so that I can hop in and see if we are indeed at the right place, at the right time, on the right day. This is one area in which we are entirely opposite; he is apologetically early, while I am notoriously late.

And so, one week later, we're at the real memorial service for our friend, who died of brain cancer at 47-years old. The parallels of her life with my sister's are too obvious: their prolific travels, their loyal friends, and the courage and grace they showed throughout their illness in the face of death at such a young age. The ten speakers are wonderful, all of them poignant, funny, and heartbroken at having to say goodbye. I stand quietly at the back of the crowded room, empathizing with the family as they say their farewells.

I will never forget Clare's service. There were close to a thousand people in attendance, spilling out of the church nave and into the hallways and surrounding rooms, where loudspeakers transmitted the voices of the orators inside. We were only three eulogists: her best friend, Alison, her husband, Adam, and me. Alison spoke first and talked about growing up with Clare. They were born a few months apart and grew up only a few feet apart as neighbours. Our mothers were close friends, and the two girls became inseparable and remained so throughout their lives.

Adam's eulogy was short and filled with heartache and humour. He needed no script. The words just poured out of him like God speaking passionately and eloquently through an evangelist at the pulpit. He was mesmerizing.

I had been writing her eulogy for the long years she was ill, both in my head and in my journal, and it took many incarnations for it to end up where it did. Here is a small piece, which is integral to this book:

But I was still her sister, and like any respectable older sister, I felt obligated to keep her in line—keep her humble. There is always

93

a time in every young person's life when she feels like she's the center of the universe, and there were times when Clare would get a little self-involved. I remember on one occasion I had to say, "It's not always about you, Clare. The world doesn't always revolve around you." Clare was so sensitive and really took it to heart because soon after that, we were on the phone one evening and after ten or fifteen minutes, we said goodbye and hung up. A moment later, the phone rang; it was Clare, somewhat frantic, saying, "I'm so sorry! How are you?" From this point on, it became a running joke that we tossed back and forth. Clare grew into an amazing person with whom to talk. She had a way of disarming people with her own vulnerability and wonderful, self-deprecating humour, which immediately put people at ease. She could listen and comment without judgment, and for a person of few years, she could offer sage advice. Regardless of the circumstance, we always went away from a conversation with Clare feeling lighter and better.

I think the thing I am going to miss most about Clare is her sense of humour. No matter how absurd, ironic, or tragic the situation, we always found a way to laugh. And her ability to laugh at herself was perhaps the best part of her humour. Many of you here today watched Clare carry the Olympic torch last year. She strode across the red carpet and climbed onto the stage. Throngs of people were cheering her. The MC was talking about all the wonderful things she had accomplished. She was waving to the masses with one hand and holding up the Olympic torch with the other. I was part of the audience, crushed against the front of the stage. Clare panned over the crowd, and eventually, our eyes met. She gave me her biggest and cheekiest smile and mouthed the words, "It's all about me!" I laughed and cried and blew her a kiss. I was so proud of her on that day because I knew she was really struggling on the inside, yet she looked like she could have competed in those Olympics.

Sometimes, making it all about you doesn't have to make you feel guilty or selfish. Making time for yourself makes you feel better, and when you feel better, you are better. And while this is an extreme example, waiting for illness, or worse, your funeral, for permission to be the center of the universe is too late. I don't want to be a martyr. All I want to do is to get excited and do some Japanese Hot Pilates. For just for a few hours, it's all about ME.

Clare was very good at making it all about her, and it's something that was laughable and admirable. She always did what she wanted to do and never made excuses for it. So, when it came time to tease her about it, she took it all in stride.

When Clare and Adam were married, Peter and I (and six-week-old Satchel) were Masters of Ceremonies at their reception. It was hard to be entertaining as we were severely sleep-deprived with our first child. Our formal wear was not red-carpet worthy—me in a breast-milk-stained dress, nursing a newborn between speaking responsibilities, and Peter with a boutonniere rose oozing spit up on his lapel. Somehow, on our way to the wedding, we composed a song about Clare and Adam. The lyrics are only a slight exaggeration; however, everyone knew Clare well enough to see how this part of her spontaneous character, which could be seen as inconsiderate, just made her that much more endearing and loveable. And the apparent nearness to the truth brought the house down and saw Adam mirthfully falling off his chair.

So, halfway through my eulogy, Peter joined me on the pulpit, a Fischer Price mini-keyboard in hand to find our first note, and we brought back that song, twelve-years later, which continued to out Clare as a free-spirited, female version of Peter Pan, who often had no consideration for the chaos she left in her wake whenever she chose to pack up and fly off on another adventure. As a subtext, we mocked her husband for continuing to love her and support her, despite being left to cover her tracks and finance her expeditions. If you've ever seen the movie The Princess Bride, you'll understand that Adam and Clare were the modern-day Wesley and Buttercup. No matter what Clare's desire, no matter how far-fetched, Adam's response was always an unconditional, "As you wish." Here is the song, with me singing the part of Clare and Peter singing the part of Adam, sung to the tune of "The Major-General's Song" from the Pirates of Penzance:

Clare: Oh, Adam dear
        My paper's due
        I fear that it may be too late.

Adam: I'll type it up
        And check your notes
        And make sure that you graduate

Clare: I drove you home
        In my dad's car
        And flipped it on the 401

Adam: I pulled you out
        And crossed four lanes
        And waited for some help to come

Clare: I got a call
        About a job
        Except it's in Malaysia

Adam: Good thing you have not
           Yet unpacked
           From your trip to Australia

Clare: We'll choose a dog
Adam: I'll clean and feed
           And pay for all the surgery

Clare: And teach him how to speak and sit
           And take him when he needs to...stroll.

Clare: Oh, Adam dear,
           Come right away
           The tax collector's at our door

Adam: I'll be right there
           As soon as I've cleaned up
           The flooded basement floor

Clare: Oh, Adam dear
           I have to get to work
           Up in Algonquin Park

Adam: No sweat, my sweet
           Eight-hours drive will get
           Me back just after dark

Clare: And by the way
           I have a job
           New Zealand's where I'll call my home

Adam: I'll stay back here
And work each day
To pay off all your student loans.

Clare and
Adam: These are the very reasons why
We know our love will never die
We thank you all for coming here
To celebrate among the dear.

At Clare's service, it was a total surprise to us that that this song, sung at her funeral, had the same effect as at her wedding, as the quiet solemnity of the attendees were brought to their knees by roars of laughter. We had to pause several times to wait for the chuckles to die down, and at the end of it all, we were stunned to receive a standing ovation. I'm sure that God in His humility never sought out a standing O, but I have to admit, it was very surreal standing in His house, feeling a bit like rock star. I almost felt like throwing myself into the first few pews to see if the mosh pit would accept me. I know Clare was watching and enjoying the laughter that was all about her.

The song worked, twice, because we all knew her so well, and those aspects of her hadn't changed in her 37 years. She had such a zest for life, and people loved to please her and encourage her because of the reaction they received, similar to watching a child open the gift you've given her and squeal with delight at its contents. She rarely sat still, and if you were game to climb aboard her magic carpet, you were welcome—as long as you were aware that this particular carpet was not equipped with brakes.

26.

It Only Looks Like I Was Shot in the Face

One of the perks of being on approved leave of absence is that, while I don't get paid, I do get to keep my health benefits. Because of my family's ominous medical history, two interesting things occur: first, I am rejected for life and critical illness insurance, and second, each year I am flagged for all kinds of potential health hazards and have to go to numerous check-ups while doctors look for signs of DNA doom.

Undoubtedly, every year after my mammogram, I am called back for another look because a doctor saw *something*, which turns out to be *nothing*, but it always makes me neurotic. Here's a little haiku I wrote in the waiting room after the first look. Maya Angelou, eat your heart out:

Mammogram
Lean, twist, pull, place, prod
Clamp, squish, gasp
Release, breathe, repeat

At the moment, I am living with what looks to be a giant zit on my face, which is really the remains of a liquid nitrogen treatment used to burn off a pre-cancerous spot. Pre-cancerous doesn't scare me anymore. I have one those spots removed every couple of years. Last year was different though. Last year, my dermatologist examined my face and told me he suspected a basil-cell carcinoma, once again, on my cheek. It shook me when he didn't use the "pre" word. He used the actual "C" word. I left the office with a similar zit on my face, that time, the residue of a biopsy.

Given my mother's fatal run-in with malignant melanoma, I quickly and responsibly went online to learn about what can happen to people with basil-cell carcinoma *in very rare cases*. The answer to that question, if you dig deep enough, is always "You could die." But in most cases, the worst scenario is that, if not treated within a reasonable time, it can lead to disfigurement.

Despite confirmation of said "C" word, my prognosis was good. The treatment involved applying a topical cream daily for six weeks that would basically burn away layers of afflicted skin, allowing the skin to repair itself once the treatment stopped. This was a far better option than having it surgically removed, and leaving a permanent scar ... or was it?

Over the course of six weeks, the hole on my face grew daily, like a flesh-eating disease, which was the technical behaviour of this cream, until I finally had to apply a large bandage over it, looking like I was covering up a gunshot wound. My students had mixed reactions to the horror show, but it was my special-education students, particularly the younger grade threes and fours, who were most greatly affected. Some of them had low-impulse control and difficulty interpreting social cues, so they rarely used any kind of verbal filter. They stared at it like it was a golden-toothed serpent sprouting from my cheek.

"What is that?" they asked.

"Why do you have it?"

"How long will it live there?"

"I just can't even look at you anymore!"

Many of them had short-term memory issues too, so we had to go through this same ordeal frequently. I adored all of my students, but as a core-French teacher, I had up to five classes a day stream in with a multitude of students staring, pointing, recoiling, and demanding an explanation or suggesting I take some time off so I wouldn't make them sick.

Everyone found it hard to look me in the eye when speaking to me. It was the third eye—the eye of a raging storm swirling on the right side of my face—that drew their unintentional attention, similar I suppose, to how men gaze downward when speaking to large-breasted women, except for the minor detail that my face made them want to wretch. People on the street took a second look, and I realized what it might be like, if only for a few months, to be afflicted by some kind of physical deformity.

Because this small continent was on my face, it couldn't be hidden and made me feel very self-conscious. As much as I wanted to call in sick each day as my condition worsened, I had to face it (pardon the pun) and live through the repercussions of spending too many days in the sun. At the end of it all, I consider myself very lucky. And I'm glad I rejected all those solicitations from the Ford Modeling Agency; otherwise I would have lost oodles of income those last few months. I'm totally kidding. It was actually Elite Models. I'm still kidding.

27.

Piano Man

Peter came home the other day with his tail between his legs. "I think I just bought a piano," said he. How one can be unsure if one has bought a piano is unclear, but his defence was thus: Our neighbour had had no luck trying to sell his piano through an ad in the local paper and seemed ready to give up. It sounded to Peter like he just wanted to unload it to a good home.

With this concrete assumption, Peter expressed interest in the piano, at which point, according to Peter's story, the neighbour pulled the "bait and switch" and said he would happily let Peter take it off his hands—for only $250.

Now, it's not just the money that we're lacking at this particular time. The five of us live in approximately nine-hundred-square feet. Between us, the balls, the cats, the furniture, and the furniture for the cats, we don't have space for a vase, let alone a piano. But the next weekend, we spend an entire day moving, purging, and cleaning the main floor to create space for a piano, which I fear will be a large and expensive baseball-cap storage rack.

This decision, to me, is like acquiring cats. It's long-term and comes with more expenses, like lessons (because I'll shoot myself if I have to listen to chopsticks for the lifespan of this instrument, which is getting shorter every minute). Peter hates that I've sat down on the stool, lowered the fallboard, and used it as a computer table. It's actually a convenient office for me once the kids have spread out their homework across the dining-room table. Then I used it as a Tapas bar, and then a display table for the kid's smaller stuffies, and then a place to hold my cookbook open to whatever recipe I'm using because the only place with enough space for this new, eighty-eight-fingered elephant in the room is, of course, the kitchen, which creates a sort of saloon-type atmosphere. I can just see a casual game of rock, paper, scissors going sour and a barroom brawl breaking out.

I love preparing dinner to the soothing sounds of "Heart and Soul" in every major and minor key. When I ask Cole, subtly, if he would like to take some piano lessons, he says, "Why don't you just teach me?" I suddenly realize that, even though he likes to question my worth at every turn, he still believes I can do just about anything. Bless his naïve little heart.

28.

Cottage Industry

Peter is a writer of lists: To do's, top tens, Christmas presents, not to mention the reams of pages lying around listing baseball players who are eligible for his fantasy baseball team, along with their positions and price tags. Even something as small as choosing a pizza joint merits a list and more gameplay; Peter will write down the names of the five closest pizza shops in the area, and we all have to individually rank them, one point for first place and upward from there. The place that accumulates the least number of points gets our business for that evening.

Today's list is not so much fun. It's titled: Ways for Jane to make money. Ugh. Tutoring is already on the list, but where do we go from there? Since we both quickly agree that the prospect of selling my body is decades and stretch marks behind me, we look for other, better-kept properties to turn tricks.

"What about our cottage?" suggests Peter. Hmmm. We rent it out over most of the summer but never really thought about the winter market. Until now, we really weren't looking for extra income.

I research cottage-advertising rental sites and decide on one that offers the greatest exposure with the lowest membership fee. I add photos and some alluring text and submit it to the site. Four days later, there are weekend renters in our beach house, enjoying the frozen waters of Lake Erie, and we have to turn down another couple for that same weekend. Success! Now I spend part of my day answering inquiries, submitting rental agreements, and playing siren, luring others toward our house above the waves.

Peter's next list is even less fun: Ways for Jane to Save Money. Which is something I've already been attempting to do. For instance, in an effort to spend less, since September, I have not bought one item of clothing for myself. Well, that's not entirely true–I bought a toque last week, but that doesn't count because I'm Canadian. Canadians wear toques. It's not shopping. It's just being patriotic.

Also, because we're watching our dollars and cents now, my usual cross-border, back-to-school shopping trip in June was a different experience this year. Every summer, I go with Heather, an old friend of mine, who currently lives in Thailand, across to the States to buy back-to-school clothes from the outlet malls. She's a school principal and takes advantage of the end-of-summer sales here because it's always summer in Thailand. I usually buy a few items for my family to start the school year off fresh, crisp, and clean, even if these only last for one day. Despite my new vocation (or lack thereof), we went again this year, because it's an excellent time for Heather and me to catch up on our year. We shop, stay in a hotel, go out for dinner, shop some more, and talk for most of the forty hours we're together.

This year I couldn't justify clothes for myself. I mean, as a stay-at-home-mom, what did I need more than track pants and t-shirts? I now have a few pairs of everyday track pants as well as my formal track pants for special occasions. Perhaps

I can compensate for them with my fancy hair and make-up (not). My wardrobe is undoubtedly looking dull. I am expecting costume designers from Les Misérables to come knocking, looking for inspiration.

And, now that I don't need to present a professional façade, I look in the mirror and am alerted to the fact that I am totally letting myself go. Case in point: It is a Sunday morning, the second week of November, and I am standing at the cosmetics counter in the drugstore when this really young thing in lots of makeup (too much make-up in my conservative, old lady, what's-wrong-with-the-youth-of-today opinion) pops up from behind the counter, brushes her pink highlighted hair away from her purple-lidded eyes, and strides toward me, breasts leading the way, in an over-confident, annoyingly youthful kind of way. Or perhaps I'm just envious.

I'm clutching my purchase, watching the dramatic arrival, when this Miley Cyrus asks if I'm a senior citizen. Excuse me? I take a quick glance in the mirror on the counter and observe that I am looking a little frumpy in Peter's winter coat (it was the first thing I saw on the way out the door), along with my toque (naturally). I am weary-looking, on the mend from a restless sleep, and holding a bottle of wrinkle cream. But despite all the circumstantial evidence, I do not look or feel like a senior citizen. I am 47—a young-ish 47—and now a pissed-off 47!

"Why would you ask if I'm a senior citizen?" I snarl.

"Because it's Seniors Day and they get 20 percent off all purchases."

"And how old does one have to be to be considered a senior citizen?"

She loses a slight step at hearing the tone of my voice. "Uh, I dunno, 60 or 65?" Her voice trails off as she sees the expression on my face change from utter disbelief to total disgust.

"And do I look 60 or 65?" A dangerous question. This can go either way with this tactless tart.

"Um, well ... the last lady got mad at me for not telling her it was Senior's Day, so I thought I would just ask everybody...?" This interaction is actually starting to fluster Miley.

This is what gets to me about some young people today. In fact, I am so pissed off I wonder what's up with my hormones. Surely, I can't be pregnant! Certainly not at 60 or 65. Never mind. Young people, they're like animals in their inability to reason. They are part of a universal Pavlovian experiment and have devolved to the point where they only respond to the sound of their phones announcing an incoming text or Instagram alert. There are no grey areas of thought interfering with the wasting grey matter of their brains, and so everything requires a blanket answer—just something to get past the cerebral obstacle in front of them so they can get back to their IMSB (I am so bored) messaging.

Time for a little grandmotherly advice: "Listen, sweetie, if you're going to offend someone, it's better to err on the side of caution— 'to err' means to make a mistake—and assume she's younger than she looks, not older. If a lady gets mad at you for not telling her about Senior's Day, tell her you wouldn't have guessed she was a senior because she looks so young. You'll make her day. Which is the opposite of what you've done for me."

'Um, okay. That sounds good. Have a nice day."

"Not likely."

As I shuffle out with my vial of wrinkle cream, I think to myself, Crap! I could have shut up and got 20 percent off this overpriced stuff.

Luckily, despite the obvious evidence of maturation, Peter still thinks I'm cute, but I'm not sure he means cute it in the way I want him to mean it. He tells me I'm cute when he finds my gloves in the fridge, and the TV remote in my purse, and when I go ape-shit worrying about early onset Alzheimer's. For some reason, to him, that's cute. But I'll take a compliment any way I can get it.

Now, with all of these anecdotes, I've distracted you from thinking about Ways for Jane to Make and Save Money. It's the same strategy I use with Peter when he starts questioning our commitment to our budget. Except with him I just come up with, "blah, blah, blah, baseball, blah, blah, spring training, blah, blah, trade deadline..." and suddenly we're talking player salaries and injury lists. Which is far better than listing my personal (lack of) salary and tally of vacuuming injuries.

29.

Bagging Candy with my Bitches

Our November ME date arrives, and seven of us pile into Stephanie's minivan, laden with coffees, teas, and enough conversation to fill our four-hour shift together. The Habitat for Humanity offices are nearby, and before we know it, we're hauling heavy boxes of candy in -14°C from a storage unit to the offices above the Habitat store. Our orders for the morning are to create small bags of sweets from the bulk boxes, then put a variety of these bags, along with icing, into larger bags so that each bag holds enough candy to decorate a beautiful gingerbread house.

It is brainless work and having a bunch of moms, experienced at making assembly line lunches every day, makes for quick work. It also makes for lots of time for hen talk, and we cluck and cackle non-stop.

The four hours pass quickly, and I get to know some moms even better, one of whom is Laura—a kindred spirit. We have an immediate connection and share many of the same values and experiences. We are around the same age, which makes us the more senior members of the pack. She is very diplomatic, doesn't sweat the small stuff, and is always game for a good adventure. And she's a football player, which earns my immediate respect. Then there's Shannon, a firecracker of a gal, who, along with Laura, is co-president of our school parent council. Shannon is passionate, fiery, says what everyone else is thinking, and has little time for small talk. Her outlet is distance running. This dynamic duo had their work cut out for them last year as they tried to repair the damage done by a year of teacher protests and government pushbacks.

As an important note, it was because of this discord in the education system that I met with my headmaster to see if I might be able to bring Tanner and Cole to school with me at the privately funded school where I worked for the following year (at 15, Satchel was already too old to attend this K-8 school). Eventually, I got the okay from Admissions and was sent to the Director of Finance to discuss what that would look like from a money perspective. "Well," he said, looking at the numbers he had assembled, "if you'd like to break even at the end of the day ... you'd have to choose your favourite son to attend." This led to the conversation about taking a leave of absence. If my boys couldn't be at school with me, then perhaps I could be at home with them.

And now here I am, bagging candy with my bitches.

After our shift, I help bring all the completed bags into a storage room, where other groups had assembled their bags earlier. Our supervisor eyeballs our loot and congratulates us on an estimated two-hundred bags, the same amount as the group from the previous day. I am a little surprised at that low number, and so, being the competitor that I am, do a quick count and come up with well over three-hundred bags. I don't correct the supervisor because that would be gauche. But we totally win at charity. And Stephanie's day is a great success that motivates others to find their own outing.

30.
That's All I Have to Say About That

Some people talk too much. They are better talkers than they are listeners. It's the middle of November, and that is my unique Observation of the Month. I sometimes fall into the "talking more than listening" category, but it's only when I'm really, really excited about something, and can't stop myself from blurting out my news. It's a very unselfish act, to listen, and it's a skill that needs to be taught and developed. So many people don't commit themselves to the simple act of giving of their time and attention, if only for a moment. We often get our hearing tested, but I think we should all have our listening tested from time to time as well.

What offends me is that some people assume that what they have to say is more important than what others have to say, and they impatiently interrupt, loudly and rudely. Then there's that person who indiscreetly stops listening—you know this because they are looking over your shoulder for someone or something more interesting than you, or they suddenly contribute something to the conversation going on beside you, the one to which they've really been listening.

I notice that I'm doing it myself as I stand in the playground on this crisp November day with another mom, who is relating a story about her weekend, although I can't remember what it's about because I am not really listening. I can barely wait for her to finish what she's saying. In fact, I stop listening in order to prepare what I am going to say next, and just wait for an appropriate opening. I tell myself that at least waiting for an opportunity is better etiquette than interrupting, but it really isn't if you've stopped listening.

Perhaps it is particularly hard for SAHMs, whose dumbed-down dialogue with young children makes them feel a little starved for adult interaction. When they are exposed to other grown-ups, they have so many pent up multi-syllable words that they explode verbally to anyone who will listen. I get it.

And so, I start my next social experiment: to be not just a good listener but an active listener. I want to not only hear what people are saying but to genuinely interact with them, too. What a revelation! In doing so, I decide that, when talking to someone, I will ask at least one question about what they are saying before adding my own two cents. Try it sometime. It's not easy to do at all, but it makes a difference. There's a great video online in which Hunter S. Thompson is interviewing Keith Richards. Both of them are so high that they are sitting face-to-face, taking turns talking, as if it's an enthralling conversation, except both of them are sequentially commenting on entirely different topics. In my eavesdropping, this is how it seems to be among many of the (sober) people to whom I listen.

Now, instead of planning my next monologue, I'm listening carefully, asking questions, empathizing. It's not insincere. It's actually interesting to dig a little deeper into another person's thoughts; sometimes it's quite rewarding to find little nuggets of insight you would have otherwise smothered with your own nattering. I think, above all, nothing makes people feel appreciated and valued more than to know they are being heard.

Probably one of the best listeners I have ever known was my friend Jan. She was a sincere listener, always ready to lend an ear and be supportive of and non-judgmental about anything you had to say. She would sit in silence until you finished talking, and then wait, giving you an opportunity to add on to what you had just said in case you weren't finished, and most of the time, you found you weren't.

Perhaps it was her Nova Scotia background—those folks are known for their incredible friendliness, warmth, charm, and hospitality—that made you just want to be with her. She was a woman of so many talents stemming from her work as a designer and artist. She was probably the best cook I ever knew, too. She poured vast amounts of love into each dish, along with a dash of her heart, soul, and Down-East sensibilities, to create masterpieces of taste and presentation. When she hosted a dinner party, we wouldn't eat all day in anticipation of the feast.

When we met, in 2000, after our first-born sons were both 2-years old, we immediately became great friends, co-conspirators, and confidantes. She had a beautiful, adventurous spirit and was game for anything, so our field trips sent us all across our neighbourhood and far beyond. She was so thoughtful and generous that even the kids benefited from a rainy day with a carefully planned tea party, with tea served in real china, along with cakes and finger sandwiches, set upon a blanket on the floor of her kitchen.

Jan was one of my closest friends and would have been the third woman in the ME slideshow; however, I didn't want to overwhelm my guests with a list of the deceased. After many years of friendship, and a second boy for us each, born just a few months apart, in 2007, Jan confided to me one day in the spring that she had cervical cancer, which is one of those curable cancers if caught early. The announcement came around the same time as Clare's first breast cancer diagnosis. After many bouts of radiation, Jan recovered, and life got back to normal. Then, two years later, in early winter (just two weeks after Clare had called me, crying from the hospital with her tragic diagnosis), Jan pulled me aside in her front hall as I was picking up the kids from a play date. She whispered calmly and quietly, "I have to tell you something. The cancer's back and it's bad. I'm going to die."

"What?"

She could only nod her head. The kids were clamouring to get out the door as Jan and I stood staring at each other in silence. This was no place for a scene in front of the kids, which was irrelevant because I was speechless. We hugged long and hard, and then the kids and I left. When we got home, I went up to my room and cried into my pillow for what may have been hours. It seemed an incomprehensible and cruel joke.

Jan's reaction to her cancer appeared to me to be the opposite of Clare's. She didn't seem to have the same fight in her, perhaps because her disease was more advanced than Clare's, and she attended appointments with a quiet, fatalistic resignation. Despite her husband's desperate efforts to get her every treatment, procedure, and medication available, her condition declined as the cancer invaded her stomach and esophagus.

We could do nothing but watch her slowly starve to death. In the winter of the next year, her husband called at one in the morning to say that she had passed away. I was honoured to deliver one of the eulogies at her service, but in the words of Forrest Gump, "That's all I have to say about that." Enough already.

Except that I promise no one else dies in this book. So please keep reading. And don't forget to keep listening.

31.

Honeymoon Sweet

It's only the end of November, and the headmaster of my school asks for a meeting to discuss next September's plan. Next year? I am a few months into this year, still in the honeymoon phase! He has to know fairly soon for budgeting and staffing purposes. A job has been guaranteed for my return, but it's not my old job. Instead of putting me back in the junior division, grades four to six, which is my favourite group to teach, he sees me working the primary slot: junior kindergarten to grade two!

I already know from experience that tiny, 4-year-old micro-bosses are not my people. They don't get my humour or sarcasm, and for tiny, demanding garden gnomes, they sure do cry a lot. Some of my training in Teacher's College was working this detail, and I must be honest, the little rodents ate me alive and spat out my bones right in the face of my evaluating teacher. I have been fearful of them ever since.

It takes a special person to tame these wild animals, and I have such respect for the calm, rational, structured kindergarten teacher, who single-handedly herds the little snowflakes in and gets them to learn stuff. I have proven that I am not that special. And what about all those pipe cleaners and buttons, and all that construction paper and glue? And then there's the clean-up. What if my power vac sucks in one of the little monsters?

After this wonderful gift of a year off, I can't be picky about my return, but this particular job is unnerving. All I can muster to my boss is that I'm not ready to start thinking about going back to work yet. He generously gives me more time to think about it. Great, a few more weeks of enjoying SAHM-hood where I can put off thinking about going back to work; however, when I'm in the yard dropping off my kids, I watch the kindergarteners stumbling to get into class and break out into a little sweat. So many little dramas occurring, so many patient reminders, so many random questions... Is this my future?

32.

Mandatory Maximum-
Participation Christmas

On the first day of December, my true love gave to me ... the flu. This is the kind of flu that lasts two weeks and interferes with all kinds of holiday requirements; for instance, as a SAHM, I keep hearing the term "Holiday Baking". With three weeks to go before the holidays begin, the moms around the school are saying, "I finished my Holiday Baking today."

"Can you believe I haven't even started my Holiday Baking yet?"

I watch moms bringing in huge, bigger-than-a-breadbox tins of muffins, breads, and cookies for teacher presents. There is tremendous pressure to Holiday Bake, and while I love to partake in assembling the odd Starbucks copycat banana bread, this is on an industrial-sized scale and just another reason I feel inadequate compared to the rest of the experienced, stay-at-home moms.

Still, in order to have the full experience of being a SAHM, I schedule a holiday-baking day. The pressure must have gotten to me, because my date with a cookie pan turns into two full-on flu days in bed, with many truncated days following, suffering from malaise, cancelling not only cookies but volunteering, Christmas shopping, tree decorating, present wrapping, writing, and of course, holiday power-vac cleaning. I feel like I am back at work with teacher holiday syndrome, which occurs at the beginning of winter break when teachers allow their bodies to uncoil and release the sleeping giant of a cold who's been waiting to get out for months. The beast has become impatient, ill-tempered, and huge so that when he finally escapes, he won't settle for anything less than total domination.

I barely make it back on my feet again in time for a December ME day, organized by Yvonne. I had seen Yvonne many times in the schoolyard but had never spoken to her, because quite frankly, I was intimidated. She is a former model—not a hand model, but a real, glossy, cover-of-a-magazine six-footer, who is nothing short of stunning. I would never have guessed how down-to-earth she was until she joined us for the ME adventures. I really like Yvonne, but that doesn't mean I go out of my way to stand next to her when we're all out together. If we were works of art in a gallery, I would be the deformed, confusing Picasso to her breathtaking Michelangelo.

Yvonne brings us to the Distillery District of Toronto, a former whiskey distillery turned cultural destination, complete with boutiques, galleries, restaurants, theatres, and numerous special events. With its cobblestone, pedestrian-only streets, the whole place draws tourists and locals alike, particularly for one of its best annual events: the Christmas Market. Seven of us meet for an afternoon of touring, listening to carolers dressed in Victorian-era costume, and shopping for handmade items for Christmas. We pop in to see new installations in the galleries, sample exquisite just-made chocolate and celebrate the season with decadent Margaritas and enchiladas at the

Mexican restaurant. It's a beautiful place in every season, but at this time of year, it certainly gives us another reason to get excited about the holidays.

Distillery visit aside, all the best-laid plans are pushed back, and I find myself rushing through holiday preparations a few days before Christmas, just as if I'd been working. Instinctively, I run to the liquor store and grab bottles of wine and beer for the strung-out teachers who teach my children. Hopefully, they appreciate something to wash down the homemade scones and shortbread cookies from the other more thoughtful and pre-pared moms.

As for preparations for Christmas day, my über-organized, older sister plans the day and loves to get everyone involved. When she sends out the agenda for Christmas day this year, it includes a family skate, appetizers, movies for kids, itemized dinner menu (including designated food contributions from each family member), clean up, gift game for kids, gift open for kids, gift steal game for adults, re-gift steal game for adults, dessert, and wrap up. My only question is, "Why aren't you running the Olympics or the world or something?"

By contrast, Christmas Eve dinner with Peter's family is at our house, and it is completely unstructured. Guests arrive, chat, and perhaps throw some kind of bowl football game on the TV; we eat, watch more sports or a sitcom or two, and they leave. It's all very easy and pleasant and over in a few hours, allowing us time to prepare for the onslaught of the next day's present-opening spree and my sister's tightly scheduled day of mandatory maximum-participation Christmas festivities.

33.

Frankie's Not Coming for Me

I am not a hateful person, and hate is a powerful word, but aside from making salads for dinner parties, the only other thing I hate is winter. My kids ask me if I ever swear, and I tell them the truth: I only swear at bad drivers on the road, when I injure myself, and all winter. Being a Canadian and despising cold weather causes a dilemma for approximately eight months out of the year, when the temperature drops to—hmmm, let's just look at the weather website now... Oh, it's a bit warmer on this lovely December day; we're up to a balmy -18°C. How cheery. Winter also makes me sarcastic. And it makes me swear. Shit, that's cold! A lot.

This is not a recent, middle-age condition, although it will motivate me to become a retired Florida snowbird one day, playing afternoon bridge in velour lounge pants and pastel sweaters with gold sailor buttons. This is more of a long-standing disdain, reaching back to the fourth grade when I'd watch movies like Beach Blanket Bingo with my mom, and long to be part of that fringed, bikini-clad, '60s crowd, dancing the Watusi on the sand, going on surfing safaris, and holding hands with Frankie Avalon. That was my destiny, I was sure.

By the time I reached my senior year in high school, there was still no warm ocean in sight, and my extremities thinned with each passing year, seeming more susceptible to frostbite. I had to become proactive. Frankie was not coming for me. I watched my former tennis-playing peers accepting scholarships to colleges in sunny destinations all across the United States and regretted the decision to quit the sport years earlier.

There was only one thing to do: dust off those racquets and find me a scholarship. I had been off the circuit for three years and was rusty, but I promised myself that, if I didn't get a scholarship to someplace warm, I would be off to wander Europe with a backpack and find my destiny there. My mother, who rarely interfered in decision-making (no matter how much it disappointed her), offered to help me financially by funding a budget trip to Florida to visit some schools and talk to some coaches. This was her not-so-subtle way of telling me she disapproved of Europe.

At the end of a compact period of practicing, videotaping, letter writing, phone calling, and visiting, I had a few offers from small colleges and began my four years of schooling, plus one year of work in sunny Florida, followed by friendly South Carolina. Pass the sunscreen, please.

And yet, here I am, freezing my ass off back in frigid Canada. It seems the USA will only allow you to stay there for one year after completing a degree legally, and so I was sent packing back to the Arctic outback called Ontario, where I soon met Peter, the warm-hearted man whose Caribbean blue eyes would melt me into a big, soupy bowl of stars and dreams. Our "meet-cute" (the Hollywood term used to illustrate how two characters meet before their romance blossoms) was at a tennis tournament in the summer of 1990, the setting for Scene One of our own lifelong romantic comedy.

All of this sunny history is to introduce the irony of a surprising family winter retreat (for three days) in North Bay over this Christmas break, which is even colder than it sounds. "North" of anywhere feels cold; even North Miami Beach can't be as warm as South Beach. Anne, the social director and her boyfriend, optimistically plan the family event and arrive there a day early, only to find their cottage heat turning off during the night in -40°C. After a sleepless night trying to stay warm and finding their toilet-bowl water frozen by morning, they switch cabins and welcome the rest of the extended family to a much-improved -19°C. Shit! (You may be wondering why we stay in Ontario since we dislike it so much. The answers are that it would be hard to leave our families and that Peter's client base is in Ontario, so we reluctantly embrace, or endure, winter). So, going to North Bay is a very un-Bedard-y thing for us to do. But we are loyal to family, if nothing else, and the kids are looking forward to snowmobiling, snowshoeing, skiing, and other wintery vernacular I thought I'd forever removed from my vocabulary.

Admittedly, it is kind of fun hanging with my extended family, assembling from across the country. At first, Peter and I enjoy building a thousand-piece puzzle, playing ping pong, sitting in the hot tub, and playing board games. You may notice all of these things are activities best enjoyed in warm environments. But the kids persist, and we end up shovelling the snow off the lake to create an ice rink for some hockey. We go cross-country skiing and for long walks to the ice-fishing shanty way out on the lake, which is really just a party in a closet. All in all, I still believe winter is a marginally tolerable place to visit, but I wouldn't want to live there ... for more than a few months at a time.

34.

Fifty Shades of Hooray

Here's one of the best things to happen this holiday season: Now that I have recovered from the flu, and the chaos of Christmas day and Christmas travel is over, I am falling in love with reading again. It's been a very long time since I found the time to devote to a good book, and now I have three on the go. All of them are written by humorous, female authors, chosen in an attempt to inspire me (or in some cases, make me hopelessly aware of my incompetence as a writer). These are the books I enjoy, and without having to run out the door to get to work early in the morning or make lunches and take the kids to school, or prepare for holiday activities, I allow some time to snuggle up with one of my authors each night.

A few years back, when many of us had very young children, a group of moms would host our own after-school special each Friday. We'd feed the kids, throw them into the basement playroom or into the backyard, uncork a few bottles of wine, and set out some cheese and crackers for our end-of-the-week group rehab. It often turned into dinner with the husbands, who would join us after work. The "Mama Needs a Cocktail" club didn't seem like a respectable name for our gathering, and so it became innocently known as The Book Club. We never actually read a book together, although we often talked about books we would like to read if we had the time or attention spans, so it's kind of an accurate name. And the only membership requirements were sleep deprivation and access to wine. Happily, some of those book-club attendees from years ago are now involved in ME activities.

As the kids got a little older, some of us pumped out a few more or went back to work, and the club eventually disbanded. It wasn't until years later that a new club was formed. I was invited by a friend but was immediately overwhelmed by the rigid structure and maturity of the meetings. This was a real book club, where they read real books, which was a little intimidating. I thought we were just going to have a drink and a giggle and throw out names of books that other people thought were good in reviews or that were about to be made into a movie, but this was serious parliament. "Here ye, here ye! We call to order the first meeting of the book club. All members rise and be accounted for and swear your oath of loyalty to the almighty page. Please refer to the agenda and pay close attention to the strict schedule. All works of literature will be read within the allotted time frame and relevant questions, prepared by the monthly host, shall be recognized by the group and discussed as per section 41-subsection d, paragraph 2. Failure to adhere to rules will be punishable by means of public humiliation, and in cases of severe disobedience, insertion of the assailant's hand into a jar of spiders."

Okay, so it wasn't that bad, and while the ladies were lovely people, it certainly wasn't as playful a group as I had hoped, and the discussions became a little too highbrow for my 5-year-old sensibilities. I had been entirely misled by my first encounter with a pretend book club. I tried to keep up with the reading and contribute to discussions, but it quickly became evident that this was not for me for two reasons: First, I didn't have time to read the heavy (both in weight and subject matter) books assigned by the group; and second, the books which were chosen were not anything I would have ever picked on my own. They were dark, intense, and filled with tragedy. Not only did I fall behind, when I wasn't busy teaching or parenting, I was accompanying my sister to chemotherapy or holding hands with Jan, watching her deteriorate. I didn't need to order up a platter of heartache from the menu; I already had it as a side dish with every meal I ate, and I began to resent the expectations to participate in what felt to me like a masochistic marathon. I needed light, friendly, and funny. I needed to laugh. I needed books to help me to escape to a world where there is always a happy ending.

And so, several months after the inception of the club, when it became clear that Uncle John's Bathroom Reader, Sixth Edition, would not make the short list, I sent in my resignation, thanking them for including me, but signing off with, "See you at the movies."

And that ended my affair with reading for many years. Oh sure, I flirted now and then with a hot paperback or a seductive magazine, but the romance was gone. It meant nothing to me, and I resented books for being so alluring yet so inaccessible.

Now, here I am, lying in bed with my warmest blanket (see next chapter), along with three books, and the passion is back. From limp, used paperbacks to stimulating hardcovers, the affair is going strong. I choose my titles and look forward to indulging each night in fifty shades of hooray! Because books are back, baby, and I'm all in!

35.

Happiness Is...

Ahh, a warm blanket. When I think about it, I am reminded of my happy places, and in doing so, I get to choose from three luxurious destinations. The first is sleeping in our cozy bed. "Going to bed" is the best. Sometimes I get so excited about going to bed that, when I get there, I can't sleep. I lay there, giddy, wanting to talk about how great it is to be in a warm, comfy-cozy bed such as ours. But, even if Peter were awake, he would think that was really weird, and so I lay there, sometimes for hours, thinking about it, and having my own private celebration inside my head, where there are always plenty of voices ready to contribute.

Sleeping is such an awesome thing. So much happens while you sleep—so much growth and repair (at least that's my excuse for trying to retreat to my bed at every opportunity). Peter is an early bird and questions my lack of initiative to get up and get going in the morning, but I just tell him I'm very busy growing and repairing. Both of my sisters suffer from FOMO syndrome, (Fear of Missing Out), but I'm different. I like to be adventurous and active, and then I like to sleep. I don't need to be the last one at the party. In fact, Peter and I have lived by the motto, *always leave the party while you're having a good time.* We really do adhere to it, and as a result, we're never disappointed because we don't have to watch the drunken, irreverent slurring, the spastic dancing, or worse, the stumbling, ill-fated hook-ups. And, like the exercise thing, I'm a bitch if I don't sleep. I love being awakened after a massage, drool dripping from the corner of my mouth, and massage table wrinkles mapping my face. Happy client.

Last year, Peter bought a couples-friendly electric blanket to improve our (my) bedding experience. It has his and hers temperature settings, so the temperature of each side of the blanket can be adjusted separately, and when I crawl in at night after heating it up, I imagine that this must be what it feels like to be in a womb, except I still have to actually get up to go to the washroom and get food when I'm hungry; otherwise I could just stay there for months, perhaps for the whole winter, hibernating in a warm placenta mix of soft, eight-hundred-count sheets, enveloped by a blanket that cuddles me. Perhaps if I can create a type of silicone umbilical cord that runs from the fridge to my bed, and invest in some Depends, I can actually stay here for the winter season.

Happy place number two: just about anywhere where my family is together—at home, at the cottage, in the car, in our (my) bed, on the couch, the tennis court, the beach. It's a parent thing, looking upon your flock, knowing that they are safe and happy under your watch with a prideful feeling of I did that! You just can't beat the joy that grows and pushes from the inside of your heart trying to expand beyond the cavity walls and invade every other cell of your body. It's mind-blowing.

And lastly, there is happy place number three, which is a multi-destination trip. I am out on a surfboard in the Caribbean

Sea, the small surf town of Rincon, Puerto Rico visible on the shoreline, my sister Clare on a board beside me.

"What have you always wanted to do?" she had asked, a few months after her final diagnosis.

My response was instant.

"Learn to surf."

"Where?"

"Somewhere hot, where the water is so warm I could stay in it for hours without a wetsuit."

My recurring childhood surfing dream.

"So, find that place. Book it. I'm in."

Clare's perspective, even before she got sick, was to never stop learning, never stop exploring, and recently, this perspective had more urgency than usual. I began the search for a getaway that offered tranquility, surfing, and yoga (Clare's requirement) and found it on a women's adventure website.

Here's another aside: If you're a parent of young kids, as much as you love them, you know that's there's nothing better than travelling... without them. No strollers, diaper bags, snacks, juice boxes, electronics, chargers, games, books, sketchbooks, anti-nausea medication, extra clothes in case of nausea, towel for nausea cleanup... For this trip, I packed a backpack, and that was it. The only baggage I checked at the gate was my mental baggage. This was about living in the present, enjoying time with my sister, and fulfilling a lifelong dream—all in three bikinis.

We didn't even mind the six-hour layover at JFK. We had massages and pedicures in the airport (the brilliant brainchild of some airport authority), along with a glass of wine with dinner. We were having such a good time that (as per my M.O.) we almost missed our flight, and for the hundredth time in my life, I found myself running through an airport minutes before takeoff.

Our hosts in Rincon, Puerto Rico were a couple from Ohio: Joan, a yoga instructor and chef, and Greg, a surf instructor. Joan cooked healthy meals, led our morning and evening yoga classes, and showed us around the town; it was like having a personal vacation assistant. Greg was a pure surfer dude, tanned with bleach-blond hair, who drove a groovy, colourful Volkswagen Van with surfboards stacked on top of the roof.

Greg was a conscientious instructor, drawing diagrams in the sand and using shells and sticks to teach us proper etiquette out in the surf, lest we step on local toes. He also gauged the day's weather and chose which beach to attend, depending on the height of the waves. The first day, we went to Step's Beach, named so because there was a block of cement porch steps that had found itself marooned in the sand. Nobody knows how it got there. The waves there seemed almost non-existent, maybe half-a-foot high and perfect for beginners. It was hard to believe that a few months later, professional surfers would descend on this beach and battle far-less innocent waves of up to 30 feet-high. Still, after the fact, I could let it slip that I surfed Steps and impress a few dudes along the way.

After a few last-minute positioning tips, we went out and waited for a semblance of a wave in the relatively still waters. On my first attempt, I almost got up, but lost balance and gently submerged into the warm, salty water. The second attempt had me awkwardly, but successfully, ride a wave right into the beach. Booyah! I could have packed up and gone home happy but several more days of surfing (each on increasingly more difficult waves) was in store, and we were sore, exhausted, and exhilarated after each one. And Clare, despite her failing health, was there every step of the way.

At the beginning of the third day, on mighty four-foot waves, we sat out in the Atlantic Ocean on our boards, admiring the sky and the ocean, but as luck (or bad luck) would have it, that day Clare always seemed to find herself in the wrong place at the wrong time. We'd be sitting on our boards, having a conversation, and suddenly she would be gone, swept away by some rogue wave. It was like we were on a split screen in two different oceans. Countless times I watched her get beaten up, thrown from her board, and tossed into the sea. Countless times I worried and waited, hoping to see her bob up near the last place I had seen her. My eyes combed the beach, believing that she had washed up and decided to take a break. But after a while, I'd hear her familiar, "Hey!" as she paddled up beside me from an opposite direction. She worked twice as hard as I did, and we stayed out for many hours, but there was no way she was going in before I did. It just wasn't in her to give up. And she never did.

This is a wonderfully happy place—not watching Clare get annihilated by the ocean, but sharing this experience, spending long periods of time in between surfing attempts talking or being quiet, feeling the warm sun on our skin and the rhythmic, undulating water beneath us. Neither of us was too successful that day, but she was so impressive, showing stamina and courage beyond my expectation or imagination. Clare was there because she loved the challenge, but she was also there because she wanted to push others to live out their dreams. She understood how precious our time was, and I will forever be grateful to her for encouraging this adventure.

She wore a necklace that I had given her when she started her ill-fated journey with cancer; it's a small silver pendant, which has Winston Churchill's famous words inscribed on it as he spoke to the students at Harrow School in 1941, encouraging them to always persevere. It reads, "Never, never, never give up."

I wear that necklace today, and every day, as a reminder of Clare and of the importance of appreciating each person and each day. It reminds me to never, never, never give up, no matter how many times the waves knock you down.

36.
Second Date

As December comes to a close, Father Winter's moving truck pulls into the region, and judging by all his stuff, it looks like he's going to stay a while. Luckily, I've met and married my match in terms of how much disdain I have for winter. From November to May, just as I wear my toque, so Peter dons his long johns, although they are far less noticeable or stylish. They are his winter staple, and he owns around six pairs, in case he has to double up some days.

Our perspective on winter may have been what cemented our commitment to each other. After graduating and using up my one-year work permit in the southern States, I had moved back home to Toronto. It was September when we met and our new courtship made the autumn seem more vibrant, more colourful, and more exciting. By December, however, we realized that we were the same frost-hating, snow-avoiding, winter-hibernating person. Something had to give. By January, we'd had enough. Even with our shiny, new university degrees in our back pockets, we found ourselves working dead-end, dissatisfying jobs and spending far too much time and energy avoiding the season as a whole.

We made a plan, about as impractical as all of our plans before and since: We would open up the newspaper and search the weather page; wherever the hottest place in the world was on that day, that was where we would hide out until our home country thawed. Our heat-seeking dart landed on Bangkok, at 34°C. We got our shots, quit our jobs, packed our backpacks, took what little money we had, and hoped to survive in South-East Asia for the next four months. Our relationship was still so new that we refer to this adventure as our "second date".

Travelling, in general, is a great way to get to know someone. An easy, early relationship litmus test would be to spend a week at an all-inclusive resort together. If you can't get along with someone at a fancy-shmancy hotel, with all of your needs taken care of, then it's one week out of your life; you've filled up at the buffet, ridden the banana boat, snagged a tan, and said adios at the airport. It's quite obvious you were not meant to be. But when all you have is a backpack, and you're 8500 miles away in a foreign land, where people speak another language, you'd better get along with the only other person you know.

Fortunately, we did get along—all the way through Singapore, Malaysia, and Thailand. It was fun and frustrating and exciting and scary, and we loved it all. I remember sitting in a VD clinic in a small town, Peter with a pinched nerve in his neck from an unsuccessful flip off a diving board, and me with a significant burn on my leg from the exhaust pipe on the moped we had rented. We were in that classy part of the region where STD clinics were the only places one could seek immediate medical attention. We sat in the waiting room surrounded by photos of patients' genitals in various stages of venereal disease and quickly learned to avert our eyes to the stains on the floor. The tiny Thai doctor didn't speak a word of English, so Peter mimed his diving accident, which was highly entertaining, and

I showed off my burn, after which we were effectively treated with painkillers, muscle relaxants, and topical antibiotics. We must have been such a relief for that doctor, who typically spends his days staring between the legs of ignorance, arrogance, or just plain bad luck.

We did all the typical things travelers do in South East Asia: explored breathtaking beaches; visited beautiful temples and mosques; trekked through the hills of Chang Mai with Po, our boyish guide (who killed a deer en route and prepared fresh venison for dinner); and smoked opium with the village medicine woman, who shared her pipe using a "One for Jane, one for me, one for Peter, one for me" order of distribution (at least until her 4-year-old interrupted us). We rode elephants through the jungle (fun for three minutes, then incredibly slow and boring). We ate omelets with funny mushrooms (for cool visuals) and giant flies (for protein). We sampled Durian (Dude, when did you puke in your shoe?) fruit, banned in some places for its revolting scent. Peter bravely tested an array of other local specialties but drew the line at what Han (our new Malaysian friend) was eating since his jaw extended out in front when he chewed, like a cash register opening and closing, displaying all the antennae and eyes of the exotic shrimp dish he was eating. I could only dry heave off to the side.

We got used to culture shock on every corner, like hearing the catcalls at both Peter and me, calling attention to our very blond hair. We were thrown by the attempts at translations for the benefit of English travellers, like the restaurant that offered "Fried Uterus Salad," a menu specialty item that we hoped had been mistranslated. But strangest of all was the Thai massage we sought out. Because who goes to Thailand without indulging in a massage?

One steamy night in Bangkok, we flagged a tuk-tuk (a three-wheeled taxi) and innocently asked the driver to take us to a place where we could find traditional Thai massage. Like any responsible taxi driver/tour guide, he took us down back streets and dark alleys and deposited us at the door of Lulu's Exotic Massage Parlor. Inside, we were met by Lulu herself, who led us to a glass wall, some thirty-feet long, behind which sat a pageant of around forty pretty ladies, each with a number pinned to her dress. "You choose girls for have good time," said Lulu.

We were mortified at the display and at our naïveté, but finally, Peter answered, "No good time. Only massage."

Lulu's annoyed look told us she was clearly disappointed with our request. We were now obviously tier-two customers. She aggressively ushered us to another window, much smaller, featuring seven motley-crew candidates—some heavy, some petite, some with whiskers, and all Lulu rejects—hanging out on the island of misfit toys. These girls were apparently not big window material and were likely heavily discounted for the less discerning clientele. Images of the clinic came back to my mind.

Despite the moral urge to cut and run, we didn't. We were completely uncomfortable, but we had come this far and were morbidly curious to see what would happen next. Our relationship was also still so green that we seemed to be testing each other's limits.

"You choose," said Lulu impatiently.

"No, you choose," said Peter, still bewildered by this bizarre presentation.

Lulu spoke into a microphone to announce to the folks behind the glass which girls' numbers had won the lottery, and shortly after, we were met by two oddball characters, who physically resembled female versions of Laurel and Hardy. They escorted us up a narrow staircase to the cheap seats at the top of the bleachers, passing many beautiful employees and clients returning from their completed transactions.

Once inside our assigned room, the girls motioned for us to take off our clothes so that we could be cleaned. Laurel filled a warm bath and sent me in, washing me gently with a soft sponge. Peter, however, was placed in front of a tiled wall and hosed down like a prized bull being prepared for show at the county fair. Hardy roughly scrubbed him everywhere as we looked at each other wide-eyed, and I had to giggle at his predicament. When the cleansing was complete, we were both directed to a round bed and signalled to lie down next to each other, face down. The ladies draped towels over our mid-sections, then straddled us and proceeded to converse in Thai, probably about the stupid, pasty tourists who lay before them.

The actual massage was disappointing. Hardy rubbed Peter's back while she repeatedly passed gas. He looked like he had been pinned down by a Sumo wrestler, who continued to merely prod his back occasionally, checking to see if he was still alive. Laurel, seemingly incapable of multi-tasking, could not talk and massage at the same time, and since she was the more loquacious of the two, there were long periods of time with no massage at all. For the rest of the hour, Peter and I lay there, shaking, trying to control hysterical laughter as Chatty and McFarty casually hung out on our asses, probably discussing their favourite soap operas. They adjusted our spines, chiropractic style, which made me wonder how they could work presumably long hours at Lulu's and still find time to graduate from a chiropractic college. When it was all over, they looked at us expectantly for a moment, and then left in a huff because we didn't realize we were supposed to tip them. We were equally put out because they left us no receipt for which to make an insurance claim.

When I think back to that day, I can't believe we went through with the whole thing. There is no good excuse. I have also since experienced an authentic Thai Massage, which is a wonderful thing and nothing like what had occurred in Bangkok, which was a massage from a Thai.

After our massage debacle, we headed to Bottle Beach, a destination added to our itinerary on the advice of another traveller. After a full day of travel, hiring several fishing boats and locals on motorcycles, we arrived and immediately understood why this place had been recommended. It was surreal. A beautiful, blue bay was the entranceway to a white, sandy beach, speckled with a few bamboo huts, and surrounded by a lush, green curtain of mountainous jungle. We were lucky to find one hut still available and unpacked for two days, which quickly turned into two weeks of extreme, laid-back bliss.

Bottle Beach consisted of seven raised huts and a rudimentary restaurant; beyond these, it lacked a pulse—as eventually did most of its visitors, who quickly integrated into the sloth-paced culture. We met John and Beth, the couple in the neighbouring hut, who were from the USA. They were fun and friendly and were following a similar itinerary as us, so we immediately hit it off. For our entire stay on that island, they became our comatose companions as we lounged in hammocks, read books on the porch, and sunned on the beach like lizards on hot rocks. Unfortunately for John, Beth had fallen in love with a couple of hefty tapestries a few days into their adventure, and for several months, John found himself lugging two large rugs on top of his backpack and often on top of hers as well. He looked like Atlas, carrying the weight of her world all across Thailand, which seemed like excellent preparation for what looked to be a life of carrying all of her other whimsical accumulations. He was a good guy, and I wonder if they stayed together until the end of their trip, let alone through a lifelong commitment.

In order to jump-start our hearts again, John accompanied us one day on a climb up the steep hills behind our beach. He had been idling on the beach for much longer than we had, and his fitness level had been severely affected. By the time we got to the top, John had detoured from the path to throw up from the exertion of the climb, but our efforts (and his undoing) were rewarded with an explosion of Thailand's exquisite array of flora and fauna. Colourful birds, bugs, and vegetation presented themselves from every direction, each exclaiming, "Look at me! Aren't I exotic and lovely!" At least I think that's what they were saying. I don't speak Eco-Thai.

Looking down from our perch, I doubt that many tourists from la-la land below had the initiative to make the climb, as much of the path was overgrown and sometimes non-existent. Eventually, we happened upon a small, deep pond, only about eight-feet across, which was so mystical and inviting that we removed our shoes and dipped our feet into the cool water. Within a few seconds, we were surprised by the presence of a school of small fish, which curiously swam up to nibble gently on our toes. I believe these fish are now used in spas to eat away at dead skin during an exotic pedicure. Suddenly, these playful fish abandoned their sweet kisses to reveal piranha-like jaws, and with jagged teeth, began shredding our feet. The pond turned crimson with blood!

Okay, settle down! I'm just kidding. But my imagination is always on high alert, and I pulled my feet up quickly, lest the little Nemos really were tenderizing us for their shark friends who lurked below, waiting for the signal to attack.

We survived our four-month-long "second date", passing a challenging test. But what's more remarkable was that this was only a prelude to an ongoing lifetime of questionable, and laughable, choices that have kept us together and on our toes.

Winter Term
JANUARY TO MARCH

37.

I Do. For now. Until Social Media Do Us Unfriend

After four months of being at home, I've had time to think about how being a SAHM impacts relationships and marriage. Do we have better relationships because we are more available to our partners? Perhaps we are more helpful? Pay more attention to their needs? Sacrifice some personal goals in order to nurture our offspring? It's not up to me to judge who has a better relationship because either you have a good marriage or you don't. I witnessed one marriage break up after eleven months and another after forty years, and I've been to a few beautiful fifty-year anniversary parties.

What makes some last and others fall apart? I have a theory: Either you're purposely working on your marriage, or you're inadvertently working on your divorce. It's as simple as that. From what I've seen, the culprit of most marital breakdowns, not forgetting infidelity, is complacency. Once your partner starts the slippery slope down the ladder of your priorities, there's trouble. We've all heard the counsellors and seen the shows about keeping a marriage fresh and alive instead of sitting on the couch and passively allowing the remote to change your marital channel from attentive to apathetic. It really does take work, but if you're really committed, like with most endeavours, it won't feel like work. It will feel like success.

In 2012, the highly controversial company, Ashley Madison, a dating website for cheating spouses, revealed some interesting data about from which areas of Toronto most of their clients came. Of the 400,000 members within the city's postal-code range, my community came in number one! Yay! We win at infidelity! We also held the study's top spot for cheaters who had the most children at home, so once again ... go us!

Another interesting point to come from this study was that the most significant factor found in a married woman having an affair is how financially secure she is in her career. Men follow suit, as the more affluent he is, the more likely he is able to afford the expense (hotels, restaurants, and so on) of keeping a mistress. If we follow this line of reasoning, we can deduce that a SAHM, with a salary of zero, would more likely be faithful to her husband, although television shows like to show what the bored "housewife" is capable of during her husband's working hours.

To gather more information on what my cohorts thought of this subject, and to force myself to clean the house, I spontaneously concoct an event to investigate further. Since we are in January, this post-holiday party is actually multi-themed, and the invitation looks like this:

Hello Ladies! Hope you all enjoyed a great holiday! As we all descend from the post- present frenzy, I would like to invite you to a somewhat spontaneous, multi-themed cocktail party. This Saturday Night, anytime after 7:00 p.m. Totally casual. Read on and let me know your availability.

Theme One:

P.C.S.T. (Post-Christmatic Stress Therapy.)

An opportunity to hang up your hosting aprons and vent about your mother-in-law or your drunken uncle. Come over and put your present-wrapping elbow or gravy-stirring wrist on ice and join me for a post-Christmas, come-out-of-the-cold (particularly for those of you who lost power over the holiday) cocktail. You've earned it!

Theme two:

Bring a thought.

As some of you know, I'm writing a book, memoir-based, with awkward attempts at humour, about transitioning from working mom to stay-at-home mom. Melissa said something to me last month that struck a chord and my funny bone, as she usually does. She said, "The reason why my marriage works is because we never hate each other at the same time." Ding! What a good topic! And worthy of a little investigative research.

And, as everyone knows, the best data always comes in the form of a cocktail party. So, all you have to do, should you wish to participate in theme two, and it's not mandatory, is to come prepared to finish this sentence: "My marriage works because..." Can be funny or poignant (although there should be some merit of truth to it) or just completely honest and to the point. As an extension, if you stay at home, or work part-time, do you think this has helped to make your marriage healthier? Think about it. Maybe discuss with your partner. You can write it down when you get here and even share it if you're comfortable. If you can't make the party, but would like to contribute, perhaps you would send me something by email. Remember though, this is all optional and as discreet as you like.

Theme Three:

It's my birthday the next day, and I'd like to share it with you.

Any presents will be re-gifted back to you for your birthday, so please don't buy one, or buy something you would like to have.

I send this last-minute letter to around fifteen ladies, some working, some not, some divorced, and ended up with seven of us, all of whom happened to be SAHMs or part-time SAHMs, around my kitchen island, chatting until almost two in the morning. Their perspectives are varied, they are articulate and thoughtful, and I think they are happy to have their opinions asked about the current thing at which they have become experts: heading up Human Resources in the family business (or in the business of family).

As I mentioned in the invitation, the impetus for this discussion came from my friend's comment about "not hating each other at the same time." I received some equally interesting and amusing comments from the group such as these:

My marriage works because...

- *We have unlimited texting.*
- *We want it to.*
- *He still tries to win me over every single day.*
- *He's my hero.*
- *It would be too tiring for it not to work.*

My grandparents on my father's side had an interesting marriage. They came to Canada with thirty-five dollars in their pockets and somehow managed to build a life. Grunfar suffered Gramma's curses and criticisms for his entire life, while they co-existed for almost fifty years, mostly in our Beach community. He was a gentle man who endured it all, never complaining and never receiving an iota of praise. It is no surprise that when he became a chef in a seminary, preparing food for priests in Scarborough, he spent weekdays living at the seminary and came home only on weekends. While she showed almost no affection for her husband, she adored her grandchildren and was generous with hugs, along with a few dollars discretely and frequently shoved into our pockets.

My grandmother was born in a small town near the Ukrainian border in Russia in 1911. As a young adult, she was strong, spirited, optimistic, and in love. Unfortunately, the boy down the road with whom she shared her hopes and dreams was not my grandfather. She didn't choose to marry my grandfather. Her parents did.

And so, it was arranged that strong-willed Dora (Gramma) marry Michael (Grunfar), an intelligent, kind, sturdy, reliable engineer with a future. But despite all of these fine qualities, she wasn't in love with him.

It crushed her, and I don't believe she ever fully recovered from her heartbreak. She did what she had to do and blamed Grunfar for doing the same. Even though they must have had some tender moments, resulting in two children, and persisted through devastating misfortune and unbelievable good luck in an unforgiving war, she resented him. I can only speculate that she felt devastated at having been plucked from a happy youth and thrown into a strange relationship and subsequent war. This was not the life she had envisioned; life was not what anyone envisioned once the war began, but I think she saw herself as a victim, regardless of the strength and determination required for her push on.

She became hardened and bitter, so often in survival mode, from hiding in Russia, to living on the front line, to incarceration in Austria, to relocation to Belgium, and finally to emigration to Canada in 1951. She seemed forever surrounded by circumstances she was able to endure, but not to change. After so many years together, it's hard to believe she didn't learn to love, or at the very least respect, the man who not only provided for her and her family but who, quite literally, kept them alive. They were, by all accounts, a formidable team, one that should have bonded over their adventurous and fortuitous journey, and I'll never understand how she couldn't come to appreciate her companion in life. My father believes they stayed together for the sake of the children, and then just stayed together out of habit.

Gramma put the final nail in Grunfar's coffin, thirteen years after his death, when we attended her Orthodox funeral. During the two-hour service, the priest circled her coffin, chanting and waving an amulet which emitted incense, after which we went to the cemetery to her final resting place ... and here's the kicker:

I will never forget that bitter, cold February day, walking out to the double grave where Grunfar resided. The headstone was there, with his name on one side and an empty space on the other in anticipation of a partner in perpetuity, but the ground in front of the stone was curiously untouched. We stood there, quizzically looking around until the priest arrived, walked past Grunfar's plot, and with a subtle nod, gestured for us to join him *on the other side of the road*, where Gramma had secretly purchased her own plot. She had remained angry to the end and opted for separate sleeping arrangements for all eternity.

There's a marriage that did not work, ironically, for almost a half-century. Nowadays, if a couple can't agree on what colour to paint the living room, it seems justifiable to divorce over irreconcilable differences. Interesting fact: The original marriage vow, "Until death do us part" was first published in an English prayer book in 1549, when life expectancy was about 34-years old. Yes, they committed for life, which was at most twenty years, but it also included a socially acceptable amount of infidelity. These days, how many people are ready to commit to a 51-year plan (given the average age of marriage and death)? Add to that a decreasing attention span, unrealistic expectations of relationships, and a progressively easy road to divorce, and this is an antiquated proposal for most. As an aside, I read that the average Canadian wedding costs $23,000, and an engagement ring comes in at around $5,431. How many times in your life can you pull off that kind of party? It depends on how many of those in the approximate 41-percent divorce rate (before their thirtieth anniversary) decide to do it all again.

I think vows need to evolve with the times to include "... in sickness and in health, on Instagram and Twitter, until Facebook do us unfriend."

My parent's marriage, like most, had its ups and downs. I remember them waltzing together in the kitchen, and I remember them arguing when they thought we were asleep. They had their ups and downs, raised four relatively normal kids, and stayed together for 33 years—until death made them part.

Does a SAHM's marriage last longer than a duo-working parents' marriage? It depends on the couple. From my limited perspective, when your family functions better because there is someone there making sure everyone is okay, and more importantly, you have a husband who appreciates your work at home, then life is good, less stressful, and everyone is richer for it (except, of course, in a monetary sense, but it's a choice you make). But if you're a mom who requires adult companionship, or a stimulating environment, or a paycheck, then staying at home may make you feel empty, while going back to work may bring the exhilaration of putting in a good, challenging day's work, earning some independent income, and having something interesting to share with your family over dinner. The best advice I've heard regarding marriage is to choose well and communicate often. In our case, I chose well, and Peter communicates often. Our biggest strength? We can find the humour in anything.

On the heels of these conversations, I ask myself a few questions: Is my relationship with Peter better now than when I was at work? Are we really benefitting from having me at home? Am I being fulfilled? Would the kids be just as well off with me being at work most of the day? Wouldn't it be nice to have a little more money?

But as I look closely at life as I currently know it, I can say with confidence that, yes, life is better now. Looking back to me as a working mom, I know I put on the façade that we were functioning just-fine-thank-you-very-much. But when I was living within that tornado, I couldn't necessarily see the storm swirling around me, leaving a path of broken promises and lost hours that could have been spent with my kids. My son had a birthday party to celebrate turning 10-and-a-half because it took six months before we could find a suitable date. Perhaps some women really can do it all, and there are indeed women who have no choice but to do it all, but I think there are also women believing, as I did, that frantic is just the new normal.

My own mother was a SAHM for almost my entire childhood; however, I do remember that she went back to work in a bank, for a short time, when I was in half-day kindergarten. I remember it distinctly as I had to spend afternoons with our elderly neighbours and their humongous, smelly, extroverted Newfoundland dog. They fed me oatmeal every day and put me down for a nap. I remember succinctly, even at 5 years old, that there was no one at home to take care of me, and I felt quite alone. When I hit grade one, my mom had another baby, and suddenly I could come home for lunch every day with my brother and sister and watch the Flintstones, and the first half of All My Children before going back to school. After school, I could bring friends home or play outside, knowing that I always had backup close by. It wasn't until Clare was in high school that Mom took on a series of part-time jobs again; however, she earned the dubious reputation of being the town jinx because every store at which she worked closed down, went bankrupt, or moved locations, which perhaps foreshadowed the demise of our small community.

38.
What Do I Do All Day?

Now, don't get me wrong, staying at home hasn't been perfect either. Here's where the bubble burst in our assumptions of this year: Peter and I thought that, since I used to be the only person in the family who had a restricted face-time schedule when I was teaching, that once I stopped, we would be able to take advantage of off-season travel prices, instead of travelling with the herds at Christmas and March Break. We naively thought that, perhaps, we could go to Peru and hike the Inca Trail up to Machu Pichu, or go to Italy and experience the incredible culture and taste beautiful, authentic Italian cuisine, or catch a football game in Barcelona. What great adventures awaited us!

Oh yeah. That costs more money than we have, even in February. Travelling is always pretty high up on our list of priorities, so it's hard to swallow that we won't be heading out anywhere this year while I'm not working. Our disposable income is sparse. Travelling has always seemed like more of a necessity than a luxury, so I will have to work on a different mindset. But then the guilt sets in again. Is this a selfish thing

I'm doing? Would the kids quickly trade in my daily presence in their lives for a week at Club Med?

The other part of the frustration I'm feeling is that I'm not writing enough. This is priority number two of this year, and it has been pushed to the back of the line. Many days go by when I can't seem to fit in even an hour. How can that happen? What do I do all day, I ask myself. Here's what I do: Beyond all the regular chores (laundry, dishes, food shopping and preparation, cleaning, home maintenance, etc.), there is skate tying and skating Friday afternoons for Cole and Tanner's classes, class "walking buddy" for Cole's class's "Out of the Cold" initiative, bringing lunches to the church for homeless people, field-trip volunteer for day-long visits to City Hall and theatres, driving lots of kids to school sports, driving some kids to after-school programs, bringing the kids and their friends home for lunch, helping with homework, preparing for tutoring, tutoring, going to Fun Fair committee meetings that I've recently signed up for, managing cottage rental, etc.

I feel like I'm back on page one. I have misplaced myself again, only in a different context. I have stuck my fingers in too many pies and am not doing anything particularly well anymore. It's time for a kick in the ass—my ass!

I put on a t-shirt given to me by Peter, that reads "Ask me about my book" on the front. It was actually a book-reader shirt, but it was meant to be an inspiring book-writer shirt for me. My reminders need to be less subtle and more frequent. I also need certain websites blocked on my computer during productive hours, like travel sites and the addictive Realtor. ca listings, where I search for greener grass in the form of two bathrooms and a yard. This search begins at locations within an hour's radius of us and extends to South America depending on how cold it is outside that day.

My cheerleading husband always manages to calm me down when I question this decision to stay home. Today he said, "Even if this is only sustainable for one year, it will have been the best year. How can you be disappointed with the best year?" His glass is always half-full. But half-full or half-empty, these recent distracted days really only mean one thing: It's time to top up. Time to shake the Boggle letters and start a new game with better focus, fewer interruptions, and hopefully no surprise letter X's, which have a way of showing up and stifling creativity every time.

39.

A Visit from Bridget

I've been reading, Bridget Jones, Mad about the Boy, and it's hard not to get caught up in her comedic writing style, so I thought I would give it a whirl for a morning:

January 20:

Number of containers of non-fat cottage cheese in fridge—3. Number of containers of mouldy, non-fat, cottage cheese in fridge—3. Weight—130 pounds. Weight last night at bedtime—127 pounds. How can one gain weight while sleeping? Number of hungry cats following me around house—2. Temperature—-34 °C. Number of sweaters layered—3. Mood—chilled.

6:35 a.m. Hit snooze on alarm clock.

6:42 a.m. Hit snooze on annoying alarm clock.

6:49 a.m. Turn off fucking alarm, get out of bed, put on toque, and go to washroom, stopping on way to wake up 15-year-old son, whose morning voice is deep and otherworldly, like Sigourney Weaver's demonic character when possessed by demon in Ghostbusters.

6:55 a.m. Put on long underwear and fat PMS pants, which fit over long underwear. Follow up with extra sweater, wool socks. No point combing hair while toque in place—perhaps next week. Waddle downstairs, stopping to revive possessed boy again.

7:05 a.m. Do not say good morning to husband as husband away on business. Prepare today's morning cocktail, consisting of frozen strawberries, apple with skin on, banana, Greek yogurt, orange juice, alfalfa, water, and flax oil. Blend and pour into four glasses hoping that, unlike every other morning, no one complains about disgusting concoction.

7:10 a.m. Listen to Satchel chew through breakfast smoothie; wonder if concoction can be called smoothie given chewy texture. Make Satchel boring lunch; unable to be creative given vegetarian and taste preferences. Run outside to turn frozen car on for morning warm-up and hope it is not stolen while back inside.

7:20 a.m. Rouse younger boys. Avoid temptation to crawl into bed with them, so warm and snuggly, but resist.

7:25 a.m. Add more layers of clothes until marshmallow-man metamorphosis complete and walking like 1 had good romp in the sack night prior—but alas, husband away—settle for marshmallow-man metaphor. Drive sleepy Satchel to tube (calling subway "tube" for authentic Bridget Jones effect).

7:40 a.m. Arrive home to two scallywags in standoff position at breakfast table, pointing Nerf guns at each other's faces. Discretely place smoothies in front of boys and remove Nerf guns so as not to be shot in face as punishment for being smoothie messenger. Ignore Cole dramatically holding nose while drinking smoothie so as not to throw up due to smell. Ignore Tanner questioning why oil is floating in drink.

8:10 a.m. Send giggling monsters upstairs to brush teeth and change shirts, which monsters have worn for many days for everything, including soccer practice. Wonder why teeth-cleaning device is called a toothbrush and not a teethbrush.

Clear dishes. Pass by liquor cupboard, surprised at thought crossing mind at such early hour.

8:15 a.m. Send sneaky schemers upstairs again to change shirts, having concealed dirty shirts under sweaters. Am not understanding attachment to dirty, stinky shirts by boys. Girls would not think of such a thing.

8:25 a.m. Explain, as do each day, why hats must be worn in -34 °C weather. Sign agendas, check for exposed skin, leave house at last possible second to allow for minimal time outside. Driving at this time is a complete nightmare due to traffic. Walking it is.

8:35 a.m. Deposit kids at school. Walk home, shoulders hunched, head down, fighting urge to swear out loud at winter so as not to sound like crazy person.

8:45 a.m. Arrive home and stand in disbelief at disaster area called home. Must avoid cleaning and focus on writing. First, make tea. Too cold to walk to Starbucks. Must save money anyway.

9:00 a.m. Open computer to begin writing. Check email first. Respond to cottage inquiries, reply to friends and tutoring questions, check out online sales.

9:40 a.m. Quick peek at travel sites, drooling at warm destinations. Must begin writing.

10:00 a.m. Momentary look at Realtor.ca, after which will begin writing immediately.

10:40 a.m. Perhaps write later. Must get to market to buy lunch items for kids. Pack on clothes for walk to shops as parking is a nightmare. Roll eyes and growl at people in shops who optimistically applaud temperature that has risen to -20 °C.

11:10 a.m. Walk to school for pick up.

11:35 a.m. Feed boys. Listen to stories of bullies, tests, and teachers.

12:10 p.m. Wrap us all up in winter gear and head back to school. End of entirely unproductive morning. Will write this afternoon. Absolutely.

End of Bridget Jones detour.

40.

Being Excellent to Each Other

Walking through the unfinished basement to the laundry area is similar to an art-thief maneuvering through a gallery, armed with motion-detecting moving laser beams. I bob and weave my way under low beams and hanging cables, over cat litter and storage bins, and around a furnace, mattresses, and boxes. It's a choreographed, coordinated dance. If Peter has to spend any prolonged amount of time down there, he wears a hard hat to avoid crushing his skull on the low ceiling and ventilation ducts (this strategy stems from experience and not theory). We're not exactly disorganized but more laissez-faire if you believe that. I would even venture to say that our home, from my point of view, is organized chaos.

Other people apologize for how messy their homes are because there is a sweater draped over a chair back or a vase that is off-center on the dining-room table. Really? I have walked into my home with a friend who has taken in the scene and quickly exclaimed, "Oh my God! You've been robbed!" because it looked like the place had been sacked by gangs or FBI agents searching for hidden drugs. Nope, that's just how it looks most of the time.

When I was young, my room was always a mess, especially, and not surprisingly, during those teenage years. Clothes were strewn across every surface area (some dirty, some fresh out of the laundry), mugs of half-drunk tea, schoolbooks, notebooks, shoes, sports equipment everywhere—like the contents of an extra large and neglected school locker.

My brother and sisters were the same way, and Mom would give us that disappointed look and quietly request a clean up now and then, but my dad was less gentle. Occasionally, we'd hear him stomping around upstairs, and the alarm was sounded: "Dad's on the warpath!" That meant either you cut your losses and got out for a few hours until the tirade was over, knowing that you'd arrive home to everything you owned tossed about, mattresses heaved off the frames, drawers emptied, a sea of all your crap forming a three-foot-high layer on the carpeted floor (clean up was a bitch), or you'd make the grand sacrifice by running upstairs and throwing yourself between him and your stuff. You'd take an ear-full of condemnations, filled with words like "disrespectful" and "spoiled rotten" and "pigsty" and you'd have to dodge a few flying books and boots, but in doing so, the dragon would run out of fire more quickly and clean up time would be reduced significantly. It's something we have a great laugh about now.

On other occasions, if we'd leave a mess in the kitchen, we'd find all our dirty dishes on our beds, under the covers, runny eggs, spaghetti sauce, and all. I guess these kinds of things didn't happen often enough to change our behaviour for long, because as I look around my room right now, I could very well be back in high school.

Unfortunately, Peter is not a clean freak either, and things often get out of hand. I used to have a cleaning lady come over every other week, but (and I know that every woman who's had a cleaning lady understands this, and almost every man doesn't) tidying up for the cleaning lady became more stressful than trying to keep the place clean on my own.

I am also wary of cleaning services. Once, I waited for a woman to arrive from a cleaning service for over an hour. Finally, I called the service and asked what the delay was. "She's already there. I dropped her off myself right on time," was the supervisor's reply. We finally arrived at the conclusion that she had gone into the wrong house, which happened to be unlocked, so my neighbour came home to a sparkling kitchen. How nice for her.

My friend Jan was saying goodbye to her cleaner at the door one day, and when the cleaner bent over to tie up her shoe-laces, Jan was shocked. "Are you wearing my pants?" Jan asked. The cleaner, who was approximately the same size as Jan, had stashed a pair of jeans under her own. She quickly confessed, stripped down, returned the pants, and was never seen again.

My last cleaning lady complained about the mess we left, and not so subtly, judged me to my face (and via sticky notes left around the house) for not training my kids to be more accountable for their share of the work around the house. You'd think that this would be counterintuitive, given that this why she gets paid, to clean my house, kids and all. I didn't hire her to comment on my parenting skills. That's when I decided to go it alone and find a strategy to keep the house in some kind of respectable state, which can officially be recorded as another "progressing with difficulty" grade.

The answer to my lack of cleaning motivation, as always, is to throw a dinner party. Inviting friends over guarantees I'll put in a good effort to create the façade that at least the main floor and our one second-floor bathroom look presentable, even if the rest of the house is a hidden mess. And this way, Peter gets more involved, and we can team up against the kids, delegating and dusting our way to temporarily acceptable living conditions, while closing the doors to rooms that hide our true selves.

In this way, we've managed to do a pretty decent job of staying on top of things, but there's still a major flaw in what the kids and Peter see as acceptable on a day-to-day basis. There is garbage left around—not like a leaf that's been trailed in off someone's shoe, but a candy-bar wrapper, or an empty plastic bottle, or a chip bag, or a beer cap. These kinds of things seem to go unnoticed on the floor or on a table for extended periods of time.

Perhaps it's time for another small social experiment: Today I left a piece of garbage (an obvious throw away) on the floor at the entrance to the living room from the front hall. It's unmistakably trash. It's a foil chocolate-bar wrapper, and it sits near the boots, where it lives unnoticed for the next five days when I pick it up again.

I know this is as incriminating for me as for them, and it may prove that my cleaning lady was right, and I'm an irresponsible mom for not setting higher expectations for my boys. But then again, what's wrong with adhering to Bill and Ted's life strategy while on their Excellent Adventure, who simply preached, "Be excellent to each other." I would rather my kids learn to be excellent to each other and to everyone else than learn how to push a vacuum around.

And invariably, if they are genuinely being excellent to each other, they might eventually find themselves helping out by pushing a vacuum around. The two are not mutually exclusive. I think that, after this experiment, I'll remind them more frequently to be more Bill and Ted by picking up their crap, lest one day they find it on their beds, under their covers.

41.

Wherever I Lay my Toque

In the twenty-three years I have known Peter, we have lived in twelve different places. Seems like a lot, and sometimes it seems that, when things get too disorganized, or we accumulate too much stuff, the most natural thing to do is to purge and move rather than to clean up again.

After we moved into our current place in February of last year, I was still working, so it was a while before we really got fully unpacked. We decided to host a party to pressure ourselves into finishing the job. We invited fifteen family members over for Easter lunch, and I scoured the place, bought flowers, rearranged furniture, and generally had the house in tip-top condition when Satchel walked in, scanned the picturesque surroundings, and exclaimed, "Are we moving again? When were the stagers here?"

Has our restlessness ruined our children? I think not. We have been in our rented home for almost a year now, and already they are itching to move, this time to somewhere with more of a contrast from the three-block radius in which we've lived for most of our lives as a family. They have it in their heads that they want to move to the country of all places! They want space. They want a trampoline. They want ... a dog.

Over the years, they have begged for a dog because many of their friends have one. There's always been an easy out: It's not fair to have a dog in the city, especially while I'm working. All of their friends with dogs have moms or dads who don't have to go to work every day—who can take the dog out for a walk or hire someone to take their dog for a walk. I'm not paying someone to walk our dog, and I'm not taking it out myself when it's -25°C.

Now they have conspired. Satchel, our free spirit, loves the feel of small-town living and pastoral scenery. Tanner desperately wants a dog and a trampoline, and Cole, who is joined at the hip with his best friend, has since learned that this lovely boy may be deserting him to attend a private school next year. Peter has always wanted to live more rurally, which is the way he grew up, in a small town north of the city in the province of Quebec. There is no reason to stay in the city anymore. No reason that they can think of—as usual, I am the wild card.

I am an urbanite. The city is in my veins. I bleed exhaust fumes. And now to add to that, I have something I haven't had in a long time: friends—friends who are becoming better friends every day. I've been complaining about how this small community is no longer small, about the parking and the crowds and the number of dogs per square foot, about the road-rage and the construction and the unstoppable growth that has to occur to support the influx of newcomers and city-seekers who flock to these areas so close to downtown. But somehow, amid all of that, finding friendly faces and becoming involved in the community makes it easier to overlook those negative attributes. We have a "We're all in this together" mindset.

And now my family wants to move to a small town, not even a suburb. Whenever we visit our close friends who spontaneously made this kind of move two years ago, my kids are in awe. Our friends have a pond, a trampoline, a vegetable garden, a dog ... and a horse. And they walk to their downtown. It's intriguing, to say the least. The pull factor towards the country is a lot more romantic than the push factor to head to the suburbs was.

Time to go back to my real-estate porn, this time with a reluctant but more realistic approach in mind. Perhaps if we found the perfect place, with friendly neighbours, who like to spend time outside, a nearby Starbucks or facsimile, a dog and a built-in dog-walker, or a yard big enough to let the dog out by itself in cold weather, perhaps a pool and a built-in pool boy, close to good schools and funky shops, and a horse... On second thought, better to stay in the city. There's no way I'm picking up gigantic paddies of horseshit. The rest of my family, horseshit notwithstanding, remain unconvinced, and I half-heartedly search for properties, not believing I will actually find the perfect place.

42.

Girl on a Train

After much preparation to have the children taken care of by no less than four different people during the thirty hours we'll be away, we board the train to Ottawa.

It's nearing the end of January. Peter has been spending time in our nation's capital recently, due to the acquisition of a new client, and has been trying to get me to come with him on one of his trips. I can only manage to be away for one night of his four-day stay. We would take the train, a four-and-a-half-hour journey, during which he could work, and I could write, uninterrupted.

After two hours of travel in business class, where food and drink are included, the only thing I complete is three glasses of wine. I really don't get out much.

Eventually, in a bit of a haze, I open my computer and begin to tap out some thoughts, hoping that, when I read them the next morning, there might be something coherent to latch onto.

The train is a great way to travel, by the way. No security, no taking off your shoes and belt, no arriving two hours before departure, and no squished-together, dollhouse seats— just lots of time to watch the landscape go by. The scenery, which starts out as a few, pretty little snow-covered towns, becomes (yup) many, many snow-covered towns. How do people live so close to the rails? Their front doors seem like they are only fifty-feet away from the tracks. I can see into their kitchens.

I have always wondered how so many people manage to get hit by trains. How does that happen? Are the trains not loud enough? Are the tracks not visible enough? Are these people just not smart enough to make that critical connection between a train track and a potential train? Do they confuse the road rule that we learn as kids to "Stop, look, and listen" with the clothing-on-fire rule to "Stop, drop, and roll?" Trains do not suddenly make a right turn off a side street and catch people off guard.

So, I look it up. In Canada, in 2014, there were fifty-one crossing fatalities on railway tracks. Trains are getting quieter, but people aren't getting smarter. Some are killed because they are walking (trespassing) on the tracks while listening to music on headphones. There is no respect for the track. In the safety-tips section of railway operations, two tips stand out to me: First: Stay off the tracks! And second: Always assume a train is coming. There are many more tips, which wouldn't be worth mentioning if people only paid attention to the first one.

Authorities claim that there needs to be more education where train safety is concerned. The only education anyone really needs is to stay off the goddamn tracks! Period! The internet reveals that some people follow a different set of rules: Try bungee jumping from a bridge that supports train tracks. Do not check for oncoming trains. Try posing your entire wedding party on the train tracks. Smile. Do not check for oncoming trains. Take that shortcut over the train tracks. When your grocery cart gets stuck, wrestle with it. Yes, there is an oncoming train, but is it really moving that fast? These are all things that people have really done, and not all of them have survived.

Back to our train ride, which is (fortunately) fatality-free. We arrive, quite tipsy, at our hotel, in the dark, and immediately grab our skates and head to the world-famous Rideau Canal for a chance to skate on this winding, 7.8 kilometre ice rink. If there is a bright spot to winter, then this is it. This experience has to be on every Canadian's bucket list. Skating along the river, watching the scenery go by, instead of in a crowded, enclosed circle at our home rink in the park, is exhilarating. Of course, we move constantly and dress appropriately, so that even in -24°C, we stay surprisingly warm.

After skating, we eat some greasy pub food, enjoy a few more alcoholic beverages, and then retreat to the bar in our hotel. Another couple of drinks later and we are warm and toasted. I haven't had a steady stream of alcohol like that in many years.

Once in the hotel room, we face the prospect of Obligatory Hotel Sex. Like most couples who have been married for a while, my husband and I have slightly differing perspectives on the purpose of a hotel room. When I walk into the room, I think, Wow, cleaned sheets that I didn't have to clean, a made-up bed that I didn't have to make, and a sparkling bathroom that I didn't have to sparkle (or wipe away urine from around the toilet and on the walls, left by distracted boys). And wow! A remote control, which I now have a one-in-two chance of holding, instead of one in five! Not to mention the possibility of a long and undisturbed sleep. This hotel room, in particular, has a friendly, skinny mirror, which magically takes ten pounds off my frame. I really like this hotel room.

When my husband walks into a hotel room, he sees a venue for frequent, uninhibited sex. No kids in the next room who might hear or interrupt, no early morning alarm, a house-keeper who will clean the room, and his remote control. There is absolutely no excuse not to have sex in a hotel room with his significant other—it's just a no-brainer.

Unless, of course, you've both been drinking steadily for the past ten hours, in which case, you pass out. Sorry, no gratuitous sex scene here. Which is too bad, because it definitely was a missed opportunity for Peter to erotically paint my toenails like in Bull Durham, the best romantic comedy he never knew he watched. Or wash my hair like in that romantic scene in Out of Africa—you know the one I'm talking about ladies: Redford, Streep, shampoo, raw African landscape... Need I say more?

In the morning, Peter leaves for some meetings after break-fast, a little worse for wear, and I wander around downtown Ottawa for a few hours before my train departs for home. Something strange, however, occurs on my little walkabout. About an hour in, I suddenly feel warm, really warm. Whether I've stepped into a shop or I'm standing out in the cold, my body is heating up at an alarming rate. I take off my gloves and hat and unzip my coat. On the street, I am the only one not wrapped like a scientist exploring penguin behaviour in Antarctica.

By the time I get back to the hotel, I am drenched in sweat. I remove many layers of clothing, which were necessary an hour earlier but are now restricting my breathing. I can't get my clothes off fast enough. I shower, change, and head downstairs to hail a cab, coat open, t-shirt billowing in the wind. How had the weather changed so drastically and why had nobody else noticed?

Once in the taxi, I mention to the driver about how nice it is that the weather is finally improving. He looks at me perplexed, "Mademoiselle?" He is a French-speaking driver.

"The temperature. Do you know what the temperature is?" I ask, irritated and fanning myself. "Quelle est la température?"

He plays with his phone for a moment then shows me the screen: -15°C.

What? Oh my God!

Can this be...? Is this a ... hot flash? When I complained that I wanted to go someplace warm, this is not what I had in mind! This was Mother Nature and Father Winter conspiring to bite me in my freezing/sweaty ass.

Back on the train, calmer and cooler, I reflect on my episode and decide that what I experienced may not have been an authentic, pre-menopausal symptom. At my advancing age and unpracticed at partying, it could have just been the effects of a delayed hangover, triggered by the extreme heat and cold from going in and out of stores, along with a touch of dehydration. Yes, that must have been it. I will be one of those women who manages to evade the stifling grip of hot flashes because I'm ... I'm ... oh, God, please don't let me get hot flashes. I apologize for every wicked thing I've ever done. I promise to stop complaining about the weather. I promise to eat brussel sprouts without dry heaving (actually, I can't promise that). But I do promise to call my dad and change the cat litter more often. Just let me donate a kidney—anything that would be less interfering, less uncomfortable, less mood-altering than having to go over the treacherous precipice into menopause. I do not wish to spend years wading through alligator-infested waters in search of the secret exit, which marks the end of our reproductive cycle. Why can't I just receive a gold watch, a commemorative trophy, or a certificate which says, Congratulations Jane Bedard, for successfully enduring the reproductive period of your life.

At home again, the overnight adventure is a blur. I am back to standing in piles of laundry, as if the trip never happened, except now I see my skates parked at the front door among the boots, cleats, and running shoes that clog our entryway, so I know it wasn't a dream. I sit quietly for a moment, watching the clock, trying not to think about the crazy schedule that awaits. Then I bundle up to pick up the kids from school and start all over again.

43.

Ice Capades

I head straight into busy-mode because upcoming is a ME day, which means cleaning up for the ME day (hosted partly at my house), some tutoring, a dinner party for a friend's birthday, and Peter's birthday, all in two days.

I go into attack mode, cleaning up dust and dirt from every nook and cranny. I wash the floors, clean the bathroom, kick the balls to the basement, remove and roll up hazardous chargers protruding from every socket, buy some cheese and crackers, and hit the shower, emerging just as Marg knocks on the door.

For our January ME outing, Marg organized a simple, free of charge, group skate at the outdoor rink in the park, followed by hot drinks at my house, which is conveniently on the way from the rink to the school for child pick-up.

Marg is kind, generous, and one of the more practical women in the group. I mean this as a sincere compliment. She is extremely sharp and quick-witted, with a sense of humour so deadpan she could have dried my flooded basement with just a few off-handed comments on the current government. She stands up for what she believes in and is unafraid of controversy.

She used to work in sports-and-recreation administration and is now an excellent mom to her two children.

The winter-weather gods are smiling down on us, and the present temperature is a balmy -3°C; however, make no mistake, with the wind factor it feels like -15°C. Six of us skate, chat, and try to stay warm. We last a good half-hour, which is a valiant effort, and then head back for the yummy, après-skate treats Marg has brought for us, along with tea in my pseudo-clean house.

Marg has organized a prize for the person who has the best/worst winter-holiday story, based on the freezing conditions, ice storms, and power outages that rocked the province. Yvonne would have won hands down had she been able to come to this ME event. Two days before Christmas, Yvonne had a flight cancelled, then a train rerouted, and eventually endured a sixteen-hour bus ride, followed by a long car ride, to meet up with her family in Nova Scotia in time to deposit the presents under the tree before the children awoke Christmas morning. She eventually trained, planed, bused, and automobiled to her destination, but not without a lot of frustration directed at uncooperative and uncommunicative train, plane, and bus officials. Since Yvonne is unavailable for our skating outing, Marg leaves the prize of Lindt Chocolates in my care and renames them a co-hostess gift.

The afternoon is fun, relaxing, and free, and forces those of us who had not just skated on the Rideau Canal to get back out on skates after a long hiatus. Another successful ME day.

44.

That's the Way We Found Her, Officer

The morning after the ME day skate, I am attacked by the flu and my period at precisely the same nanosecond. It feels like I've been hit by a truck, and then the driver of that truck got out of his rig, picked me up by the scruff of my neck, and punched me in the uterus sixteen times. Also, what a fun birthday for Peter!

It is all a bit of a blur, but I remember lying semi-conscious in bed all day Saturday, downing Nyquil, and making the odd trip to the bathroom to check my "equipment", as my mother would say. At one point, I am so weak I can't get up at all, yet I am suddenly hungry, not having eaten since the day before. I can hear the music playing downstairs and Peter and the kids playing poker and blackjack. Then the TV goes on and a movie begins. All of these things are distracting my clan from discovering that Princess Jane is 911 hungry. I am waiting for anyone to come upstairs to use the washroom so that I can wave him down from my bed, which overlooks the hallway. A full bladder is my only hope.

Many hours go by with no rescue. I am too weak to even shout over the noise of the TV and am about to give up hope when I see it: the box of Lindt chocolates on the floor, beside my bed, dropped there during a quick clean up. Hours later, the kids find me, looking like some kind of strung-out addict, passed out, surrounded by red-foil Lindt wrappers, with a bottle of Nyquil resting in my limp hand. Foul play is quickly ruled out.

Once vertical again, I complain to the boys, "Why hadn't anyone come up to use the washroom? There's always a steady stream of kids using the washroom! Someone should have come up and seen that I needed help!"

Peter (giving me his most charming and innocent bystander look) explains, "That's probably because I haven't fed or watered them. They're empty."

Suddenly it's Monday. I am forced back into reality and the morning starts abruptly. Get sleepy Satchel ready for school and realize, due to my sick leave for the past few days, that there is almost no food in the house. Make him a bowl of oatmeal, and sprint down the street, in the dark, to the bakery (which is open early) and buy a couple of spinach and feta croissants for his lunch. On my way back, I slip on the ice and go down, ass over teakettle, the bag of croissants flying so high in the air that I pick myself up, check for injuries, and still have time to watch it rain croissants around me. Zero casualties, no back injury, and croissants splayed across the clear ice and not the dirty snow or the mucky, slushy road (but somewhat near the spilled coffee remains from the day before, where Peter performed a similarly graceful move).

I drive Satchel to the tube (taken to calling it that since my Bridget Jones days) and come home to Tanner and Cole sitting at the table with dry cereal. No milk. Sprint to the corner variety only to find they are also out of milk. Dash back to the bakery to buy some bread to make French toast, sans lait. Arrive home to only one egg for French toast. Prepare it anyway, with watery egg mixture merely dribbled over bread, but with loads of maple syrup to make up for dryness. Miraculously get kids to school with seconds to spare. Working-me would not have survived this morning.

45.

There's No Place Like Home

Two weeks into January, I receive an email from my headmaster again. There is a staff meeting later that day, and he'd like to announce my retirement. Judging by our previous talk and my silence since then, he made the assumption that I would probably not be coming back, so why put it off any longer? I panic, and he offers me yet another week to think about it. Peter and I talk it out and weigh the pros and cons, which are considerable on both sides. Then I make an appointment with Maurine.

I have avoided mentioning Maurine because I don't want to scare anyone off who might think I'm some kind of crackpot who believes in psychics or ghosts or other aspects of the paranormal. But I kind of do. Maurine has been working as a partner in Peter's company for over ten years as an accountant, advisor, and co-coach. She is smart and practical and uses these attributes to help guide Peter in many aspects of his consulting business. She is also an intuitive psychic. It's not like she can pick the best horse to bet on in the Triple Crown, but she can assess a situation and find the best approach, according to the mood, the players involved, and the environment. Sometimes she can sense how things are going to turn out and help others prepare for it.

Her talents extend to healing practices, and she has proven time and again the effectiveness of her abilities. As an example, her husband, who is the oldest living Canadian with a rare heart condition, has had many close calls in the operating room. On one occasion, he was rushed into surgery for an emergency procedure. After several hours, the surgeon met with Maurine in the waiting room to tell her that things looked dire because her husband's blood was not regulating and was so thin that they couldn't contain it. He was going to bleed out, and there was nothing they could do.

Maurine sat in the waiting room and prayed, calmly sending waves of healing toward her dying husband. Within the hour, the surgeon came out again. "I can't understand it. His blood has thickened. It became almost too thick, but it's levelling out now, and he's going to be okay."

Coincidence? Maybe. Perhaps she has performed miracles, perhaps not, but that aside, she has sound judgment, is a straight shooter, and a caring person. She calms us when we're anxious and alerts us when rough waters are approaching. She helps us figure things out, see new perspectives, and de-cloud our foggy brains.

Every now and then, I book an appointment with Maurine to receive a Reiki treatment and to talk about what's weighing on my brain. Reiki is a hands-on, healing treatment, in which a practitioner places her hands lightly on or over a patient's body to facilitate healing and relaxation. It combines the Japanese and Chinese word-characters of "rei" (spiritual or supernatural) and "ki" (vital energy). Having someone listen so attentively to my body and mind, with the goal of helping to ease my burden, is an incredible feeling, like having a natural high or even my own fairy godmother.

Once, after a treatment, I was driving home and had to actually pull over to the side of the road because I was too damned happy to drive. I actually cried tears of joy for no apparent reason. On another occasion, I was feeling pretty healthy, so I went for a maintenance visit, as opposed to my usual low self-esteem or life-crisis babble visit. During my extended monologue, she suddenly stopped me and said, "Stop! Clare is here. And Jan. And your mom. There is such an outpouring of love for you from them right now. It's raining love on you."

Whether you believe in that stuff or not, the warmth I felt at that time emanating from deep within me and spreading outward toward my skin and beyond was unlike anything I have felt. Yes, it could have been the power of suggestion, but why not believe that it was three of the people I loved dearly and missed so much looking out for me and sending showers of love? It wasn't hurting anyone. It was just ... good.

Now I have to make a life-changing decision, so I go to see Maurine for a little guidance. I lie fully clothed on my back on her table, and she puts one hand on my belly and the other under my back. I feel them heat up as we talk. Eventually, after I chatter on for a while, she interrupts me somewhat impatiently and says, "Stop. What does your heart tell you to do?"

Without thinking it comes out: "My heart says to stay at home with my kids."

"Then listen to your heart, and it will all work out."

And in my head, I continue the conversation: "How? How will it all work out?"

And my heart answers: "I don't know. It just will."

Sounds cliché, like all I had to do was click my ruby slippers together three times and find myself on the other side of this dilemma. Maybe my mission isn't a one-year search for connection and adventure. Maybe my goals to regroup, rediscover, and reconnect are leading me to the conclusion that (like Dorothy) there's no place like home.

46.
What Does S.E.X. Stand For?

"What's sperm?" asks Tanner innocently from the back of the van. Satchel and I exchange nervous looks. Time to bring out the book. When Satchel was 10 and pulled one of my tampons out of his school knapsack that I had borrowed on a weekend, I quickly declared the tampon to be a "fancy pen", which (of course) he wanted to use. I bought a book called, Let's Talk About S-E-X: A Guide for Kids 9-12 and Their Parents. Satchel, always the academic, took the book to his room, shut the door, and read it cover to cover. The only question the book didn't answer was, "What's a tampon?" but he got the gist of everything else.

Tanner knows about the book as we have been posturing about reading it together for a few months but hadn't got around to it. My delay-response tactic to the sperm question is this: "That's a question that will be answered when we read the book." A few hours after the sperm question, we are watching television, and a maxi-pad commercial comes on. "What's a period?" asks Tanner. Definitely time to do some reading.

We sit on his bed, taking turns reading about sperm and erections and ejaculation and semen (or "goo" which is our scientific term), and pubic hair, and all those other fun things you enjoy discussing with your 10-year-old son. Cole, only 8 years old, considerately gives us some space but eventually arrives as we are finishing a chapter. He looks at the title quizzically and asks, "What does S-E-X stand for?"

Soon, I'll be reading with Cole, but I'm so pleased that these conversations are happening now, instead of being condensed down the road into a big, threatening ball of "Just stop it!" the way my dad educated my sister all those years ago. I'm also happy that my kids are still holding on to that rare innocence so hard to find in children these days. Through the media, they are exposed to so much on a daily basis, it's difficult to tell the difference between what they've heard and what they understand. Add to that what the government deems necessary for them to know by implementing a new Sex Education curriculum, which (in my opinion) addresses some overly sophisticated topics at too early an age, and soon they'll be teaching me. We used to complain about the New Math; is the "New Sex" part of our future curriculum?

I remember in fourth grade when Lucy Redding accosted me into her bathroom to tell me the big news about the birds and the bees. I stared at her wide-eyed, listening, speechless, while she waited for some kind of reaction. Finally, the only conclusion I could draw was, "Well, maybe your parents did that, but my parents absolutely did not!"

It wasn't until Betsy Mather pulled me into her bathroom (which seemed to be the universal classroom for these lessons) to show me her dad's stash of Forum magazines when I truly started to believe the rumours that had been swirling around. I couldn't even look my parents in the eye for days. How could they do that? Why would anyone want to do that? None of it made sense to me, but I had no one with whom to talk about it.

Which is why I totally get where my 10-year-old is coming from when we read about all this "goo", and I can only imagine that he tries not to picture his parents engaging in this deviant behaviour. We read a few paragraphs, and then he looks at me, trying to get his bearings. We are his obvious points of reference on this, so I am on shaky ground because I don't want to gross him out. And how do you explain that people do this with each other because they love each other and/or because it feels good? He feigns maturity, and I am so impressed by his efforts not to giggle or gag. I'm sure he'd like to think that maybe other people's parents might be doing that, but not his ... except we read the book together and I don't deny any of it. Wasn't it just yesterday that he was working through the whole Santa Clause thing and now this? It's all just too fast.

47.

Mommy-fied

There is ten inches of snow on the ground, and it's still falling. I finally slip into some kind of winter coma. I'm in a state of disbelief that there can be this much condensation in the atmosphere. Luckily, I remember that I have my mayday, call-up-the-Special-Forces winter coat stashed away for serious winter combat. This coat is enormous, goes down to my ankles, and is filled with down feathers. I look like a walking sleeping bag, shuffling along, oblivious to passersby and hoping that my little ducklings are imprinting behind me as we waddled to and from school. I am sure they're there somewhere, although I can't see them through the snow squalls and the tiny opening in my hood.

I'm also wearing a belated birthday present from Miriam, a close and crafty friend of mine: it's a handmade toque, patched together from old cashmere sweaters, with a polar-fleece lining. It's pink and grey with a big grey flower on the side, and in Canada, giving someone a toque simply means, "I love you." So, this makes me feel warm in two ways.

The weather today has also broadened my MLS search to include Victoria, B.C., the only place in Canada with above zero temperatures. After my dad met and married his second wife, Vicky, they moved out there instead of snow-birding it to Florida (yes, Vic and Vicky moved to Victoria). He called from his balmy 8°C the other day to see how we were faring during a particularly harsh patch of January and just before we hung up, he added, "Don't be like me. Don't wait until you're 70 before you realize that you don't have to live in that weather." He's wrong, of course, in that I don't consider this living.

To cheer myself up, I find the spa gift certificate I received from my in-laws for Christmas and book a facial at the spa in my gym. Perhaps I can fit a workout in if I can get there early enough—if I can get there at all. The roads are looking pretty grim. There is a mountain of snow on my car to be brushed off, and I have to shovel the driveway after the snowplow barricaded me in. Taking the kids for our Wednesday after-school skate has already been wiped from the schedule. I feel oppressed, my every move conditional upon the weather.

I am looking forward to going back to the gym, even if I only glance at the cardio machines on my way to the spa. Winter hibernation has prevented both Peter and me from getting out there lately, so we started a new diet to counter the comfort-food-infused winter insulation we've added to our midsections. Our inspiration is the recipe book for Wheat Belly that I bought him for his birthday (I'm soooo sweet that way). What we've discovered since starting this diet is that almost our entire food intake, minus the chewy, morning smoothie, is comprised of wheat, especially in the winter: thick, cozy soups with bread for dipping, grilled cheese, pancakes, French toast, quesadillas, crackers, cereal, chili, spaghetti, Paninis, and Ah Caramels! (spongy white cakes coated in a chocolaty layer, overflowing with luscious caramel and pastry cream—a veritable kryptonite for our family). And, of course, as you soon as you deny yourself something, it's all you can think about, so on that first day of dieting, I limited my wheat intake to a chocolate croissant and a carrot muffin. It will be a weaning process for sure.

The other problem with this diet is that replacing all of these doughy delicacies with gluten-free substitutes is expensive. After tasting gluten-free bread, my recommendation is that it should be marketed as glutton-free because it tastes so bad you'd never want to overindulge in more than one slice. Open-faced, gluten-free sandwiches are now au courant around here, which only makes my culinary creations even less inviting.

Adding wheat-free to meat-free makes Peter's choices severely limited. I'm not sure this is sustainable, especially since he was informed that beer is made from wheat, so beer has made the shortlist of things he won't give up. This diet for him consists of wheat-free with a side of ale, and mine is wheat-free with a dash of croissants. I believe there will be space on our bookshelf for Wheat Belly, somewhere between the dusty Atkins and Dukan diet books.

Eventually, my wheat belly and I make it to the spa, where I have my face expertly washed. Actually, it is definitely much more than a face wash; it is a parfait of paradise. A most delicious concoction of layered pastries smeared across my chapped and dry visage (and given my mostly abstinence from these delicacies, I want to lick gobs of these creams right out of their jars).

I don't often indulge in luxurious pampering, so when I do, I feel I have to come clean about my absence like I've missed confession: "Forgive me, Esthetician, for I have sinned. It has been two years since my last facial."

Esthetician tries to look patient while I scan the spa menu, focusing first on cost.

Prices range from what I would pay for dinner for five at McDonald's to a weekend for five at Great Wolf Lodge. Yes, these are my points of reference when budgeting for extra-curricular activities, which may explain why it has been two years since my last facial.

My eyes glaze over as I read the descriptions of each treatment. The number of options is overwhelming: hydrating, purifying, anti-ageing, soothing, collagen, detoxing, micro-dermabrasion, brightening, refreshing, and enhancing—not to mention a list of "sides" to accompany my main entrée, like eye treatments and brow waxing. I just want the one that will return my skin to the soft and wrinkle-free state that my neighbour's eight-month-old daughter has. Which one is that?

I look helplessly at Esthetician and ask her what she thinks. She pretends to scrutinize my face from many angles and distances, but her reply still comes way too quickly. She delicately recommends the Anti-Aging Facial. Ugh. Memories of last year, when I found my first grey hair and was given my first prescription for reading glasses on the same day. Yes, I'm ageing. I get it. Give me the Anti-Aging Facial.

Then, to add insult to injury, she recommends a side of brow wax. For some reason, she believes I should have two eyebrows. What will these crazy millennials think up next?

The next thing I know, I'm on my back while an onslaught of stuff is smeared on my face— layer upon layer of creams and ointments, intermixed with steam. At one point, Esthetician actually puts a large piece of gauze over my entire face, mummifying me, then tops it with what I can only assume is sweet-smelling formaldehyde to preserve what is left of my 40-plus skin. I can't really turn my head or see very well, but when I hear Esthetician moving about, I imagine she has left the room to borrow a hand sander from the maintenance room to exfoliate my decrepit cells.

After the embalming, she protects my mouth and eyes with cooling pads, then applies a thick layer of what feels like Elmer's White glue all over my face. Thoughts of how my kids would paint my mask would have made me giggle if I were able to smile without breaking the setting plaster. Would they create an evening (or late-afternoon) post-chardonnay, happy mommy or an early morning, pre-caffeine, scary mommy?

While the miracle glue tingles and rejuvenates my dehydrated epidermis, my weary body relaxes into the table. My eyelids grow heavy. The room gets darker.

Mmmmm...

Suddenly, Esthetician interrupts my bliss by asking if she can massage my neck and shoulders. It is shocking to me that she has to ask, but she explains that some people don't like to be touched, other than on their face. This baffles me. Who are these people? Throughout the day, I caress, massage, shampoo, and gently clean off the dirt of the day from my children's bodies. I rub antibiotic ointment onto cuts, tape up injuries, and wet down horn-like clumps of hair. I cut finger and toenails, and wipe away snot and tears, often without a tissue. I am committed to countless tactile acts throughout the day, and now someone is asking for permission to massage me? It doesn't bother me that she is being paid to do it, I am still almost moved to tears. "Yes," I answer. "You may massage my neck and shoulders."

A little later, she startles me again by asking if she can massage my feet while a vitamin-C mask sets. I am compelled to say, "Listen, without trying to be suggestive of anything inappropriate, not one part of my body would be offended if you tried to rub it, so next time, don't ask, just surprise me."

Off I go again to that puffy, cloudy, floaty place filled with harp-playing angels wearing lavender and eucalyptus-filled amulets—until she surprises me, and I bolt upright because Esthetician has lit my forehead on fire. She swiftly dabs at the freckles of blood oozing from my freshly waxed eyebrows, plucks at a few stray hairs that have avoided the bushfire, then extinguishes the whole area with an après-burn ointment. She performs the assault as efficiently as a trained assassin, and before I know it, I'm lying supine again, wondering if those last few moments were real or just a fleeting nightmare.

And then I close my eyes, try to relax what's left of my eyebrows, and go on a quick trip to my happy place: on a surfboard in the warm Caribbean Sea, my feet dangling off the board, while underwater scuba-spa staff polish them with a ticklish loofah. I almost have a happy ending right then and there, which (for a busy mom) means that I almost fall asleep.

Mmmmm...

48.
You Can't Afford Me

It's only the beginning of February, but as of this coming August, I am officially without a job and quitter's remorse is setting in. Even though I chose it, it isn't sitting well. Even though I am being rewarded with what I think I want—to stay at home with the kids, do some writing, continue on with ME, and enjoy the pace—I'm now thinking of what I don't want: to lose our benefits and pension, limit our travel, eliminate non-essential shopping, colour my own hair, self-pedicure, and eliminate restaurants and take-out.

Oh shit, what have I done? My mind plays out the consequences of how to feel: "And here comes Confidence rounding the bend! Confidence is lengths ahead of the pack! But, oh boy, look out for Self-Doubt! Self-Doubt is gaining quickly! They're neck and neck! And down the stretch they come! It's Confidence and Self-Doubt! Self-Doubt and Confidence! Battling it out as they approach the finish line! And it's Self-Doubt by a nose!"

Time to prepare a resume.

Re-doing my resume is what I do when I'm nervous about the future. When we moved from the suburbs back to the city, I felt I had to get back into the workforce in order to afford our urban lifestyle. But the point of not accepting a position back at my school this time is so that I can not work, and that feels a little too permanent. A few weeks ago, I could relax about the idea of staying at home, knowing that I had a job in the real world waiting for me when my year ended, and we could get back to our standard, hectic lifestyle with money and no time, instead of time and no money.

And what about when I might be ready to return to work? My profile would match that of an antique: old and expensive. How does one market oneself after a prolonged absence from the workforce, going up against so many youthful, childless, go-getters, fresh out of college, with nothing but time on their hands and low-pay expectations?

I have great admiration for a friend of mine, whose daughter's disability falls into the very wide net of autism. Michelle's beautiful, 14-year-old daughter, Tennyson, is non-verbal with limited cognizant and fine motor skills. She requires constant care and full assistance with feeding, bathing, and all other daily rituals. Today her health is good but scoliosis has set in, and the fear is that it will progress rapidly, sending her into a wheelchair in the very near future.

Tenny's parents have been tirelessly fighting the good fight for years with the school systems, the medical community, and the layers of bureaucracy to find better and more accessible treatment, along with more funding and recognition for the thousands of girls who have Rett Syndrome, along with other kids who fall on the spectrum. Throughout the day-to-day therapies and accommodations for Tenny, and the countless meetings, protests, and interviews, Michelle, her husband, and their two other children have tried to maintain as normal a life as possible. And around her passion for her family, Michelle, has even managed to pursue her dream of building a successful photography business. Like Peter, owning her own business (where she is the face of the company) is more tenuous than working for a larger, more-established organization, but the tradeoff is that it allows for a certain amount of flexibility in her scheduling.

The idea of working for myself is intriguing but daunting to me, mainly as my self-confidence is so low that I can't even think of what business I could do. I've heard this concern from other SAHMs before, but this is the first time I am confronting the question myself, and I don't like the silence that engulfs my answer.

The resilience and courage of Michelle and her family astound and inspire me. Like many families, they have been thrown onto the field, ill-prepared, and life has become less about following a plan and more about calling audibles along the way. They work hard, enjoy the good moments, deal with the frustrations, support each other, and plan for a retirement that will include three people.

When I think about Michelle and others like her, sometimes I feel guilty that perhaps I am not being the role model my boys need me to be. Will they expect their future partners to leave their careers and stay at home to raise children? My kids joke with me all the time that I wasn't a real teacher, I was just a French teacher, which fell under the category of other fake teachers, like Physical Education teacher, and Library technician (no offence to teachers of Gym and Library, but we're not kidding ourselves; we know where we stand in the hierarchy of essential subjects).

I knew my children respected that I went to work every day and that I had responsibilities, even if they were the fake responsibilities of a pretend teacher. And they knew that I received a paycheck each month and that I don't anymore. But

I hope they remember the kind of bitch I was when we couldn't get it together in the morning, or how I couldn't give them any attention some evenings because I had evening duties or coaching responsibilities.

Up until now, it had been easy to tell people who asked that I am on a leave of absence for a year. (And by the way, what does that mean, "leave of absence from work"? If you were leaving your absence at work, wouldn't that make you present at work again?) But now, I say that I stay at home with my kids and have to overcome a hypocrisy that has me judging myself for not being out in the field working, as opposed to out in the field playing soccer with my kids.

I would love to say that I'm also a writer, but I think that in saying that there's an assumption that I'm paid to write, and so far, I've written a lot of words with very little to show for it. What I am is the CEO of Bedard Inc., a highly complex organization, which has more than doubled in size in the last decade. I am proud to say my position as CEO has had a very high employee satisfaction rating since it's inception twenty-one years ago, when Peter and I got married, and that the company has had zero turnover, for which we are all very grateful.

The choice to stay home, however, is now mandating absolute frugality. We can't let things slide anymore, because if everything had worked out as initially planned, I'd be back at work soon enough, and we'd be able to patch-up those areas that had been broken by incidentals during the year, i.e., a new mattress, Christmas presents, new snow tires, etc. This is it. My "retirement" as my headmaster put it, is not the sparkly, gated community in Florida I'd once imagined, but more of a murky consignment shop on the edge of town. Besides, I'm way too young to retire, despite what Stupid Cosmetics Girl at the drugstore says.

Time to reassess the situation and find perspective again. The decision is made. I'm at home. There's no turning back. We operated before with the safety net of me going back to work, and now that net is gone. Working mom, stay-at-home-mom ... we both make sacrifices. Trying to live a life free of regret is the fine balance. Our family is taking a leap of faith that this is what will be best for us, but only time will tell.

During this new perspective search, I notice an article online about a survey conducted on a site called Salary.com. Fifteen-thousand working and non-working women were asked to list their top-ten most time-consuming jobs, and a dollar amount was assigned to represent what each task would cost per hour, were it to be performed by a paid professional. For instance, a housekeeper was listed at $11.18 per hour and a cook, $15.01 per hour. The categories were: housekeeper, cook, day-care teacher, van driver, janitor, psychologist, computer operator, facilities manager, laundry operator, and CEO. The working mom, in this scenario, puts in less overtime as she may have other people helping to provide services like cleaning, cooking, and childcare: for example, stay-at-home moms listed cleaning at 14.6 hours per week while working moms listed it at 8.3 hours. SAHMs listed daycare teacher at 14.3 hours, and working moms suggested 5.6 hours.

Here are the statistics:

Stay at Home Mom

Base salary:	40 hours	$48, 509
Overtime:	52 hours +	$94,593
Total:		$143,102

Working Mom

Base Salary:	40 hours	$52,685
Overtime:	19.4 hours +	$37,538
Total:		$90,223*

*Add in Mom's actual working salary for total compensation.

I'm not mentioning this survey to pit working moms against stay-at-home moms. I just can't believe there is that much work to be done by anyone, regardless of her employment status. I do appreciate that not every working mom can afford to hire outside help, which makes her a veritable supermom. As a working mom, whenever I was at the end of my rope, I used to think to myself, It would be so wonderful to have someone to stay at home and look after things. Where do I find Alice, from The Brady Bunch?

Some families keep their nannies to fill in gaps, even when the kids are in school all day. Nannies stay on to drop off and pick up kids, do light housework, and stay with the kids after school. When the kids are in school all day, there's not much for the nanny to do to justify the fulltime paycheck. How do they resolve this discrepancy? Get a dog of course!

49.

Been Der Done Dat Disney

On the heels of those thoughts fraught with financial uncertainty, February is passing swiftly, and everyone around us is planning Winter-Break trips. As we watch temperatures continue to rollercoaster between -10°C and -20°C and listen to friends talk about their Caribbean holidays, we go into vacation-envy mode. We dwell in deep, white snow, our thoughts bathing in warm, white sand.

Before I know it, I'm surfing the travel sites, looking for something cheap. I just can't help myself. There certainly are sunny destinations, which are reasonably inexpensive, but those deals are all created for families of four. The travel world is built for families of four. Even hotels claiming to be family-friendly can only accommodate two adults and two children in one room. Every grand-prize family adventure that's advertised stipulates A Trip for Four! I give up on online travel shopping because I always get the same message: "The maximum number of guests for this room is exceeded".

Of course, the exception to this rule (and just about every rule when it comes to customer satisfaction) is Disney. They totally get families. However, if you're a hard-core Disney fan, skip this section. I have a lot of friends who swear by the Disney World in Orlando and visit frequently. They've learned to navigate the forty-square-mile labyrinth, which is the size of San Francisco. For me, it is absolutely overwhelming. Unfortunately, I didn't know about the book titled: Walt Disney World and Orlando for Dummies, which offers strategies on how to book and survive a successful trip to Disney. How I wish we'd known about that book!

Wearing my guilty mom, first-world-problem hat, I had it in my head that a child did not have a proper childhood if he did not visit Disney. Some friends of ours had a vacancy in their vacation rental home in Orlando last year, removing the task of searching for accommodation, and so we went during March Break. We were completely ill-prepared for what awaited us when we arrived at the grand gates of Walt Disney's House: a well-organized, massive line-up and the first of many to follow. No, we didn't buy our tickets in advance, because (duh) that would take planning, and we don't usually plan for having fun. We just have it. And besides, it's Disney! Fun is supposed to land on our laps and tickle our tummies from the moment we arrive in the parking lot.

After an hour and a half in the ticket line, with my brother-in-law, Adam, and his son, Nathan, in tow, we were able to purchase our tickets and stood on the grounds looking at signs and arrows pointing in a myriad of directions. Everyone else seemed to have read the guidebook and knew exactly where to go and what to do, like in a Manhattan rush hour where you must keep up with the pace of the crowd, and jump on or off the moving conveyor belt of people, or risk being carried away in the wrong direction or trampled by pedestrians trying to get to work on time. There is no stopping to look at a map or a street sign. This is how we felt on entering Disney. We stood dumbfounded, like a stranded bumper car being jostled by strollers and stray kids, feeling pressured to make up for lost time spent in the ticket line, but what to do first? Where to go?

At eleven o'clock in the morning, we wandered toward a ride we wanted to go on and asked an employee about the Fast Pass, which is a concept only Disney could have implemented on such a grand scale. For those of you who have not visited Disney (yet), a Fast Pass is a free card that you have stamped with a ride time at the entrance to each ride. After you visit each ride and pre-book it, you can return during your designated time period to enter a Fast-Pass line, which expedites you to the front of the longer line. I always said that, when the H1N1 Virus hit Toronto in 2009, they should have hired Disney to orchestrate vaccination stations, thus avoiding the days-long wait that people endured in the cold, wet weather.

Once we figured out the Fast-Pass strategy and pre-booked our rides, we began the game of plotting what to do in between ride appointments. The widespread consensus was to eat. Given that everyone was doing the same thing as us, timing movements around ride schedules, there was a lot of eating on the go. And what consumption there was! The number of gigantic turkey drumsticks being inhaled by all ages and weights was a little disconcerting. Some enthusiastic eaters had two of them, double-fisted, dripping with grease and waddling about with their Oompa Loompa kids in tow, who were also bearing down on their meals like lions after a fresh kill.

And speaking of drumsticks, here are some interesting and fun facts gathered from a Corporate Disney website:

- More than 1.6 million turkey drumsticks are eaten every year in four Orlando Disney theme parks (Magic Kingdom, Epcot, Disney's Hollywood Studios and Disney's Animal Kingdom.)

- More than 75 million Cokes are consumed each year at Walt Disney World resorts.
- The Giant Big Wheel in the 1970's courtyard of Disney's Pop Century Resort can accommodate a rider weighing up to 877 pounds. (I think I saw that guy at the turkey drumstick counter.)

We found an empty patch of grass and unpacked our bagels with cream cheese, bottled water, fruit, and granola bars and chowed down. There would be ice cream and cotton candy later, but for the time being, our kids looked enviously at the decadence surrounding them. I'm not one of those moms who are completely anal about what goes into their kids' mouths. Take one look in our cupboards at home, which are filled with boxes of Ah Caramels! and Oreos, and you'll know that I understand carcinogenic food additives are unavoidable. I just don't like to be extorted and have to pay top dollar for them. I mean, really, if I want to go to the cinema, should I have to pay ten dollars for a movie ticket and then twenty for popcorn and a drink? I think not. For this very purpose, I own a concession purse. My concession purse is big enough to hold five juice boxes, five small bags of chips, and one family pack of licorice, without which the cost of the movie experience quadruples.

After a full day at the Animal Kingdom, we'd had had enough. We rode three good rides, petted some hot, tired animals, and waited an hour to get on the Riverboat Ride to see prehistoric dinosaurs, all the while feigning excitement so that our children's brainwashed minds wouldn't question the Disney cult and our entire March-Break mission.

But I was finished. The next day, Peter and Adam took Cole, Tanner, and Nathan to the Magic Kingdom, which I gather was a greater success than the Animal Kingdom. I'm convinced the big draws for Disney are the princesses. All the little girls want to meet, be photographed, and dine with the princesses. My boys don't do princesses—at least not yet. But the castle, the rides, and the fireworks were apparently enough to make them happy with their day-two experience.

While the younger boys were at the Magic Kingdom, Satchel and I spent the day at Universal Studios, where we could up the scare factor on the rides, but more importantly, so that we could be swept away by our ultimate destination: The Wizarding World of Harry Potter. This was like meeting a Disney princess for us. The life-sized Hogwarts Castle loomed over us as we walked the familiar, cobbled streets of Hogsmeade, recognizing all the landmark shops and characters from the books. This was a very special trip for Satchel and me. I had read all seven books to him over the years and seen every movie multiple times. We were giddy as we slurped our Butter Beers while waiting our turn to enter Ollivander's Wand Shop. Once inside, Satchel was chosen from the crowd to participate in the choosing of a wand, or to be more exact, to see which wand would choose him (because as every Potter fan knows, the wand chooses the wizard). It was all meant to be.

Because we purchased the Universal Express Pass, we went to the front of every line, without even having to pre-book. We went on exhilarating rides, back-to-back-to-back until the day-light faded, and I thought I might be sick. That was a good day.

I do apologize to hardcore, mouse-ear-wearing Disney fans. I have great admiration for the Disney Empire and the joy it brings to so many children and their grown-ups. For me, however, I'm just not prepared to invest my soul into the whole Goofy culture. The box has been ticked, my kids have seen it, done it, and I'm happy to move on to the next big item on my list. I understand that even Machu Pichu has a Fast-Pass option, which provides the option of riding a train to the top instead of hiking and camping for days; however, the hike, in my opinion, is part of the experience. Chomping on turkey drumsticks between ride appointments may be part of the Disney experience, but it seems daffy to want to indulge in them, and everything else, more than once.

50.
Ain't That a Kick in the Head!

To warm us up as February comes to an end, we have a ME adventure emerge that is worthy of an Epsom-salt bath. When Stella's mitten-making expedition fell through, Jenna stepped up and brought us all to a kickboxing class, run by a mom in the schoolyard who is a competitive kickboxer. You just never know whom you might find in the yard.

On the scheduled day, we show up to the workout room—six newbie kickboxer and two veterans. This class makes me realize how pathetic my workouts have become again. I have missed so many boot camps and weight classes recently that this, literally, kicks me into gear again. Just the initial warm-up, beginning with skipping and jumping jacks has me ready to slither into a corner with my tail between my legs. There are a variety of conditioning and strength-training activities, followed by boxing (with cute pink boxing gloves) and kicking, all aimed at a partner holding thick pads, which act as targets and a way to absorb the force of our supermom strength.

We are eight somewhat feminine Rocky Balboas, punching and kicking, doing sit-ups and skipping, and jumping over and crawling under each other. It is exhausting and energizing.

After the initial shock of "Are we actually working this hard?" wears off and we get used to the fact that there will be no breaks, we dig in and enjoy it immensely. It is the perfect ME day: fun, cheap, and local. It is also a great way to get people out to try something new without them feeling self-conscious—another goal of ME. I observe that there seems to be a core of women committed to making every event, but there are also a variety of others, filling in the gaps, coming and going if the timing and their interest intersect.

We finish the hour-long class and are invited back to Jenna's for sprout smoothies and scones. By the afternoon, I feel stronger and weirdly taller. Perhaps after so many months of curling up to stay warm, I am actually standing up straight. This workout, along with the appearance of warmer weather, gives us a brief window into the evolution of humans, as we all slowly peel our shoulders back and transition from our simian, hunched-over winter positions to completely vertical postures. Makes me feel like building a fire or etching some hieroglyphics into my coffee table to prove that I not only existed but also survived the cruellest of winters and lived to carve about it.

51.

Rise of the Cave Dwellers

The very best thing about living in negative-degree temperatures for three months is marvelling at that very first day that the thermometer's mercury raises above the frosty 0°C-tree line. March second is that day. At 5°C, with the sun shining, people stop in their tracks on the street and stand, facing the sun, absorbing its warmth, greeting it like a long-lost friend who has finally found its way home. Without judgment, there is just a universal, unspoken moment of appreciation for that warm, tennis ball in the sky, which says, "Thank you for coming back. We're glad you're here. We've missed you." Heads are exposed, eyes squinting at the daylight as if we'd all been living in evacuation mode, deep inside a cave. Holding hands becomes a tactile experience, without the interference of bulky mittens. An email is circulated with a picture of a green blade of grass erupting from the earth with the caption: "Have you seen this?"

Is this why we tolerate the extreme winter? So that we can better appreciate the opposite conditions of spring, which gives hope for a warm summer? Does this feeling go on the list of expressions like: How can you appreciate peace if you have not experienced war? How can you appreciate trust if you have not experienced betrayal? How can you appreciate love if you have not experienced loss? How can you appreciate spring if you have not experienced five months of the coldest fucking winter in twenty years? How can you appreciate Happy Summer Jane if you have not experienced Hostile Winter Jane?

This window of temperate weather will be short-lived, but it does offer hope that spring is around the corner and that we can look forward to the adventures that flooding brings when all this snow begins to melt. I'm not being facetious this time. I really do look forward to grand puddles and backed-up sewers, because they are signs that the warm weather sprites are making their way northbound from community to community, spreading heat, happiness, and wet basements.

52.

Me, Myself, and I are Narcissists

All this talk about watching our budget has me reflecting on the time when I had a paycheck coming in. I had worked at several private schools, where some of the families had no shortage of money, and I remember hearing a conversation in which one girl shared that her father's car was keyed outside her home, and another girl asked if the culprit was caught on any of the security cameras. Because we all have security cameras watching our homes. Another time, I was speaking with a father in the parking lot who showed me his latest toy: a new, bright-red pick-up truck. "Don't you have one of those already?" I asked.

His reply: "Not a red one."

And one grade-five girl described my engagement and wedding rings as "cute." Which is fine. It is amusing to think that my rings remind her of a bedazzled trinket from My Little Pony.

My friend Miriam and I went to one of the fundraising galas together. Before we knew it, the night was ending, most guests had left, and we realized that we were all dressed up but had not had a picture taken together. The room had almost emptied out, so I ran over to the first person I saw and asked him if he would take our picture. That person happened to be the lead singer in a hugely popular Canadian band and a super nice guy—so nice that I don't want to exploit him by using his name in this anecdote. You can imagine how he must have cringed, seeing me running toward him, brandishing a camera until I asked him if he would take a picture of Miriam and me, to which he happily obliged.

This was when it occurred to me what a funny and narcissistic photo album that would be, featuring pictures of me taken by various celebrities. "This one of me was taken by Liam Neeson. Here's one of me taken by Gwyneth Paltrow. Oh, and look, Roger Federer had such a cute smile while he was taking this picture of me. And here's one of me taken by Russell Crow." But then everyone would know that I was lying because Russell Crowe doesn't seem like the type who would indulge in helping out a mere fan take a picture of herself. But Drew Barrymore and Prime Minister Trudeau, they would do it for sure. I'll have to be very selective about who I ask to take my picture.

53.

Falling off a Mountain

It seems a mean irony that, even as the weather begins to turn to something more palatable, we are looking for a quick escape. A friend just got back from Florida, where she said it was more saturated than usual with Canadians who just packed up and left like they were running from the law. March Break is getting closer, and the only thing we're sure about is that we won't be going to Disney. Our agonizing discussions revolve around our eclectic desires for a vacation: Peter wants some culture; I crave adventure. We both want warm weather and a reasonable price, which takes March-Break travel out of the running. It would be cheaper to travel pre or post-March Break, except Satchel doesn't want to miss classes. Tanner and Cole remain happy little elves, content to tag along. But I can pretty much guarantee that these elves would not be too interested in architecture and museums.

I enjoy exploring other cultures, and I'm delighted to tour around and look at museums, architecture, and ruins, and to experience the local gastronomical offerings, but I also feel like we'll be doing that sort of thing when we're old(er) and grey(er.) Whereas I'm not sure how much longer I can ask this old body to climb a mountain or bungee jump from a hanging bridge, or rappel from a cliff top ... that sort of thing.

An ideal trip for me includes a cocktail of offerings for the mind, body, and spirit, and when Clare, Anne, and I went to Costa Rica, we found the perfect mix of these activities. It was the early spring of 2010, and Clare was in between clinical trials, meaning all of the standard methods of cancer care had failed, and so she volunteered to become part of several studies, which were attempting to explore alternative treatments. She went through painful procedures, putting her body through more than she had to, all in the name of cancer research.

It had become a waiting game, watching the cancer advance with no line of defence. It slowly moved through her body like an invisible army invasion, overthrowing one organ, regrouping, and then moving on to the next. Every appointment brought news of another fallen region: liver, lungs, bones, eyes, brain. And yet, she soldiered on, taking the best that each day had to offer. It became harder and harder to say goodbye after each visit with her as if we were rehearsing for the final one.

After her psychologist told her to begin her "final preparations," I called her up and said, "I think it's time to go surfing again."

"Book it, Dano."

This trip had to be really special. While Clare's spirits were still up, her body was tired from the beatings it had taken from four years of medications, therapies, needles, and IVs. She had been having radiation on her brain and in one of her eyes and was slightly inflated from the steroids mixed in with her chemo.

I dove into my research with determination. Honing in on Costa Rica, I looked for the perfect mix of yoga, surfing, and exploration, but based in a quiet retreat, hidden from the rest of the world. I emailed and interviewed the owners of smaller boutique hotels, which offered the kinds of things we sought. I told them about our unique circumstances and concerns and about what we wanted to get out of this trip. They patiently answered all of my questions, but one, in particular, seemed to stand out. Her name was Jill, a co-owner of a new hotel, and we made an instant connection. Even though this place was so new that it had no reviews or ratings, Jill's warmth and commitment to making our time there worthwhile made it feel just right, and we booked for a week. Before long, my sister Anne was on board; however, our brother Peter was unable to make the trip, and so the three sisters touched down in Nosara, Costa Rica in late June.

When we arrived at the stunning, mountainside yoga spa, our hosts, Jill and Ben, came out to greet us, along with Rosie the Rottweiler. Immediately, I knew this had been the right choice. Jill and Ben gave us welcoming hugs, then took us to our accommodation, which was a large, high-ceilinged room made from local materials and decorated with native art. The whole resort was eco-friendly and designed to camouflage itself into the landscape of the lush, hillside jungle. We walked into the open-air yoga pavilion, which looked out over the green rainforest and then beyond to the azure sea. It was breathtaking. We could hear a waterfall nearby, the squawking and chirping of tropical birds, and the grunts of a chatty howler monkey hidden in the trees.

Paradise.

Jill and Ben took care of us, fed us healthy, local vegetarian fare, and treated us like family—the kind of family that you could choose. We were the only guests for the first few days, and we all ate meals together and got to know each other well, staying up late and exchanging life experiences. Through our numerous emails prior to the trip, Jill and I already had a good rapport, and her warmth and nurturing nature that came across in our correspondence turned out to be completely genuine. She quickly got a sense of the three sisters and our dynamic and managed to form a special bond with each of us. Jill spent time with us and listened empathetically to our stories without judgment. She became our therapist in one sense and our mother in another. It had been a long time since we'd had a mother, someone who knew each of us and who wanted to take care of us. It must have been interesting for her to hear three different perspectives of the same story—the story of us.

From me, she must have sensed the weariness that stemmed from working, raising a family, and worrying about Clare. I had been on automatic pilot for a long time. Then something happened that made me stop in my tracks, speechless. Jill walked up to me early in the morning, took my hands in hers, looked me square in the eyes and said, "What would YOU like to do today?"

Her question became key to my presentation to the ME group. It's a powerful question that evokes such a strong response from strung-out parents of young children, working or not. Think about it: What would you like to do today? How would you answer?

I was stunned. My eyes even welled up. What? Me? Choose? This simple question made me weak in the knees, and I realized how negligent I'd been with myself. Of course, I got to do things for myself at home, but there was always an imminent deadline looming nearby—an hour here, an hour there. Free time is not in the invisible contract you sign when you decide to have kids.

I was overwhelmed. Then I was nervous; what if I don't choose correctly and waste this opportunity? Suddenly, it was obvious. It was one of the reasons I was there: Put on your suits, girls! We're going to the beach!

The jeep was loaded with surfboards, along with our driver, Darrin, another co-owner of the resort and mastermind behind its unique and eco-friendly design. The long stretch of beach along Playa Guiones, another world-class surfing beach, greeted us for our surfing adventure. The waves were BIG! Bigger than me! I wondered if the sharks in these waters were also big? Then I realized something: If there really were sharks in these waters, did it matter how big they were? Darrin seemed convinced that the fins I thought I saw out in the distance were merely dolphins playing in the waves. Clearly, these dolphin-size waves were too much for me, but I went there to surf and was determined to surf, regardless of how intimidating the swell. Anne and Clare took one look at the waves and wisely took a pass, choosing two boogie boards on which to frolic closer to shore. The surf, however, was so large and relentless, even close to shore, that they were thrown around and spit out onto the beach time and again. They had an absolute blast.

Meanwhile, out on a longboard with Darrin, I struggled just to paddle out. I was pummeled, over and over by waves way beyond my level of comfort, sending me back and forcing another approach. I was not sure that Darrin had worked with many beginners before, as our perspectives of what was an acceptable wave differed immensely. Waiting for a ride-able wave, I'd hear him say, "Here comes a fun one!" whereas I'd look back and say, "Holy shit!" His "fun" wave was a wall of water about to swallow me up. I did manage to stand up a few times and gave it my best shot. After a couple of hours, I was spent, and Darrin's hatless head was torched bright red from the sun.

An afternoon siesta was followed by sunset yoga and dinner with our hosts. This was so good for all of us. Clare needed physical healing and Anne needed emotional healing. Anne had been struggling to recover since separating from her husband several years earlier. After twenty-five years of marriage, she was depressed and hiding behind a reckless schedule. This wasn't the banana boat, booze-fest she thought she wanted, but Costa Rica gave her time to be quiet, reflect, and finally begin healing—something she desperately needed.

The following days found us kayaking on a beautiful river, learning about the environment and the culture of Costa Rica, reading, napping, yoga-ing, writing, playing scrabble, eating beautiful, fresh food, dancing at a local bar, gazing over the jungle, and listening to an unrehearsed choir of animals and insects, alerting us of their presence in case we got lost in our own thoughts and missed one of them. One of the best days, however, was the canopy tour in the jungle. Clare and I went on our own because Anne is not keen on heights.

When we arrived at the zip line headquarters at 8:00 a.m. sharp, we met eight other women of varying ages standing in front of a small, wooden building, each wearing a harness and helmet. There was an immediate common bond between us, because (for some reason) each of us was there to throw ourselves off the side of a mountain and swing across a valley, attached to a cable. It was a sisterhood of adventure seekers, but our chatter was quickly stifled when we were joined by four of the cutest young Chicos (native Costa Ricans) who were to be our guides for the day.

Marvin, a muscular local with blue-green eyes and a wide smile, introduced himself and his three compadres. We began loading up onto the back of an open-air truck like soldiers being transported to camp. Cito, a lean, athletic treat with a mischievous grin and long, shiny hair pulled back in a ponytail, sat with us in the back of the truck. Next to Cito was André, and in contrast to the others, he was a quiet, thin young man with multiple tattoos and piercings. He was shy and self-conscious about his English but always had his camera ready for that great, spontaneous shot. And finally, there was José, who showed up when we least expected, playing practical jokes, preparing our next launch location, or just unabashedly providing eye-candy for his all-female guests.

The truck ascended the windy road up the mountain, the red dirt softened by the nighttime rains. We learned that our companions on this adventure were all missionaries from the USA, taking a break from spreading the Good Word to (literally) hang around in the jungle. After a few minutes of bouncing around in the truck, I had a feeling these Southern gals would have traded in their bibles for cushions and seatbelts. But they were good-natured and optimistic and having all those people representing the Lord put our minds at ease as the truck groaned to make it up the hills.

At one point, midway up a steep incline, the truck slowed, its wheels spinning deeper and deeper into the earth; the engine panted, and we came to a standstill. Our rock-star guardians jumped into action, two of them jumping up and down on the back end of the truck, trying to bounce the wheels free from the nest of dirt, while one pushed and shovelled, and the other worked the clutch and accelerator of the truck. Eventually, Marvin said, "I'm berry sorry, but joo hab to get out and walk a leedle bit."

Our tribe de-trucked, hiked up the steep hill, and watched the truck show from the top. And what a display it was! These boys bounced and pushed and shovelled and clutched until the unresponsive truck lurched back to life, to the great cheers of the church ladies.

Just minutes later, as the truck began to slow again, our congregation broke out into song, praising the Lord and asking Him to nudge the truck up the hill, just a little more. As it turned out, God was also good at practical jokes, and out went the guides with their shovels and clingy, wet t-shirts (praise that Lord). This happened only once more, after which the truck became possessed and seemed to be pulled up toward the heavens and over the last hill.

Clare, meanwhile, breathed hard at the back of the procession, frequently stopping to catch her breath. I knew she'd never turn back, but it was worrisome to see her struggle, and thoughts of how quickly we could get her to a hospital always lingered, no matter what we did or where we were.

As we exited the truck at the summit, it was not lost on our Spanish-speaking heroes that they had acquired a gaggle of giggling overage groupies. This was further evidenced by the fact that they all stripped off their wet t-shirts and wrung them out in plain view, revealing etched abs and swollen pecs. We swooned accordingly.

Jumping off a mountain was not as difficult as we thought it would be. Our gear was solid, checked, and double-checked, and before we knew it, we were swooping two hundred feet above the rainforest, dangling by a system of ropes and pullies. It was thrilling. At one point, I let go of the harness, hung almost upside down, and flapped my wings as I flew spastically from one end of the valley to the other. We crisscrossed the mountains ten more times over beautiful rivers, waterfalls, curious monkeys, and birds, then removed our harnesses and walked through the jungle to a beautiful oasis where we could eat lunch and swim.

A gorgeous lagoon with a sparkling waterfall, which cascaded into a cool, clean lagoon hosted our sojourn. Cito ran into the trees, reappeared in swim trunks, and dove into the water. Clare and I quickly followed suit, except with a far less dramatic reveal (ageing bodies in sagging swimsuits ... or was that sagging bodies in ageing swimsuits?). Even though Clare was younger than me, her body had been altered by the long fight. She'd lost her hair, but she'd lost other stuff too, stuff that the rest of us always lug around: her vanity, her pettiness, even her worry. She was just one big grin as she leapt off that mountain, whooping and hollering and just loving it.

For our last zip, Clare and I went tandem, laughing near hysterics as we flew down the mountain. I held her as tightly to me as I could, and she hugged me right back. Then we were ushered back to the truck and revisited the red road that had tried to swallow up our vehicle earlier that day. We were exhausted and sweaty but feeling so alive. Gracias, beautiful Chicos, for this unforgettable day with my sister. Gracias.

The following days found us enjoying a fine balance of local explorations, yoga, rest, and reflection. An aura of inner-peace began to emanate from all of us, and the feeling of Pura Vida, Spanish for "Pure Life" slowly infiltrated our psyches as we parted ways with those stressed-out sisters who had arrived a week earlier. One day, as she swung from a hammock on the deck, overlooking the jungle and the sea, Clare said, "I think, if I just stayed here, I could get healthy again."

When I think of Clare now, this is where I picture her. In Costa Rica. Healthy again.

54.

Cuba or Bust!

Whoever said there are only two certainties in life, death and taxes, was wrong. There's a third: laundry. It's true. Wherever you go, whatever you do, even if you walk around the circumference of the earth with only one pair of underwear to your name, you will eventually have to wash that meagre garment. I'm looking at piles of laundry on the floor of our hotel room in Cuba.

That's right, we're in Cuba. During March Break. Because that's the kind of people we are. Forget logic. Forget budgets. Forget responsibility or discipline. Forget strength under adversity. There's only one priority: warmth.

It's my friend Kerry's fault that we're in Cuba. Had I not met her for tea one morning and listened to her plan her Cuban March-Break vacation, I might be gritting my teeth through the late-winter/early-spring polar vortex that had suddenly descended upon much of our part of the world.

Our flight made it out during blowing snow and plummeting temperatures, and now I'm sitting on a patio, listening to Cuban music, with the background pinging and ponging of Tanner and Cole at a nearby table. Yes, I had been looking for a way out of winter, but I look for a lot of things I know I'll never find, like four inches in height, a body that is less like Sponge Bob Square Pants, and fashion that doesn't scream "STUDENT LOAN!"

When we finally booked, we were too last minute for even a last-minute bargain, which put us in the desperate category, falling prey to vacation extortion. We might have been better off (and made the news) if we had been the first people trying to escape from Florida to Cuba in a raft. CUBA OR BUST!

We arrive at our resort in Varadero in the evening, weary and hungry, and are quickly acquainted with vacation buffet dining. Resorts like these definitely make money off of people like us who don't eat or drink a lot, but there are certainly others who make up for our scaled-down appetites. I witness one couple, obviously no strangers to the dinner bell, who have food piled six-inches high on their plates. Either they don't understand the concept of the buffet, or they do, and this really is just the first round. They are kids in a candy shop. I also see a man who can't even be bothered to get a plate. He eats straight from the buffet tables, hand to mouth. So much for five-star Cuba.

The next morning finds us back at the buffet, where it becomes clear that breakfast will be our primary source of fuel and where our Wheat Belly book has no business showing up (not unlike our four-hour Paleo diet). Skinny, little, bone-rack Tanner arrives back at our table with a plate piled with: one waffle, one pancake, one croissant, one French toast, one donut, two bacon slices, and French fries. All of the children in my family can benefit from gaining a few pounds; we joke with them that they each have a six-rack (of ribs) instead of a six-pack (of muscles) in their abdominal sections. I, on the other hand, continue to play a never-ending game of dieter's dodgeball, trying to evade fast-moving balls of calories and fat targeting my body, except I feel like I am the last one left on my side of the court and am pelted relentlessly. It doesn't help that I miraculously continue to gain weight while I sleep. It's almost as if the truffles I eat nightly in my dreams show up on the scale the next day. It occurs to me that I may be sleep eating in the middle of the night and should ask Peter to put a lock on the fridge and snack cupboard or install a camera to catch the whole dismal act on film.

As the week progresses, each visit to the buffet has us carrying lighter and lighter plates back to our table. Through trial and error, or just plain eyeballing, we are identifying foods that won't sit well with us. I like fish but not the kind that can look back at me, and the line for fresh-grilled fish fillets is so long that it becomes unappealing anyway. Thinking I'm being smart and healthy, I stick to large plates of salad for lunch and dinner until I'm sick of them—or should I say sick from them? I forget about the fact that raw fruits and vegetables are not necessarily washed with filtered water, and near the end of the week, I go down with stomach cramps and other wicked bodily functions. We should have remembered that "all-inclusive" includes an optional/accidental excursion to Montezuma, with all its revengeful side effects. Peter signs on for what he calls the Triple-B Diet: bread, butter, and beer, which leaves him feeling safe, if unsatisfied.

Having stomach issues, however, somehow doesn't seem so debilitating in 28°C with ocean views. I sit on our balcony overlooking an ocean so blue that I swear it's been photoshopped. I hear the leaves on the palm trees swishing in the breeze and watch the pelicans gracefully skimming across the water, my rum-drenched Bahama Mama within reach while Tanner sits next to me drawing in his sketchbook. Could I live here? No. Could I wait out the rest of the winter here? Si Señorita.

Our trip also provides the serendipitous pleasure of accidentally booking a resort right next to where my sister Anne and her partner, Frank, are staying. She quickly becomes our sixth player on the tennis court, making even teams, as well as another playmate on the beach, not to mention an estrogen-carrying companion with whom I can chat. She is also a travelling pharmacy and has any remedy I have forgotten. Frank pops in and out of our routine but mostly enjoys sipping frosty cervesas and reading on the beach.

Our days evolve into a pattern of breakfast, tennis, lunch, beach, and dinner, followed by a variety of evening activities consisting of hotel performances, card games, ping pong, and giant chess. Any gaps in the day are filled with drawing, napping, reading, writing, drinking, and frequent trips to the washroom.

Near the end of the week, my buffet plate holds a few teaspoons of rice and a few morsels of boiled chicken, which would have been quite palatable had I not found a few feathers still embedded in one piece of poultry. I realize then that I can't eat anything that looks back at me, or that still has its feathers, like it may still be considering an escape. Vegetarianism is looking more and more like an option again.

Each day we increase the time spent in the ocean. I love the feeling of coming back to the room after an afternoon at the beach. I love licking my lips and tasting the salty leftovers of the sea. I love that gobs of sand spill out of my swimsuit into the shower as I wash away the remains of the day. My nails grow faster, and my hair is softer, and the kids are always shiny and clean for a change.

One of my favourite memories is sitting on the balcony, listening to Peter trying to teach the kids to play Euchre. I can hear Peter's patience waning as he coaches, "No, you can't play that card... No, you can't play that card either... No, that's a trump. You need to play the diamond you tried to play a minute ago... You're so annoying... Pay attention... You still can't play that card... You know, you're quite useless at this game... It's just called a trick. There's nothing magical about it!"

Even though Cuba lifted its travel ban in 2013, the criteria for which Cubans can travel (to where and for how long) are still very stringent and inconsistent. Those professionals deemed necessary to ensure the health and safety of the Cuban population, such as doctors, scientists, and engineers, would not be able to leave. Some may be detained for reasons of national security. Others must still obtain a passport, a document that would cost around five-months salary, along with purchasing an expensive visa from the destination country. The average wage per Cuban is eighteen dollars per month, so even if they could afford a plane ticket, unless there were family to receive them at their destination, they would have nothing to live on when they reached the other side.

What is shocking for us to learn, while staying at our fancy-pants resort, is that because of the low wages paid to even the most educated of Cubans, many of these professionals are better off working at hotels such as ours. We learn from repeat guests who are friendly with the staff that our maid is actually a lawyer and the bartender a doctor. The tips that they receive from tourists provide a far-better wage than working in jobs for which they are trained extensively. With that knowledge, it is difficult not to wonder what the back-story is of every employee we meet for the rest of our trip. None of the staff openly reveal anything about their situations. They work hard with dignity and a smile, and count on the kindness of others, despite the multiple degrees and licenses hidden away in dusty frames at the back of their closets.

At the end of the week, once we're packed and ready to go, like many visitors, we discretely hand out bags of balls, bats, toys, personal hygiene products, and children's clothing to the staff we had met. Before we know it, we're in our jeans, waiting for the bus to take us back to the airport, where we realize that the only thing worse than eating the food in Cuba is trying to get out of Cuba, starting with the massive line to check-in at the airport. This is followed by a monster line at customs, followed by a gigantic line to pay the tourist tax. We're lucky we make it on the plane, even though we arrived five hours early, much to Peter's relief.

At home, I bring the laundry down (in multiple trips) to our matrix of a basement. As I am about to put each article of clothing into the machine, I press it to my face and breath in the smells of sweat and sunscreen, reminders of warmer, happier times. I've read that the sense of smell evokes the strongest recall of memory, and I believe it. A particular smell can put you back into a room, a garden, a street, a restaurant, or with a specific person whose fragrance lingered. Whenever I smell a particular kind of pipe tobacco, I am immediately transported to my childhood home, where my English grandfather, who passed away more than thirty years ago, stayed with us and took smoke breaks throughout the day. I smell my children's hair each day, hoping to get whiffs of sun and salty air, about which they are annoyed but tolerant, given the option of showering.

A few days and six loads of laundry later, we are under a fresh siege of snow and Cuba is just a distant memory. Ahead of us are the realities of the decisions we have made and their uncertain outcomes. Could this be our last trip south for a while? Would we land on our feet again? Or had our luck finally run out?

Spring Term
APRIL TO JUNE

55.

Spring Has Sprung

It's the very end of March, and for the last four months (minus one Cuban escape), we have been hibernating in our shelters and foraging for food in the cupboards and freezer, because it's been an unfathomable walk to the grocery store. I know, I know, life is just so unfair, and poor us, and all that. But we felt like victims of our surroundings for an extended length of time, and it was sometimes hard to find any lightness in life. This got me wondering about Seasonal Affective Disorder, or S.A.D., and about how people in countries within earshot of the Arctic Circle handle their lack of light.

When the sun doesn't appear for twenty-four hours, it's called a Polar Night. In the northern part of Scandinavia, for example, they may have up to sixty Polar Nights in a row! Sixty days without sunlight! Holy night goggles, Batman! How do they manage? Cod-liver oil for one. It's loaded with good omega-3 fatty acids, vitamin A, and vitamin D (commonly referred to as the sunshine vitamin and one of the coolest vitamins out there.). And training. Populations that experience extended periods of darkness are prepared for it and are taught to embrace it. They learn from an early age about S.A.D. and proactively do things to prevent it. They treat darkness like daylight; children play outside after school, and everyone is encouraged to get exercise and fresh air. When summer does come, they take full advantage of every sun-kissed second.

It seems that we, however, are in a perpetual state of unpreparedness, always hoping for the best and avoiding preparations for the worst. That winter is dark and cold is always a bit of a surprise for us, and sometimes it's for good reason. I remember two winters ago, the year we went to Florida for March Break, where we found the twenty-plus degrees we'd been looking for, only to hear the temperature was also twenty-plus degrees in Toronto. I, for one, have a selective memory and like to assume that all winters will be as mild as that one. And I, for one, am always shocked and disappointed when they are not.

And now, we're one day away from April, and we have temperatures soaring into the six-degree Celsius range. The sun is shining. People are outside for the sake of being outside. The coffee shop has a lineup; grocery stores display tulips (the signature flower of springtime hope) for sale in bins on sidewalks in front of their stores. Hats are off, and spring coats that thought they'd never see the light of day are splashing the streets with colour. Vitamin D is flowing freely to exposed skin everywhere. And it's easy to be appreciative. "Thank-goodness," I overhear someone say. "We can talk about something other than how bad the weather is."

It's like all those blades of grass, peeping up from under the snow, are reaching up and shouting, louder and louder, "We are here! We are here! We are here!" like the wee Whos down in Whoville, desperate to be acknowledged for their survival, and showing us that we must have blind faith that spring exists.

March thirty-first looks like it's going to be an awesome day. The sun does shineth. The kids have an all-day field trip, for which Peter has enthusiastically volunteered. Satchel is at school. I have the place to myself, which seems to happen less than one would think, given the circumstances. I spend part of the morning with administrative duties, including cottage correspondence, bill paying, banking, reuniting lost mittens and socks with their forlorn partners, and then (of course) there's always a laundry category. But having the house to myself doesn't always mean productivity when it comes to writing, and this serene setting is, once again, hijacked by the usual voices: "Clean me!" says the kitchen floor. "Pay attention to us, so that we can ignore you!" say the cats. "Look at how many of us there are!" squeak the many balls scattered all over the floor. They have the most annoying, condescending voices because they think they're more powerful than me by sheer virtue of their numbers. One day, I will kick all of their ball asses to the basement, where some may end up bouncing into the kitty litter. Take that, you over-inflated, arrogant bastards! And so, even though I am alone, I pack up my things and head to the coffee shop for some "quiet".

56.
Open-Door Policy

One of the best parts of being at home with the kids is being there when they arrive home from school. I remember coming back from work some days, after they'd already been home for a while, and bustling through the door, dropping my bags, kicking off my shoes (tripping over their bags and shoes), and on my way to the kitchen, asking distractedly, "How was everyone's day?"

To which some of them may have reflexively replied, "Fine," without taking their eyes off their iPads.

What else were they going to say to someone whom they knew wasn't really listening? If they actually still cared enough to pay attention to that fly-by greeting, they might feel offended by the emptiness of the inquiry.

Having the door open for communication means having it open often, not just during certain times of the day or even week. Kids won't talk when you want them to talk. They talk when they want to talk. And if the door happens to be closed at that particular time, the opportunity can be lost. Having the door open often allows them the freedom to wander in and out when the urge strikes, spill bits and pieces here and there, testing the waters until they feel comfortable enough to tell you what they really want to say.

Each day, I pick up the two younger boys at school, and we make our way home. Sometimes we meander, sometimes they are like puppies, rolling around and tumbling over each other, roughhousing and giggling, but as soon as we get in the door, they start talking all at once about their day. It's like Lucy flipping "The Doctor Is In" sign in the Charlie Brown comics. The clock has started ticking, and they have to get the details of the day out before "The Doctor Is Out." Each of us holds on to the anticipation and excitement of sharing an experience with the others. Without an active audience to set the mood, the moment could dissipate into one of apathy. If someone tells a story, and no one is there to hear it, is it still a story?

When Satchel comes home, he, too, has been waiting to tell us something that happened during his day. Often, it's about a bizarre incident on the subway; sometimes, it's about an exciting assignment at Film School. Occasionally, he drops hints, trying to appear ambiguous about his subject matter, until I take the bait and press him for information so that it seems as if it's me who wants to talk about the girls in his school, or the suit which he really doesn't want to wear but probably will, so he can go to the semi-formal, which he really doesn't want to attend but probably will, so as not to hurt someone's feelings, and then the conversation can really begin.

My friend Sue decided to go back to being a stay-at-home mom when her two daughters were in their teens, because as she said, "Their problems are fewer, but they're bigger."

And getting most teens to talk openly requires a lot of patience, and patience requires time, and time is the precious commodity I am so grateful to have right now.

On those days when I was the last one home, I missed all of that. The door was closed and may not have opened again until I was having goodnight snuggles in bed with my younger boys. They thought that they wanted to tell me something, but they couldn't remember what it was, or by that time it was hard for me to listen anyway as I was struggling to stay awake. I'm not implying that working parents don't communicate with their kids. Every dynamic is different, and I would have said that my family had as good a relationship with each other as any other family, but now, in my new situation, being at home has allowed me to be so much a part of my kids' lives that, even if they haven't spoken up yet, I often have a pretty good idea of what's going on in their congested worlds, and I can steer the conversation into the proper lane before we've missed the exit.

57.

A.D.H.D. Yoga

Arthritis, planter's fasciitis, and sesamoiditis are the diagnoses of the podiatrist who examined my feet. It's April, and I have backed off boot camp and weight classes because my knees and right foot are bothering me. It turns out that problems and solutions really do start from the ground up. Orthotics have been ordered, but in the meantime, I need a new outlet that has less impact on my poor, pained tootsies.

As it happens, the next day I pass a sign for a new class at the gym called Yoga for Jocks and sign up. Why I put myself into the jock category repeatedly is a mystery, but I show up with my mat and place myself in the dark, back corner of the room, among seasoned yoga folks, who are already contorting their bodies in Gumby and Pokey warm-up stretches.

Our instructor, Shayne, is a young, hip, tattooed, former-basketball player, who oozes positive energy and enthusiasm for his craft. His style, he says, is a mix of yoga and something called Tabata. Tabata, I learn, is relatively new to mainstream gyms and incorporates short, intense workouts, mixed with recovery periods.

And so we begin our yoga/Tabata class, but instead of the usual mellow, mystical pipe and flute music that accompanies yoga—the kind you hear during an Animal Kingdom episode featuring "The Wonder of Eagles" as you watch them soaring over forests and mountains—Shayne puts on an some upbeat, motivational-type tunes, the kind you might hear if you were watching a movie about a hockey team heading toward the ice in game seven of the Stanley Cup Finals, ready to fight for their injured teammate, who took one for the team in the previous game. It's all very cool and urban and fast. That's what I like about it: It's A.D.H.D. yoga for those of us who have trouble sitting still and calming our minds. Shayne likens his teaching philosophy to playing with puppies. "They won't necessarily sit for you if they're wired, but if you play with them for a while, they'll get tired and eventually settle down."

Another thing I like about Shayne is that he uses his team experience as a motivational tool in his yoga teaching. Yoga is usually a very personal journey, so quiet and mindful, but Shayne is yelling, "Come on! Hang in there! Nobody quits! We finish this together! Nobody quits!"

Had I been on my own personal yogic journey, I could easily have curled up into child's pose at any point during the class and napped my way to the finish line, but the team player in me could never let my squad down.

And so there we are, his litter of puppies, wagging our tails, looking to play and expend some energy. And we move, changing postures, sometimes quickly as if they are all part of one smooth choreographed dance, sometimes slowly, holding painful poses for a while, all to the beat of a rhythmic drum, pushing us onward towards our destiny.

At the end of the class, Shayne gives the usual yogic parting spiel, offering appreciation for our time together and wishing us a healthy and happy week, then he adds, "Thanks for the hustle." Which is what we really want to hear.

With Jock Yoga occurring only one day a week, I have to supplement my fitness with something else that won't hurt my feet, so I thought I'd try Hatha yoga, which is a slow-paced stretching class with some breathing and meditations. It's challenging in a whole different way from Jock Yoga. It's supposed to align my skin, muscles, and bones, as well as quiet my mind, which (as I already mentioned) is not my strength. In fact, as soon as I try it, lying still on my matt, with the Tibetan pipes playing, it's like someone breaks open my brain piñata and all the 6-year-olds in my mind go psycho, as they attempt to amass the most amount of candy. Go away children, I tell them. Go find your sugar coma and leave me alone... Good, they're gone. Quiet the mind. Empty the thoughts. Quiet the mind. Empty the ... garbage. It's garbage day tomorrow. Don't forget to take out the garbage. Put the bottles in the recycling bin but not the wine bottles cuz they can go back to the liquor store... I'm out of wine... And yogurt. What time does the Liquor store open? Maybe I can go on the way home from Yoga. When does Yoga end? What time is it? Ooh, I like that Lulu top on the woman under the clock. I wonder if Lulu has anything on sale? I should drive there. But first I should get my snow tires removed. Must call dealership to schedule appointment. Tires. If you replace the s with a d, you get tired. I'm tired. And bored. What time is it? Maybe I should get a sundial. That would be cool...

Looking around the room at all the very still bodies, I imagine I can't be the only one in the room doing this, can I?

This is definitely the hardest part of Hatha yoga and something I may not master any time soon. I finish the class feeling not very enlightened or clear-headed but antsy, like I just spent an hour on hold, waiting to speak to a customer service agent from the cable company. The fact that this was such a negative experience tells me that this is an area of potential growth for me, and I should pursue it. But for now, I'd better get to the liquor store before it closes.

58.
Leaving the Nest

At 15-years old, Satchel has inherited the travel gene in a big way, and right now, that itch needs to be scratched. He's frustrated. He wants to move. He wants to travel. He wants to expand out of the city—out of his high school. We look into a variety of ways he can travel, including school exchanges, adventure camps, or camp counselling. But he's not much of a Kumbaya guy, and he's somewhat introverted, so those campy options really aren't for him. Then it all comes to a halt during a conversation with my friend Heather, the principal at the International School in Thailand. "Send him here! He can spend a semester at my school and live with us!" she says.

Heather's husband, Mitch, is a high-school social-sciences teacher and their son is in grade ten, the same grade as Satchel, while her daughter is three-years younger. And now, a few weeks later, I am filling out forms for his four-month stay in Pattaya, Thailand, to begin grade eleven from August to December. How do I feel about that? Excited, apprehensive, and somewhat nauseated. Four months is a long time for someone (who has only experienced the occasional sleepover at a friend's house down the street) to be away.

But he's ecstatic. He's learning all about Thai culture, history, language, currency, etiquette, weather, and geography. He already knows to never touch a Thai's head (it's the most sacred part of the body) and to never show the sole of the foot (it's the filthiest part) or point a foot at someone, even if it's because you've crossed your legs and your one dangling foot is pointing in another person's direction. Peter and I learned these kinds of things the hard way as we meandered through the country, checking in occasionally with the Lonely Planet's Guide to Thailand. We were quickly and strictly accosted once by a police officer for hugging on the street, where apparently public displays of affection are strongly discouraged.

What appeases my anxiety is that Satchel will be staying with Heather and her family. There is no one outside of my family I would trust more with the well-being of my child. Heather and I have been close friends since we were 12-years old. Growing up, she was considered the fifth child in our family, and we have remained close despite the geographical distance between us. Every summer, Heather and her family come back to Ontario for the summer, and our families come together. Her husband is a great guy, and her kids are happy, worldly, and grounded. We will sign over guardianship for his time there, which means he essentially becomes their ward and therefore attends school for free (normally a $20,000 price tag).

This is such a generous offer and so awesome an opportunity that we can't say no. I know how much he wants to go. I know how he feels, being so ready to explode out of the mainstream and find adventure in faraway lands. What I don't know is how I will handle the huge void that will be left once he's gone. He really is one of my rocks, and I depend on him in so many ways, which is why he deserves this so much. Perhaps this is a good test drive for when he leaves for university in a couple of years. Once he's had this experience, however, there's no telling where he'll end up for university and beyond. This is the beginning of a relationship of emails from foreign places and brief visits home. I am already so proud of him for the kind of person he has become and for what he has yet to accomplish, and it selfishly breaks my heart to have to share him with the rest of the world.

59.

Looking Up at the Sky to See Who Answers

With the void of a March M.E. outing due to the March Break, I feel a little like we have let ourselves down and lost some momentum. On a whim, I call Maurine and asked her if she would consider coming in to deliver an afternoon of Reiki, a sampler for the group to try out, and she agrees. I am reluctant to mention to the group that she is also an intuitive, as some people have strong opinions about that kind of thing, as well as about the type of people who believe in it. I run it by a few people whom I think might be open to this kind of experience to get a sense of how well it might be received.

My brother is a chiropractor and has discovered that he also has an intuitive gift. He uses this sense, with great success, to help treat his patients, but we don't live close enough to each other for treatments. From a small-poll sampling, I have enough positive feedback to put the invite out, introducing Reiki to those who may not be familiar with it and adding (although downplaying) the possibility that Maurine's psychic skills could observe the appearance of other "guests" during the treatment.

It is surprising to find nine quick responses to the offer and the day is planned.

My friend Stella offers to host the event at her home, which (coincidentally) she believes houses the ghost of the previous owner who died there from falling off a ladder. When Maurine arrives, her immediate impression is that the spirit is definitely there but doesn't realize he is already dead. This makes sense to Stella, who observes that the ghost shows his agitation by stomping around and slamming doors whenever she changes the paint colours or when her husband criticizes the DIY electrical work he discovers.

Personally, I have only ever seen what I believe was a spirit once. I was awakened one night to find my mother's figure, standing next to my bed, soon after Satchel was born. She was wearing the same ugly green tracksuit that she used to wear too frequently, and we communicated without speaking. She was there to say that she was watching over us. I felt extremely warm and safe. Then, as she turned to leave the room, she said, "I'm just going to check on Satchel," and I watched her walk down the hallway towards his room, comforted by the thought that he had a guardian angel keeping an eye on him.

I lay in bed for a long time after that, intentionally moving one leg, then the other, then wiggling my fingers to prove that I had conscious control over my body and mind. This was no dream. Nothing about the experience was unsettling, but rather the opposite; I felt contentment over the connection. I had always been disappointed that my mother would never know my children, but now I know that she does.

When Satchel was younger, he and I used to go to my mother's grave on occasion, where we would have a picnic and leave flowers. As we prepared to leave each time, Satchel would look up to the sky and yell, "Bye, Grandy!" as loud as he could, so that she could hear him all the way up in heaven. It was so sweet to watch, but I wonder if all that yelling actually startled her, because she was already standing right next to him.

Stella creates an appointment schedule for the nine curious ladies who sign up. She puts out tea, coffee, and snacks so that the women feel welcome to linger before and/or after their appointment. One by one, they slip away upstairs to the room Maurine has chosen, specifically because that's where the ghost is also hanging out, probably wondering why all of these strangers are invading his abode. They all come downstairs again displaying varying degrees of relaxation. Some are reasonably unaffected, while others are limp and have to sit down for fear of losing their legs. Lan has been suffering for years from whiplash, the effects of a car accident. She comes down glowing and relaxed, so loose she can barely feel her inflamed neck. Several of the women sit at the table, slightly dazed and grinning, like they'd just smoked some great weed and had not a care in the world.

Maurine is cautious about bringing spirits into the short, twenty-minute sessions. She tells me beforehand that she doesn't want to upset or frighten anyone. Before Jenna heads upstairs, she quietly confides to us that she will be fine as long as her beloved dog, recently deceased, doesn't make an appearance. Of course, during her session, Maurine innocently says, "Hey, I hear a dog barking," at which point Jenna immediately gets teary, and Maurine redirects her focus on Jenna's relationship with her kids.

All in all, this is another great afternoon, made so by wonderful, open-minded people. Melanie, a recent divorcee, tells me that every time a M.E. invite goes out, she tries to convince herself that she doesn't have the time or the money to commit, and yet, she just can't resist. She is planning an awesome May adventure. I'm so happy it has had this effect on people. My sister Anne, who lives an hour and a half away, has started her own adventure club. I know there are women's adventure tours that take them far and wide to experience once-in-a-lifetime encounters, but they are so far out of reach for so many, both geographically and financially. If we can get it into our heads that we only need a few hours a month, maybe we can spread the word.

Each time we complete one adventure, I wish we could start another right away, but I realize it shouldn't be overdone and risk losing its allure. Once a month makes it something special to which everyone can look forward. In this particular case, whether you believe in the after-life or not, it's always intriguing to mentally take that leap into the regions of the unknown. For me, I've seen, felt, and heard too much to dispute it, although I certainly understand why others do. There's no science to it, which is what makes it so interesting. And as long as you don't have some psychotic poltergeist hurling brass candlestick holders at your head, making a connection (real or perceived) with someone whom you loved dearly can bring on some bliss-ful feelings. Just yell up at the sky and see who answers.

60.

Why I Don't Buy Into Mother's Day

"I don't want anything for Mother's Day. That's right. You heard me."

My children didn't believe me. They thought they were being set up. What's the catch?

A few years ago, as Mother's Day approached, a YouTube video was forwarded to me. In it, a fake company posted a phony job opportunity. The job title was listed as "Operations Manager" and the job description included things like:

- Must be mobile and be agreeable to being on your feet most of the time.
- Must be willing to stay up all night with clients if required.
- Hours are 24/7/365 days per year.
- Workload increases during holidays.

Oh, and the salary? Nothing. Zero dollars.

The end of the video stated simply, "It's Mother's Day on May 11. Make her a card." Seems like a weak offering given the previous presentation; however, the sentiment is historically accurate.

According to the website mothersdaycentral.com, Anna Jarvis wanted to honour her mother and the contributions of mothers around the United States. In 1905, after her mother's death, she began campaigning to try to have a special day declared, which would recognize the dedication of mothers. Her project gathered steam, and in 1914, President Woodrow Wilson proclaimed Mother's Day an official national holiday. Today, countries around the world join in this celebration.

Within a few years, however, Anna's objective had blown out of control, and she resented the commercialization of the day. Her idea had been that people could show their appreciation for their mother through simple gestures such as writing a letter or sending a single carnation. But the train had left the station (stay off those tracks!) and Anna spent the rest of her life (and most of her inheritance) fighting the exploitation of the day by big business.

As the mother of three boys, I had already been feeling uncomfortable with the consumer-driven concept of Mother's Day and decided to join Anna in her protest. I didn't want my family to feed into the artificial frenzy of it all, so I politely asked them not to give me anything. Instead, I made cards for my children thanking them for making it possible for me to love my job. My sons each received a card featuring either a Batmom, a Supermom, or a Spidermom, all wearing Disney-like princess dresses like transvestite action heroes, each offering up a superhero quote like "With great kids comes great responsibility." Cheesy stuff, but they were impressed by my ability to find the graphics on the Internet and to colour inside the lines.

Society, however, told them they had to do something. Sheepishly, they brought forth their gifts, trying to be as minimalist as possible. Cole gave me a box he had made out of paper and tape. It was too delicate to hold anything that wasn't also made of paper and tape, but it was a lovely paper box; Tanner gave me a beautifully painted ceramic butterfly, which was an art project at school, along with a poem, which he said his teacher forced him to write; Satchel brought me a no-fat, no-foam Earl Grey tea latte from Starbucks, along with a hand-made greeting card; Peter, gave me a pot of flowers, which I will quickly kill by forgetting to water them—I can only handle so many dependents at a time. The day came very close to what Anna Jarvis had envisioned.

Don't let me mislead you, however; just because I don't want my children to treat me especially nice on Mother's Day doesn't let them off the hook. I expect that they treat me especially nice every day. When they do, there is no need to disingenuously condense all of their love and gratitude into one day while potentially letting the other 364 days slide. If we all just show respect and appreciation for each other as a part of our every-day existence, there would be no need to force it upon like an annual make-up class.

Frequently, one of my kids will approach me while I'm making dinner and ask what he can do to help. It warms my heart, and I wouldn't trade these consistent small gestures for a month of spa days. What if one of your offspring made you a thank-you card or bought you flowers just because she was thinking about you? And what if that happened to be on a Wednesday, any old Wednesday, in February? Just because she was thinking about you! You might faint.

Furthermore, my opinion (and I understand it's not a popular one) is that I don't need to be celebrated for something I had the luxury of choosing to do. I wanted (and struggled) to have children, and while nothing could truly prepare me for the sacrifices of motherhood, I never questioned any of it, from the first thirty-three hours labour and subsequent C-section, to the all-night stomach flu's, to the back-to-back forehead stitches in the emergency ward. Yes, sometimes it's hard, but it's what I signed up for.

The reality is that I am personally rewarded every time I see my kids conduct themselves using compassion, kindness, and respect. That (before my very eyes) they are growing into global citizens who show resourcefulness, integrity, and humility is baffling to me, and my husband and I often joke that these traits must have skipped a generation. At the end of the day, however, this is my job and I am doing it, like everyone else, to the best of my ability and not for some guilty yearly bonus built into my contract.

After all, as my kids made strides to becoming self-sufficient, like learning to use the toilet or to dress themselves, each became one less thing I had to do, and I felt like I got a small promotion—kind of like going from working on the factory floor to a supervisory position. As they get older and become helpful to me, there is another promotion, this time to manager. Eventually, grey-haired and wizened, I will end up sitting on the board of directors, watching from a safe distance and offering advice on how to maintain the family's vision and values.

After the awkward gift exchange on the morning of my "boycott", it was business as usual: Peter left to run a 10-km charity event, Satchel went out, and I took the two younger boys to soccer practice, then prepared dinner for Peter's family. When my boys asked why I was making dinner for other people's mothers on Mother's Day, I answered in terms they could understand, cape flowing in the wind: "Because I'm Batmom."

To me, the Batman metaphor is more relatable than, say, Superman or Spiderman, because Batman doesn't have any special powers. Sure, he has some cool gadgets, but ultimately, he just works really hard and does the best he can with what he's got without seeking recognition.

Yes, I am Batmom, the one in the Dark Nighty, signing field-trip permission forms in the shadows of my kitchen, while my people sleep safely and peacefully, knowing that their world is protected by a phantom watchwoman. I may not be the mom they need, but I'm the mom they deserve. It's what I signed up for.

Cue Batmom exit music.

61.

The Sky's the Limit

I have traded in my toque for a beanie at the moment, hiding my roots again and foregoing another morning comb. But there are others who, despite their patience and optimism, have not survived this extended winter season. They are the small shop owners who have struggled to stay afloat when there are no customers. Even the most popular stores have had no pedestrian traffic for most of the winter, as shoppers opt for indoor malls or shopping centres, or in some cases, just going without. Even Christmas this year saw a considerable decrease in foot traffic in lieu of online shopping from the comfort of home. Many shops in our neighbourhood have already closed down because tenants were unable to afford the rent in this area without the support of locals and tourists. They can't survive in this high-rent district in the best of times, and slowly they close down, one by one, and are replaced by chain stores. It's sad to see them shut their doors as we watch our hidden oasis be swallowed up by the city, one boutique at a time.

Some stores mysteriously put up signs that say, closed for renovations, which makes us falsely optimistic that things may be going well and that there's a bit of a facelift going on behind those butcher-paper-covered windows. But when the shop next door also closes, we are prepared for the announcement of another condo development and all the havoc that a construction site brings to the neighbourhood.

Construction signs begin to emerge way before the flowers have had a chance to creep out of the ground. Orange really is the new black in the city. As the cranes arrive and detours are created, our little sanctuary is turned into bedlam, with more cars and commotion than the small streets can accommodate. And with that congestion comes the increased of commuters who can't get in or out, and tourists who can't find parking spaces and decide to take a chance and park illegally on the main street, or (incredibly) blocking access to private driveways on side streets. I challenged one such person who was about to tiptoe away from his car, which was completely blocking my car, nestled in its little parking pad. Once confronted, he had the audacity to ask if it would be okay if he left his car there, just for a little while. "Sure," I replied. "But it will cost you twenty bucks, and you'll have to leave your keys in case I have to move it. That's a deal. A parking ticket will cost thirty bucks or $225 if you get towed. "

He left, as others have done, in search of that elusive, parking spot in the Beach community, their cars eventually discovered, sitting awkwardly in the street, out of gas, with skeletal remains inside, still waiting for a spot to open up.

The city of Toronto sits on the shores of Lake Ontario. The major artery into the city, called the Gardiner Expressway, snakes its way along the lake, providing access to the downtown core from the east and west. It is one of the worst planned highways in urban history and has earned the nickname The Mistake by the Lake (not to be confused with the other Mistake by the Lake, the old Cleveland Indians stadium). Similarly, the Don Valley Parkway, which is the highway arriving from the north, intercepting the Gardner at the lake, has aptly been dubbed the Don Valley Parking Lot. Every other major city with a water feature, it seems, realized the value of land along the shore and had the vision to create beautiful parks, quaint shopping districts, and low-rise residences so as not to block the views of the water. Instead, Toronto decided to use this valuable, waterfront land for a highway that was too small to accommodate the growth of the city, flanked by high-rise condos, each one taller than the next. The whole thing is one big, ugly, congested eyesore.

This year, the old Gardiner Expressway continues to succumb to the symptoms of age, weak from the wear and tear of an overused, poorly planned operation, and begins to break apart, chunks of it falling from the raised areas onto the roads below. It becomes dangerous to travel on it or below it, which means only thing: more orange. With the already perilous, shaky concrete and the arrival of the Pan-Am games in Toronto in the summer of 2015, it has to be repaired and have more lanes added, so construction will be ongoing for years, making commuters add sometimes hours to their daily grind. Anyone coming into or out of the city is at the mercy of lane closures, bottlenecks, and the impatient frustration of other drivers. It affects how and when we travel, and if we travel at all.

Apparently though, the city is still the place to be. The housing market says so. The average price for a detached home in Toronto continues to soar. Yet young families continue to take on massive amounts of debt to own a mini patch of ground. I understand the urban buzz they get from being surrounded by the dazzle of the city, because I've lived with that craving for my whole life. But the cost is unfathomable, and I fear for their futures if the housing bubble ever bursts. In the hot, spring real-estate market, every For Sale sign that goes up is quickly covered by a Sold Over Asking sign—or as Peter likes to correct, a Paid Too Much sign.

In our old wisdom, we finally accepted that we will never be able to buy back into the area. We will either be lifetime renters, or like many others, begin to look outside the city. I used to resent this feeling, that we've been financially bullied out of the market, but now that the urban shadows have started to steal more and more of the sunlight, I realize that we need to find our daylight elsewhere. In speaking with a city friend about the possibility of moving away to something more rural, she asks sincerely, "What would you do out there?"

At that moment, the only answer that comes to mind is, "I dunno, maybe look at the sky?"

She ponders the response for a moment, looking around at our concrete environment and up to the sliver of sky showing between buildings, then seems quite satisfied with the answer. "Hmmm," she says. "That seems like a good idea."

And the more we talk, the more intrigued she becomes at the prospect of leaving the city, but like many others, her husband's job is tied to downtown and a career change isn't in his immediate future.

I can't count how many times I've had this conversation with people, who, when engaged in this topic, discuss their disenchantment with our beautiful Beaches district (and it is still beautiful). But those urban sirens that used to sing to me and draw me in again and again have turned into police sirens chasing me away from our formerly bubbled neighbourhood.

It's no wonder that my passionate life-long affair with the city feels like it is continually being tested and that my eyes are beginning to wander. I am seriously contemplating cheating on this relationship and exploring other options. Using a Gilligan's

Island reference, I have lived with glittery, exotic Ginger, and now it's time to see what Marianne has to offer.

We've been to this rodeo before, but this time we really mean it. We have become so disillusioned by the gentrification of the Beaches that there is no turning back—no room for another U-turn. The more the claws of change take hold of our surroundings, the more we crave space, the sky, the land, the air, and the savings.

On the real-estate sites, we are discovering beautiful homes, near good schools, in small towns that are intriguing to us. Ironically, the traffic getting out of the city often prevents us from leaving it to visit these places, which only convinces us more that we need to make our exit. While I'm not one-hundred percent on board yet, I'm hoping that one day, we're going to walk into a home, and just like when a future bride looks in the mirror after trying on a hundred wedding dresses, instantly realizing that "this one is THE ONE" and it fits her budget, that's how it will be with our next house. So, we can be patient, using the theory of the power of positive parking and the wizened knowledge that the house will appear when the buyer is ready.

62.

Snow Bitch

The reluctant arrival of spring is timed perfectly with the annual charity golf tournament in which Peter and I play each year in support of a camp for kids with cancer, and in memory of Peter's dear friend, who succumbed to the disease in his twenties. I don't play a lot of golf; in fact, I play about once a year at this charity event. Expectations are always low, and there is a lot of goodwill and friendly cajoling on the course, which is part of a country club set in the beautiful cottage area of Muskoka, where the elite of Toronto and some of Hollywood come to unwind in the summer.

This course is so spectacular that, despite my attempts to (literally) deflower certain landscaped areas with my slices, pulls, and shanks, its beauty can't be scoured, nor my mood punctured by my poor play. And play poorly I do. As the organizer give us all the pre-game, low-down, he mentions that, after eight strokes, the ball should be picked up. One of the elderly ladies playing that day turns to me and says with a wink, "Down in Florida, we call an eight a snow bitch."

To which I reply, "What a coincidence! Around here all winter, that's what I'm called, too!"

Peter has been playing this event for over a decade, whereas I am relatively new to the scene. We usually play as part of a foursome with our good friend Tom, who is about as jovial a guy as you could ever meet, always charming, smiling, and friendly. With a wry wit, he works a room like no other. He is respectful of his audience but knows how to make the senior golf ladies blush with bawdy references or teasing come-ons. Tom always has an endless supply of unworthy compliments and undeserved encouragement towards my golf game. Bushwhacking through the brush with me in search of my ball, he says, "Wow, I've never seen the course from this vantage point. Thanks for bringing me here."

Unsolicited, he turns my many snow bitches into sixes, and when I don't ask for my final score, he doesn't offer. It's all for charity, and since charity is about giving, I can honestly say that I gave as many strokes as I could during this particular outing.

63.

Don't Mess with Mama

Ian was a litigator before she decided to stay home with her two boys. She has always wanted to do a self-defence course and finds that using M.E. as a vehicle to do so provides just the right motivation because she can do it with a group of friends. She manages to find a top-notch women's self-defence instructor, along with a large church basement in which we can attack and defend each other, creating May's M.E. day. Six ladies show up for a three-hour seminar, which is one of the most valuable things I've done in a long time.

Our instructor, Carolyn, is a black belt in several martial arts, works with the police and with other defence programs, and offers her own self-defence seminars for women. She is funny, informative, and knowledgeable, and after three hours, I believe that every woman, young or old, should attend a workshop of this kind. The first hour includes discussions on how to spot and avoid potentially dangerous situations. Probably the three most surprising things we learn are:

1. Most sexual assaults occur during the hours of seven and nine in the morning!

2. There is an increase in the number of sexual assaults by taxi drivers! Think about it; they have the perfect opportunity to take you to a secondary location. Young women coming home drunk from clubs and parties are easy targets.

3. 89 percent of women who fight their attackers get away.

After the oral presentation, we head into the kick-ass portion of the morning. We learn simple one-step moves in case someone was to grab our wrists, to more difficult three or four-step moves used for headlocks or choking. We choke and grab each other, learn kicking, punching, and distracting techniques, and at the end of every move, as per our instructions, we run away. Just knowing that we not only should do something and can do something, but that we must do something, was a little frightening at first but by the end of it, we felt empowered—not that any of us will go out and pick a fight at a bar.

Unfortunately, the kinds of moves we learn in self-defence do not just stay loaded in the front of our brains ready to discharge at a moment's notice. For them to be effective they have to be practiced until they are second nature. Our attacker was not going to wait for us to slow down and think through our options and the process by which we would use them: "Okay, just wait a second. Let me think ... step one: move my hips over. Hmmm ... would that be to the left or to the right? Where are you standing? Oh, to the left, so I twist my wrist counter to that. Step two..."

When Peter and Satchel arrive home later in the day, I practice my new moves on them. They are both extremely uncomfortable following my instructions, "Go ahead, choke me. Now grab me. Now push me up against the door."

Even though my responses were slow and calculated, these attackers were patient, which allowed for some very effective disarming methods. The moves really did work, and both of them were surprised at how easily I could get out of a sticky situation. These new skills could be extremely useful in the cookie aisle when there is one bag of Puffs left and two of us with a craving. Clint was finally impressed. Don't mess with Mama. And hats off to Lan for organizing a unique, fun-filled, and practical M.E. day.

64.

Life's Too Short to Stuff a Mushroom

Has my cooking improved since I left work? If I ever made the assumption that it had, and I really thought it had, my confidence is dashed by a conversation Satchel has with the mother of one his friends—who loves to cook. He had just finished one of her formidable, from-scratch meals, where she actually whipped up a Caesar-salad dressing at the dinner table (really?), and the discussion went something (exactly) like this:

Other mom: "Satchel, is your mother a good cook?"

Satchel: "Umm ... my mom kickboxes."

Me (later, on hearing about it): "Really? That's what you came up with? My mom kickboxes? Oh, Please. Couldn't you do better than that? Do you know how hard it is to feed a vegetarian, a pescetarian (a vegetarian who eats fish), and two nuggetarians? Oh, never mind. Just sit down and drink your dinner."

Okay, it's all true. I don't cook well, but it's not that I'm not a good cook— it's just that I don't like to cook. It takes so much preparation so that by the time I've chosen a perfectly unreasonable recipe, shopped twice for all the ingredients because it all looks so good in the cookbook picture but is ridiculously difficult to make because I have to caramelize this, and steam that, and then add odd ingredients like smoked paprika or lobster, which I don't have, but first I have to clean the kitchen so that I have room to work, then I'm too tired and bored to close the deal, not to mention another clean up, and five to sixteen weeks later, throw away all those weird, expensive, remaining ingredients in my refrigerator.

This week I decide to make another attempt at sneaking something healthy past the kids. I make those healthy brownies, secretly filled with spinach and carrots (steamed and pureed of course) that I swore I would never make. They look like brownies and smell like brownies and the kids eat them up, slowing down briefly to puzzle over what's different about these particular brownies. I am dying to tell them what they have ingested but don't in case I ever take another shot at them. I also don't want them to become paranoid and scrutinize everything I put in front of them for fear there might be elements of covert vitamins and minerals tucked away. It is all about creating a feeling of trust—not actual trust—but a feeling of trust. I get away with it this time but not without a lot of anxiety.

Peter continues to appreciate anything I put before him and is getting pretty good at not even subtly cringing when the younger boys get hamburgers and he and Satchel get my version of Curried Vegetable Stew. His diet can fit on a Jeopardy board in the following categories:

1. Soupy Vegetables
2. Eggstreme Makeover
3. Are Those Beans or Lentils?
4. Cheesy Things
5. Smells like Fish
6. Looks like Meat
7. Smoothie Hodgepodge
8. Curried Pot Pourri

The less recognizable the dish, the more money it's worth on the board. I'll take Are those Beans or Lentils for $500, please. Answer (according to one of my healthy cookbooks): This recipe includes a large version of this kind of vegetable, filled with these other vegetables, which are rich in manganese along with heart-healthy legumes. Question: What are Portabella mushrooms stuffed with brown rice, lentils, and parsley? On the heels of making this recipe, I was inspired to purchase a decorative sign for the kitchen, which reads, Life's Too Short To Stuff a Mushroom. Amen to that.

65.

I Am Out of the Office.
Please Leave a Message

No. No. No. I have to practice saying it. May continues to be an unbelievably busy month, and I observe that I probably wasn't this busy when I was working. The difference is that when I was working, there were things that my schedule just wouldn't allow, like volunteering for field trips, driving kids to full-day track and field meets, and joining committees, whereas now, nothing is stopping me from helping because there is no set schedule. It's becoming a problem that I rarely say no to anything.

I gave a friend one of those fun fridge magnets with a vintage photo of a frazzled mother on it, which read, "Stop me before I volunteer again." Obviously I am not alone in this hyper-helper mentality. Why do I feel so compelled to say to yes to every request that blows in my direction? I owe it all to Guilt Parts 1, 2, and 3. Guilt Part 1 is self-inflicted. It tells me I am staying at home for this very purpose, and so I owe it to my family to give them as much of me as I possibly can. After all, what else would I be doing with myself if I were not on call for their every need?

Guilt Part 2 is environmental. I was raised Catholic, so it's just automatic to feel guilty about everything, all the time. Guilt Part 3 says that I have to justify my role as stay-at-home mom to myself and to others. I know some SAHMs who have learned to refuse pleas for help without any explanation. I hear them say, "No, I'm unavailable that day." And then I see them on the specified day on the street with a yoga mat under their arm.

I totally understand that they can't help out because they have a yoga class to attend, and I admire that they are committed to their own self-preservation/self-improvement, but I find it difficult to put my individual needs ahead of my family, no matter how valid or healthy it may be to do so. And so, I change my whole schedule, cancel plans, appointments, writing, errands, because otherwise, I feel selfish.

I hate to say that it is a lack of confidence, which can come with staying at home for some of us, but it kind of is. Since there is no quantitative measure of value for being home, I personally don't always feel I am worthy of putting myself first. It would feel like going shopping on company time. I know that this bothers a lot of the other women who partake in the M.E. adventures, and it occurs to me that this was why M.E. works. There is a sense of solidarity on those days, which makes all of us feel more like members of a team and forces some accountability to each other. It is much harder to let your team down than it is to let yourself down.

If I had to rationalize it in terms of financial value, I suppose I could say that if committing myself wholeheartedly to the task of raising of my children increases the chance that they will be responsible, contributing, kind people, and decreases the likelihood that they will become a burden to society by ending up on Employment Insurance or in rehab, or (worse) jail, then the choice to stay home is a wise financial investment indeed. I understand that there are no guarantees as to how they'll turn out in the long run, but if my presence can, even remotely, help steer them toward making good life choices, then my time has been well spent.

And so, a few days of driving kids to soccer games, a few days of driving them to track meets, and to the odd ultimate Frisbee game, an afternoon with Scientists in the School, a field trip to a theatre downtown, and suddenly, the rest of my duties have slid out the back door into my weed-infested mini-yard. (The neglected yard, by the way, has bred some kind of super weed, which has crawled up the stairs of the mini-deck, crossed the floor, and inched its way up the glass sliding door toward its handle as if it will eventually find a way to open it and creep inside. It's like some kind of bizarre game of Red Light-Green Light, where every time I look away, then back again, the weed has quietly moved a little bit closer to the door handle. And oddly, it's beginning to look more and more carnivorous, which is unsettling.)

Somehow, I'll also be helping out at the school Fun Fair in June, although I don't remember volunteering. The organizing team is a force of working moms and SAHMs who put together an amazing fundraising event. It's a great time for everyone to come together, especially on the day of the event, where working parents come out in droves to spend a Saturday afternoon running activities and counting heads going in and out of the various inflatable contraptions.

Taking a confident stand when the circumstances call for it appears to be a learned skill and one I will have to foster with the help of some of my more-seasoned SAHM friends, many of whom I have also neglected recently. It's been hard to nurture my friendships, and I desperately want to do that. It's not easy with everyone's volunteering, after school, evening, and weekend activities, but I do get to hang out with some moms who are also on call for team delivery for the school or who have joined a M.E. day. A couple of times I even attended a mom's night out at someone's house or a local bar.

I am still amazed and humbled that I am invited to these soirées with all the moms whom I have recently met, who have adopted me into their busy lives. A little part of me thinks they feel sorry for me or that they have a secret society, luring me in, fattening me up with wine and cheese, waiting for the day when they need to make a human sacrifice. But so far, they have been nothing but genuine and inclusive and certainly not the type to throw a body into an active volcano.

In fact, the more I learn about these new friends, the more I realize how lucky I am to have fallen into their far-reaching web of kindness, intelligence, and resourcefulness. I am absorbing so much from them, including what it is to be self-aware and comfortable in my low-heeled mommy shoes. I need to connect more with those who already know who they are and what their purpose is ... at least at this point in their lives. They don't apologize for their choice to stay at home, nor do they flaunt its importance or attempt to justify it to those who question it. They just do it and do it all without pay raises or bonuses or recognition of any kind, except from those clients who matter most: those runny-nosed, skirt-clinging, knee-scraped, ride-needing, hungry, hot, cold, tired, wired, tie-my-skates clients who offer hugs, kisses, and snuggles as compensation. And in mommy currency, despite our snot-smeared shirts and unkempt hair, we are richer beyond belief.

66.
Moving On

With the arrival of June, the final month of school is packed with parties and play dates and soccer, some of which we miss because I made the promise to take Satchel and four of his friends (two of each gender) to the cottage as an end-of-year celebration. The plan is to head up after their exams while my younger guys finish school, but at the last minute, Peter has to go away on business, and I am caught between a promise and a commitment. After much deliberation all eight of us jump in the van for two and a half days of fun, fun, fun.

A note about young teenagers: individually, they are all recognizable as fully formed, unique, excellent human beings. I really like all of Satchel's friends and have had lovely conversations with each of them. But once they are in a group, they take on a singular shape, the form of one entity with many arms, legs, and heads protruding, which moves as a whole like cattle being moved toward their enclosure. If one of them happens to stray from the herd, it is possible to have a thoughtful conversation with it because (deep down) it is an intelligent, well-mannered, social creature. But those moments seldom happen, and it floats from room to room or down the beach, stopping briefly to refuel now and then before holing up to watch YouTube videos or a movie. I know going in that I am merely coexisting with them, and I am not wrong. I cook the food, serve the food, clean up the food, and send them to their rooms at an appropriate hour. That is my purpose. When I'm not on kitchen duty, I'm keeping the younger lads busy. It is exhausting, but in the end, I am happy to have done it. Happy that Satchel is keen to bring his friends to the cottage with his mother, and that they all get to be together for some quality time in case we end up moving away.

Seeing Satchel with his friends resuscitates the question of whether or not a move is in our best interests. We all have friends, co-workers, and teammates whom we would miss. We all have favourite places to frequent: the bagel shop, the Thai restaurant, the place for wings, the boardwalk, the beach, the park, the rink, the ravine, the bakeries, the movie theatre ... all of these are within walking distance. What are we thinking? And then, as I am driving back home from the cottage and hit a wall of traffic, construction, aggressive driving, and smoggy air, I am reenergized to hit the reset button on the house hunt.

This search is becoming exhausting. Driving a couple of hours out of the city to visit smaller towns and look at houses takes a lot out of me, but the family seems to be more and more determined. Despite the wonderful things going on around us with great coaches, teachers, and friends there is still a pull to find something simpler and quieter. Because in the meantime, the cranes rise higher around us, the road congestion, combined with the heat, seem to make people angrier. The conflicts on the street now involve cyclists and cars, and every walk to school includes the screeching of tires and the swearing of cyclists as they bang on car windows to show their irritation at drivers who have cut them off, as impatient commuters make their way through rush hour. Our friend Dave calls these people Angrians, and their numbers are increasing throughout the city.

67.
The Court of Appeal

Melanie is a divorced mother of two who has been attending M.E. events regularly. She works in administration for a soccer organization, offering grassroots programs to youth. She has been working on a M.E. idea for June, hoping to implement it before the end of school; however, the new bar in town with the mechanical bull is having difficulty obtaining a liquor license and has delayed the grand opening.

It's certainly a bold proposal and while I love an excellent adventure, I'm not sure my neck and spine would support this particular one. Perhaps this will sit on the backburner for a while, at least until we can coordinate a follow-up group visit to a masseuse/chiropractor or find an evening where we can be encouraged to participate by a few pre-ride tequila shots.

In the meantime, we have one last chance at an outing before the end of school so at the last minute, I ask a tennis instructor friend of mine, Rachel, if she will teach a clinic for us. She agrees, and we have eight women sign up immediately.

Some of our attendees have played before and are grouped into an intermediate level with Rachel, while others are still relatively new to the game and spend the time with me on another court. After an hour lesson, they hit and giggled through some doubles for another hour, and then we all walk up to the main street for refreshments. A few of the women make plans to play again, and others discuss taking lessons in the summer.

Voila. Another inexpensive, fun morning where 1 got to share my favourite sport with some keen friends. It is also the last of these adventures for a while, which makes me feel proud of what we have accomplished. Way to go, gals!

68.

The Closer

And then it happens.

I walk into a house in the small town of Fonthill with a real-estate agent and am stopped in my tracks. It is beautiful. It is affordable. It is perfect. It is the wedding dress. It's like a small version of a lakeside resort, filled with warm woodwork and windows everywhere, which bring in dramatic light and showcase the lush trees surrounding it. I love everything about it, including the pool in the backyard.

A few days later I take the kids up to look at it, and when they walk in the door their jaws drop. The boys have never been invited to look at any homes yet because we didn't want to waste their time looking at places that weren't worth considering or get excited about houses that weren't realistic, so we waited. They are used to our tiny fixer-uppers with crooked floors, carpeting on the walls, and cork on the ceilings, so when they see this place they can't believe it. Cole's eyes are wide, and he pulls me close to whisper in my ear, "We can't live here. This place is too classy for us."

"You're right, Sweetie, it may be too classy for us, but we can afford this out here."

He is visibly confused. We walk around and around, our excitement growing until we are claiming bedrooms and bathrooms and figuring out where to put the basketball hoop.

Our joy is short-lived, however, as our agent calls us on our drive home. "If you're interested in that place be prepared to put in an offer tonight because there are already three others coming in."

Nooooo! I can't believe it! One of the advantages of buying in a small town is avoiding the evil, urban bidding war. Yet we seem to have brought it with us. Our agent prepares our generous offer of over asking/paid too much and submits it with the others. At 11:30 that evening, he calls with the news. "I'm sorry, you didn't get it. They wanted a long closing, and you wanted to be in before the start of school, so they went with another couple."

This is unbelievable to me—that we lost out on a bidding war in a town of seven-thousand people!

Back to the drawing board. House after house, logging many miles, seeing many dwellings: side splits, back splits, bungalows, rural, and small town, but nothing that takes my breath away like that last one. I am beginning to get my head around the fact that we might be staying in the city, and I start exploring job options. We stay for a weekend at the cottage and make trips back and forth to the surrounding areas we like but nothing is enticing. Perhaps we have missed our chance. Our Say Yes to the Dress moment has passed.

A few weeks later school ends, and we leave the schoolyard unceremoniously, still uncertain of our future. As far as we all know, we will be back here in the fall. The kids are assigned their new classes, figure out with which friends they will be grouped, then we casually say goodbye and see you later to everyone. It feels a little odd, being non-committal to questions about our plans, but we don't want to incite drama where there might not be any.

The day after school ends, we go back up to the cottage to unwind and continue our quest for a new life. If it's going to happen, it will have to happen soon or not at all. Eventually, we come across a home that seems to meet all of our criteria back in Fonthill. It doesn't explode on the scene for us but quietly sits back, patiently waiting for the bell to go off. We take another look. Then another. The backyard is spectacular, with a big pool and still enough space to kick a soccer ball and jump on a trampoline. Four bedrooms, office, eat-in kitchen, family room, two other "formal" mystery rooms, and a double garage round out the deal. As a bonus, the owners are desperate to get out and get their kids enrolled in a new school, in a different province. From back in the city, we put in a low-ball offer, they sign back once, and it is a done deal. Peter, bless his trusting heart, hasn't even seen it. Satchel had been out with his friends when he received the email: Hey Satch, please be home by seven cuz we're going out for dinner. P.S. We bought a house.

Summer Holidays

JULY TO AUGUST

69.

Las Vegas, Baby!

Holy shit! We bought a house!

Just a week into July and the reality of the purchase and its implications start to seep in. We are moving. Away. Not blocks away but away, away. A one-and-a-half-hour drive away (two hours with traffic). It is all a bit surreal after so much talk about *maybe* moving. We are excited about what lies ahead, but each of us is also sentimental about what we are leaving behind, so the mood is quiet and cautious, all of us a little stunned that we have actually pulled the trigger. I don't think the kids believed we'd really do it. Many of our friends were already stationed at their cottages for the summer, some had gone to camps or on holidays, and so we quietly go about our business getting the kids to soccer, playing tennis, managing cottage rentals, and using our upcoming vacation as a distraction to the imminent upheaval of our lives.

It feels odd, walking along our main street, noticing the empty schoolyard, the absence of familiar faces, and the onslaught of tourists, knowing that this would be a limited view. I reflect on an entire school year without "work", and I can't believe how the time has flown. I think back to that first day of school last September and how ecstatic I was to be sitting in a coffee shop, writing. A cliché movie montage plays out in my mind illustrating the year's events: how we'd grown, what we'd done, where we'd been, and where we are, which is on the precipice of a new start— an entirely different kind of start. I think about how this would feel if we had decided that I would be returning to work at the end of the summer. Status quo. Comfortable. Predictable. That sounds nice, but it doesn't seem to be our modus operandi. Our decision is just another leap of faith with the expectation that we would land on our feet. And we will, as we always do, as long as we are together.

With an August 15 closing, we can slowly start separating our belongings into two categories: summer and Fonthill. With the number of residences on our resumé, we are adept movers and aren't daunted by the prospect of packing up. We had decided many months ago that, whether we moved or not, we would take a holiday, flying to Las Vegas, then driving a large loop for nine days through the Southwest, USA, before meeting up with Peter's brother and his family (who live in California) for a few days back in Vegas. Before we had kids, Peter and I had toured around New Mexico, where we attended a friend's wedding, and we wanted to continue to explore the region with our kids. We have accumulated travel points on our credit cards over several years and book less attractive accommodations en route, so we are able to offset much of the cost of this trip.

Just as the weather in Toronto is returning to unseasonably cool temperatures for the very end of July, we hear our flight attendant announce, "Welcome to Las Vegas. It's ten o'clock in the evening, and you'll be stepping out into a balmy 41°C, which is 106 °F for our American friends."

We wanted us some heat. We got us some heat.

Stepping outside of the air-conditioned airport onto the taxi platform is like walking into a humongous, hot yoga studio with giant fans continuously blowing more blistering air into our faces. Layers of clothing fall off us and into our bags. Each of us has just one carry-on bag for this entire desert romp. Luckily, this time around I am not pulled out of the line at security because my Clinique lipstick resembles a bullet casing on the baggage scanner. We also have one racquet bag filled with tennis racquets and shoes and we're complete. Our entire little red wagon of stuff comes in at less than a quarter of our total baggage allowance. Compact packing like this does mean that the laundry chore follows us from hotel to hotel, but it's better than lugging monstrous suitcases around.

After a night at a cheap hotel, we load up our rental car and make for our first stop at the Damned Dam, known to those outside our family as the Hoover Dam. Spectacular and terrifying are two ways to describe it. Its existence is baffling, and it's no surprise it's been included in so many disaster movies. The thought of such an immense construction being brought to rubble is frightening. My recommendation is this: Don't go on the bridge if you're afraid of heights. There is a cemetery of baseball caps just below the bridge to remind you to hold on to your hats and while there were thankfully no small children down there, I would recommend holding on to them too (it's that windy). Then, like the Griswalds in National Lampoon's Vacation, we jump back in our car for the trip to the Grand Canyon.

Spending hours at a time in the car provides time for our ongoing quiz and questions games. We play Top Three, where we have to come up with our top-three picks for a variety of topics such as: top-three animated action heroes, top-three James Bond villains, top-three James Bond theme songs, top-three ice-cream flavours, top-three instruments you'd like to play and with which band you'd want to belong, and so on. We play for hours in between stops while marvelling at the scenery, which consists mostly of dry, red, dusty desert to dry, red, rocky desert. There's a reason it's called red-rock country. It's very, very red with striations of reddish hues along the rocks.

Once inside Grand Canyon National Park, we check into our lodge and find our campy but spacious room. Hikers are returning wearily from a day on the trails, and Satchel and I can't wait to get our first views of the canyon, so we drive to the visitor's center to steal a peak while the others unwind and throw a ball around. Thanks to an unintentional overthrow, they go looking for their ball and instead stumble across ... the Grand Canyon. Who stumbles across the Grand Canyon? Just a few feet from our lodge is the precipice to a rather steep first step.

The surprising thing about the Grand Canyon is the lack of safety railings or visible signage warning of the hazards of the cliffs, perhaps specifically for those who have unfortunate aim with a baseball. For a destination that draws 4.5 million tourists a year, we expected there to be a barrage of signs cautioning of the dangers of getting too close to the edge but throughout every canyon we encounter, Grand and otherwise, there are noticeably few. In fact, we learn it is illegal to post too many signs in National Parks as they are to be maintained in as natural a state as possible. Besides, the same thrill-seeking dummies (my apologies to your male friends, but most accidental fatalities in the canyon occur to young, daredevil men) would ignore the signs anyway, no matter how obvious the risk or how big the fence constructed to prevent accidents in a few areas. We witness those dummies who climb past the few warning signs that do exist to get the photograph that nobody else is getting, and we shake our heads and turn away as they creep closer to the edge to sit and dangle their feet over the six-hundred-foot drop.

In the morning it's time for us to hit the Canyon. Unlike an art museum, where you walk from painting to painting and see a variety of subjects by a variety of artists, the Grand Canyon is one gigantic masterpiece. It's said that if you were to plant yourself in one spot, from sunrise to sunset, the light reflecting on the rocks would create an ever-changing canvas. Most people don't have that kind of time or patience, but many seem to settle for taking selfies—huge headshots of themselves and loved ones with glimpses of *something* majestic in the background.

Our trip is somewhat time sensitive, as we have a different lodging booked for almost each night along the way, so after several viewing spots and a few short trails, marveling at God's paintbrush and saying to ourselves, "Yes, this is a very beautiful and very grand canyon indeed," we jump into our car and begin the short, two-hour drive to Sedona. Grand Canyon: check.

The next morning we wake at 4:00 a.m. as we are still adjusting to the three-hour time change. This is the time we would have been picked up by the hot-air balloon company, had my secret plan come to fruition, but the expense proved too dear. Instead, we would see Sedona on foot and by car. We spend hours driving around the area, following the tourist map to get a peek at the famous rock formations named after their doppelgangers like Snoopy Rock and Cathedral Rock. Sometimes we get out and hike up the rocks or along the trails surrounding them. Even though we have a budget hotel, it has a lovely pool, and we spend our off time taking refuge from the intense heat.

After two days in Sedona, we drive to Canyon de Chelly (pronounced Shay), nestled deep in Navajo Territory. Despite it being the second largest canyon in North America, Canyon de Chelly plays the part of the younger sibling, hiding in the shadows of the elder's accomplishments. The Canyon itself is beautiful and has a far less daunting trek to its base than its grandiose older brother.

In order to venture down into this canyon in the Navajo reservation, a native Navajo guide must accompany you, and so we had previously booked a three-hour private tour and arrive at the starting point to meet Josie, our guide, who ends up being more interesting than the journey itself.

She gets out of her dusty Suburban and introduces herself. We notice the lines etched deep into her weathered, brown face, which tell of a life spent in the outdoors. She wears jeans and running shoes, caked in red dirt, and is adorned with beaded jewelry, which she tells us has not only a beautifying but powerful purpose, with each kind of bead representing something strengthening for the body or soul, or something repelling for unwanted visitors from the spirit or human world. Her hair is streaked with a colour that Revlon might call Grey Experience, but her eyes still hold the twinkle of a young, curious youth. When she smiles, she shows off only a few, remaining brown teeth.

Josie ushers us into her car, and we descend deep into the winding canyon valley, learning about ancient rock carvings, wildlife, flora and fauna, current life in the valley, and early dwellings dating back to 1100 A.D.

She invites questions and encourages our own interpretations of the hieroglyphics; however, when I offer information I'd heard about the Kokopelli, the flute-playing spirit of fertility that we see etched on the side of many rocks, she says thoughtfully, "No. No, I don't think that's true." Eek! Quashed on my first attempt with no participation badge in my future.

Josie knows every nook and cranny of that canyon because she grew up there. And just like you or I could navigate our way through our childhood neighbourhoods, finding memories at the park, or the schoolyard, or the corner store, Josie has a story about every aspect of that massive area: where she found and ate berries, hoping they weren't poisonous; where she dug for water during dry seasons; where she climbed rocks or played versions of baseball; where her parents and grandparents lived in the summer and raised sheep and farmed the land. This was her playground, and as she speaks, it is so easy to picture this wrinkled old woman as a young sprite, roaming the land precociously until there wasn't one inch of it she hadn't uncovered.

Unfortunately, talk of that innocent, carefree life is cut short when Peter asks about how long they have been on this land. (Note to reader: Do not ask a native about land ownership, even if, like Peter, you are generally sensitive, sympathetic, and politically correct.) Josie immediately pulls the jeep over to the side of the dirt road and gives us a twenty-minute tutorial on the treatment of Natives over the decades in this valley. She cringes as she speaks about how her family was taken from their land while their homes and farms were burned to the ground. When they eventually were allowed to return, many years later, there was nothing left, and they began the task of rebuilding their lives out of the red dirt of the canyon and surrounding area. As she speaks, Josie attempts, unsuccessfully, to suppress the escalating anger in her voice.

Our teacher eventually finishes her lesson, takes a deep breath, then turns and looks hard at her speechless, shell-shocked students. Her demeanour has shifted, and she says, "Now stop bombarding me with questions!" We had undoubtedly and unintentionally hit a nerve. No participation badge for Peter either. She begins the tour again as her passengers sit tight-lipped, barely breathing through the tragic, unjust remains of her past. No more questions.

Ten minutes later, Josie suddenly pulls the jeep over again. We worry that she is going to resume her history lesson, but instead, we find ourselves in front of a modest home, which is where her friend Susie lives. Susie manages to farm some of this arid land, and she also happens to make jewelry. Right on cue, out comes Susie's 10-year-old son, running across the ground, bare-footed, carrying a stick from which dangles an array of necklaces. He runs to my window and pushes the stick towards me for my perusal. "How much?" I ask.

This adorable, manipulative salesperson gives us prices ranging from $2 to $50, which prompts me to look for signs of a credit card machine tucked into his frayed little shorts. Josie sits patiently at the wheel, gazing forward, not making eye contact. We are not leaving until we make a purchase.

Once we are on the road again, I manage to change the subject matter to her family, and Josie, like any mom, brightens up. During the rest of the tour, we learn about her children and grandchildren, all of whom she is supporting. Despite the depressed economy, she is doing what she can to keep her brood together and to impress upon the younger generations the importance of preserving their native heritage.

Eventually, we pull back into the parking lot and say goodbye to Josie. Peter hands her a significant, appreciative, guilty tip, and I respectfully finger my new beaded necklace, made from ingredients which will protect my family from evil. We drive away in our rental car, humbled, kicking up dust and waving back to our weathered, old guide, another sister in motherhood who reminds me again not to sweat the small stuff.

After a couple more stops, we are all officially canyoned-out and hit the highway for one last time en route to our final destination, Las Vegas, baby. Approaching Nevada, the thermometer in the car displays external numbers that creep upwards of 108°F. The landscape transitions from barren rock to a few buildings and billboards to a full-on neon city.

We arrive a day earlier than scheduled with no room booked, and so an online hotel-auction site finds us a five-star hotel for a three-star price. Suddenly we are standing in front of the Trump Tower looking like the Clampets arriving in Beverly Hills. We look up at its gleaming, golden façade, silenced by the utter excess, especially having just left Navajo Nation. When we meet the woman at registration, she looks at haggard, dirty, weary us, and upgrades us to a suite with a view of the strip. It is a massive room with golden accoutrement shining throughout. A bathroom bigger than our last motel room invites us to please shower and bathe. This is in such contrast to the small, dark, dated rooms we've had with views of garbage cans and stray dogs. We spend the day relaxing by the pool, our ice water replenished at regular intervals by attentive pool staff.

In the morning, Satchel goes for his early morning walk-about and sees the more sinister underbelly of Vegas. There is a man passed out on the bottom of an escalator, his body on the floor while his head bounces roughly on the revolving bottom step. Another man lies on the sidewalk with a sign which reads, "Need money to get my dealer out of jail."

Later that day we meet up with Peter's brother and his family, check into the Mirage and spend the next three days touring Vegas, swimming, eating, drinking, but surprisingly, not gambling. Having the kids around creates a different kind of Vegas than we might have experienced as a couple—plus, at the tail end of a vacation, the money feels much tighter than at the beginning. The kids love Vegas and the spectacles it provides. For the previous ten days, we had gotten into the routine of efficiently checking into a hotel or motel in the late afternoon and checking out the next morning. The kids didn't need reminding about the program–same day, different canyon. It is a treat to be able to park ourselves for three whole days, and being adaptable people, it doesn't take us long to acclimatize to the overindulgences of Vegas. We spend a lot of time at the pool with Mark and Debbie and their kids, catching up and catching our breath from the pace of our previous schedule.

These are Peter's favourite kind of holidays, which resemble our own little Star Trek adventure. Our two-week mission to explore strange new worlds, to seek out new life and new civilizations, to boldly go where we have never gone before. And (I might add) to chat up the locals and be let in on that hidden gem of a restaurant known for its tacos or green chilli. As long as we include some hiking, swimming, tennis, and pizza along the way, the kids are on board. And because these trips are significantly more challenging than a beach vacation in Cuba, they are more memorable and create greater bonds that we hope will last a lifetime.

70.

Mama Bear

As soon as we return from Vegas, the first person to contact us is our golfing friend Tom who wants to know if we're coming camping with him. Tom has been inviting us to join him for years, but we've never made it. I am overwhelmed at the week's agenda, the least of which has Satchel having four wisdom teeth removed, followed by a doctor's appointment for me, followed by ... oh yeah, we're moving.

But (surely) we can fit in a short camping trip! And if we don't go camping with Tom, the kids may never go camping, at least not with me. I don't camp well. I don't think I would even glamp well. The closest we've come is the blanket fort we made in our living room when the kids were really young—proof that we're familiar with the concept of roughing it. And who knows how many more invitations Tom has for us? If I dig deep, I may be thinking of ways to keep us busy and avoid thinking about the move looming so near in the future. So, while we're still in travel mode, we repack our backpacks, borrow some sleeping bags and head out again.

When I was a kid, we went camping every year but it was car camping, where we slept in tents but had an assigned site, a charcoal BBQ, a lake with a buoy line around the shallow area, and a building that housed toilets and showers. What sticks with me is that we kids had a ton of fun, but I rarely saw my parents stop working. Preparing and cooking food, along with cleaning up without a kitchen took up a large part of the day. It didn't seem like much of a holiday for them, even though my brother and sisters and I had a blast swimming, skateboarding, and hanging out at the tuck shop. The Trump Tower Diva in me was emerging at the thought of wilderness camping, but this would be a great opportunity for the kids, and Tom is the ultimate host, even if this party would take place in Mother Nature's living room.

With puffy cheeks, the remainder of his antibiotics, and four fewer teeth, Satchel jumps in the car with the rest of us for our big camping adventure. And by the rest of us, I mean Cole, Tanner, and me. The only person less fond of camping than I am is Peter; he conveniently remains, promising to pack up the rest of the house while we're gone.

Three and a half hours in the car lands us at a boat dock where Tom picks us up and takes us to his family's island on Lake Rosseau in Muskoka. We meet our fellow campers, Tom's friend, Collin, and his 8-year-old son, Ben, who are also experienced campers.

The twelve-foot, dining-room table in the cottage is filled with food for the trip, a first-aid pack, and cooking gear along with all the incredible tools and gadgets for camping. This is the thing about camping: Whether it's one night or one month, the amount of equipment is almost the same and the preparations are formidable. Looking at all that gear, it's hard to fathom that Tom, Collin, and Ben will be out for five days while my boys and I will pack as much fun as we can into one night at

Tom's and one night camping, which is all we can fit in between Satchel's dental surgery and my appointment.

After a swim in the lake and a hearty dinner, we gather around for The Talk. Tom teaches us how to be safe out there in the great outdoors which includes a mini-course called, What To Do If We Encounter a Bear, 101. My littlest adventurers freeze at the mention of bears. They give me a look which says, "We did not sign up for bears." Tom assures us that the most likely place we would see a bear would be on the drive inside the provincial park and that it would probably only be a black bear. But we are urbanites and have no bear prejudices. Black, brown, polar, grizzly ... we are equally terrified of them all.

Understandably, the topic comes up again at bedtime. "We don't want to meet any bears," they say. "We want to go home." It's hard to convince them that we won't see any bears when we were just told what to do if we see a bear, which means there are definitely bears out there.

The next day finds us back in the car for the two-and-a-half-hour drive farther north to the launch site. In two vehicles, under grey skies, we wind our way through beautiful northern Ontario until there are no stores or restaurants, only signs for camping, hiking, and boating. Finally, we turn into the entrance for Killarney Provincial Park, known for its azure lakes and undisturbed, natural setting. Not five minutes later, right in front of us, crossing the road like he owns it, is a black bear. I react quickly. "Isn't it a good thing we got that bear sighting out of the way? Now we can relax about that whole bear thing, right kids?"

They remain unamused.

After picking up our two rented canoes, we load them up with hundreds (I'm not kidding, hundreds!) of pounds of gear. The food pack alone weighs in at around 150 pounds, plus the tents and camping gear. Add seven human beings and you can imagine that our canoes are quite low in the water. Using my rudimentary calculations, our two vessels are hauling well over a thousand pounds of camp-bound stuff— some of it reluctant.

Now, loading a thousand pounds into two canoes takes both strength and an ability to organize those pounds equally between both canoes, while also taking into consideration our individual weights (including optimistic, ballpark assessments by some of us), as well as noting our paddling skills. Once Tom is satisfied with his equation with Satchel, Cole, and Tom in one canoe, and Collin, Tanner, Ben, and me in another, we push off into the lake and begin our paddle to what I thought would be our campsite. This is my first misconception. We actually paddle to our first portage, then carry all that stuff (including the canoes this time) over multiple trips through the forest, only to load it all up again and paddle to our second portage, so that we can reach our third lake and seek out a settlement.

After two hours of paddling and two portages, Tom chooses our site and the tents go up. The lake is beautiful, and the large rocks surrounding it are smooth and heated up by the hot weather, ready for sun-seeking salamanders like myself to collapse onto them and relax. This vision of sanctuary is interrupted by camp-director Tom who announces, "Looks great everyone! Still enough daylight to go for a hike!"

My warm-rock fantasy melts away, but with such a short stay, I am game for everything about this trip. So, for a little adventure and to expose the kids to as much wilderness as possible, we jump back into our canoes and paddle to the trailhead.

The hike turns out to be steeper than I anticipate and takes us up to the highest peak in the park from which we can see for many miles. It is a breathtaking sight to take in, particularly for those of us who can still breathe comfortably after the somewhat challenging climb to the final summit. I toy with playing my Princess Card halfway up but being part of this boys' club means holding my own or hearing about it for eternity. No divas on this trip.

By the time we land back at our campsite, it is almost dark with only time enough for a quick swim to wash off the sweat and bug spray before starting dinner. The two men work efficiently in the dark, starting a fire and cooking up vegetarian burritos while delegating smaller jobs to the rest of us. With dinner comes the uninvited mosquitos, who sense a feast of their own and drive us quickly into our tents for the night.

Satchel, exhausted from the day's events and still a little weak from his surgery, falls asleep immediately. Tanner and Cole, however, have a different idea. They are sitting up, hugging their knees tightly, rocking back and forth, and waiting for the bear to attack. I pull them close, one under each arm, and lie with them until they fall asleep, at which point I spend the next few hours preparing a plan for what to do when the bear attacks. Then I watch the shadows of daddy long legs crawling across the tent, hoping they won't appear in my recurring spider dreams. I hear the raccoons rummaging through the pots and pans hanging on the trees, looking for scraps. As a grand finale, the monsoon hits. And it rains and rains and rains like God is pouring a heaven-sized bucket of water directly onto our tent. Everyone's sleep is restless, and each time any child moves in the tent I bolt up, making sure they are all okay and discovering that each fresh look around shows our four bodies in the form of a different letter of the alphabet.

In the morning, because we had retreated so quickly into our tents the night before, we hadn't prepared for rain and so everything is drenched. It takes a while to set up a tarp and make breakfast, even as the deluge continues. Unfortunately, a full day enjoying our surroundings is looking more like a hostage situation as we wait for a reprieve in the weather to make our escape. Tom, Collin, and Ben also watch the skies wondering if the forecast, which calls for rain for the next four days, will be accurate. We keep ourselves busy at camp, packing up our tent and sleeping bags, cleaning up after breakfast, and wondering if we will ever get back out on the water.

By late morning, I don't see Tanner lurking about and go for a scout around our campsite. I find him standing in front of the "treasure chest" (a wooden box, covered by a lid, which is our designated lavatory). We consider his dilemma in silence. Using a long stick, I lean in and hoist up the lid. There is a hole cut out of the top, out of which we see spiders crawling, while a cyclone of flies spins in and out. The grisly content of the box has grown dangerously close to the opening, indicating that the relocation of the box is long past due. We both throw up a little in our mouths.

"This is it, buddy. Shall I wait for you over there?" I say encouragingly.

He continues to stare for a moment, picturing the event in his mind, then retreats. "It's okay. I can wait." Which he does for the next eight hours. We can never un-see this image, and I feel a loss of innocence for both of us. I put "plumbing" on my list of things to hug when we get back to civilization.

Around midday, the rain stops briefly, and the Bedards, their gear, and accumulated garbage are loaded into one canoe, while the others chaperone us in the other towards what I thought would be our original boat launch. This is where another of my misconceptions occurs. Tom, Collin, and Ben help us get over the first portage and wish us luck on the rest of the journey home.

Excuse me? Are we heading back the rest of the way without our seasoned guides? As we float away in our canoe, clearly confused at our predicament, the boys and I watch our "friends" wave goodbye from the portage point, then disappear into the forest back to their own canoe. I had not anticipated that we would be on our own so far away from civilization, out in a canoe, loaded up with stuff, in wind, rain, and choppy water, with no cell service. As we paddle through whitecaps, upwind the whole way, I make everyone check his life jacket and constantly examine our surroundings, always aware of where the closest swim to shore will be in case we dump. Several times we are blown off course and have to paddle hard to return to our assumed route and during the whole trip, we don't see one other traveller. No one else is crazy enough to venture out in this weather. It is eerie and every awful, tragic, Titanic thought crosses my mind as I downplay my concerns to the kids—even though a capsizing feels way more real than a bear attack ever had.

We make our way through another portage and an hour later, with tired and sore muscles, we touch land, stow the boat, deposit the garbage, transfer the extra bags to Tom's car, and climb aboard our mini-van for the last leg of our journey: a five-hour-drive home. While the kids quickly fall asleep, I focus on the changing landscape as rocks, trees, and open highway slowly give way to speeding cars, roadside burger joints, and the eventual inevitability of bumper-to-bumper traffic.

Tom is a true adventure-seeker, and I can always count on him to challenge us and take us out of our comfort zone, and this micro-trip was no exception. I also know Tom would never ask anyone to do anything he thought was beyond his or her capacity. He calls them "calculated risks." But it's one thing to test yourself and quite another to watch your kids struggle, as much as we know it's good for them. We feel it's our job to keep their bicycle tires pumped and to smooth out the bumps and fill in the potholes on the trail before they arrive. But if they never feel discomfort or pressure or fatigue, how else will they get to show you how brave they can be? How smart and independent?

This particular trip was too short to accurately access our resilience and resourcefulness because sometimes with great challenge also comes great disappointment, which is a different kind of challenge altogether. But we survived and proved to our city-slicker selves that we are adaptable ... for a twenty-four-hour shift anyway.

Next time we're invited camping, my kids are on their own ... okay, probably on their own ... I guess it depends on the forecast ... and the bear situation ... and the number and length of portages ... and the lavatory ... and whether or not I can play my Princess Card without consequence. Otherwise, camping: check.

71.

Like Ninjas in the Night

When we arrive home from "The Forty-Eight-Hour Camping Super Adventure," Peter, true to his word, has packed up the house and has already brought several loads to our new house.

A few days later, we put Satchel on a plane (for his birthday) to spend a week with our good friends, Derek and Jody, in the mountains of British Columbia. They have generously offered to introduce him to pole-vaulting (our friend Derek is a track-and-field coach) and to live the life of a mountain man. To Satchel's great disappointment, his trip to Thailand has been cancelled because a military coup has occurred in Thailand, and despite Heather's assurances that "everything is fine; these things happen all the time over here," the perception from the Western world is that a military coup is not something to be taken lightly. We definitely weren't ready to send Satchel into an area of political unrest for his first solo journey. Everything happens for a reason, and someday we will find out why this will have turned out for the best, but for now, Kamloops is the new Pattaya.

While Satchel is away, the moving truck arrives and ships our lives out of the city. Most of our friends are still away on vacation or at cottages, so we slip away like ninjas in the night.

Over the next two weeks, we unpack, arrange furniture, and explore all the nooks and crannies of our new home. I sit looking out at our new backyard, at the pool, the soccer net, the tennis backboard, the trampoline, and the large deck—all for much less than the price of our little, crooked house in the big city. We have several rooms without furnishings because we don't have nearly enough furniture to fill them. We do have a ballroom—a room dedicated to housing all the balls we own, with a bare wall for them to be smashed against.

We've also already had four small pool parties with city friends and family, and we are so happy to have the space to host them all. The master bathroom is larger than our last master bedroom and each boy has his own room instead of Tanner and Cole sharing as they have always done. They are delighted not to have to make an appointment to use the one bathroom we had as they can now choose from four. I am giddy with our good fortune at finding this place and have a tough time believing it is ours. It feels like we are merely house sitting.

While purchasing this palace on one salary does not relieve us from some financial strain, we are optimistic that the savings of day-to-day living out here will help ease it. We have discovered that tennis and soccer programs for the kids are much more affordable here, even while the facilities are superior. There are fruit and vegetable stands along the side of the road, selling fresh produce at prices far cheaper than any grocery store in the city. There are only a few restaurants from which to choose, so we won't go out much. My sister even has an esthetician who charges $15 for an hour-long pedicure. With these initial cost-cutting findings, we are hopeful that we will see some savings along the way.

We have also decided that having me take one more year off to help us all through the transition is a good idea. We need to orient ourselves to our new surroundings and establish a network of sorts before we can feel comfortably integrated into our community. After that, the kids will be that much older, and perhaps then I will reinvest in my teaching career. For now, we will enjoy the last week of summer, learning about what to do when our pool turns murky green and making serendipitous discoveries in our community, like the beautiful bike path that runs parallel to the Welland Canal, starting in Lake Ontario and ending in Lake Erie, or the stand-up paddle boarding in the canal itself.

Two days before school begins, we have to make an afternoon trek back to Toronto for the last soccer game of the season. I steer around our old hood, surprised by how much I don't really miss it. I think about our new town, and the overwhelming feeling is that I really enjoy not having to fight for everything: a parking spot, a lane change, space to walk on the sidewalk. We step over dogs and keep our elbows out to hold our space in line at the ice cream shop. I ask Tanner how it makes him feel to be back in the city. "A little afraid," he says. "So many cars."

72.
Back to School

Three-hundred-and-sixty-five days ago I sat at Starbucks for the first day of "my year off". Today, I should be in my classroom, waiting for hungry learners, catching up with my co-workers, knowing a paycheck is waiting at the end of the month, comfortable and content with the familiar chaos. Yet, here I am, sitting in a quaint café, in a small town, surrounded by strangers. I have been here a few times already and met the owner, Patti, who is warm and welcoming and already knows my name and drink order. There is French bistro music playing, and I could be in Paris, France and not small-town Ontario for all I am aware. The nearest Starbucks is a distant thirteen-kilometres away. I feel a mix of wistfulness and excitement. I am trying to distract myself from these swirling thoughts by working on my writing and appreciating the time I have been gifted to work on it again, but my mind keeps jolting me back to the events of earlier that morning.

A few hours ago I dropped the kids off at their new school. Satchel walked confidently into his new high school, excited and ready to begin a new chapter in his life. Cole had already voiced every concern he could think of, from believing he might be the slowest, the shortest, and the least intelligent, to likely having the meanest teacher and so on. Tanner remained stoically quiet, absorbing all his anxieties internally as he is apt to do.

In the schoolyard they both searched for a friendly face. "Do you think one of our friends has also secretly moved to this area and is waiting to surprise us?" asked Cole hopefully.

A few minutes later they were alone, standing quietly in their class lines, trying to be brave and not look as lost and scared as they felt. I had hoped that there wouldn't be tears, but they came anyway. Oh, the sobbing, the inconsolable tears. Had the boys seen me, they might have started crying too, but I ducked away, head down, into the empty back of the yard in search of an alternate exit. Even when my boys first entered kindergarten they already had friends from the neighbourhood, from mom's groups and meetings in the park. Kindergarten was new for everyone, so it wasn't nearly this nerve-wracking. This year, Tanner would have been one of the big men on campus in the oldest grade at his former school as it only goes up to grade six. His new school finishes at grade eight, so he has to wait two more years to be a part of that illustrious group. He stood in his line focusing on the door, ignoring the chaos around him. Cole stood with his peers in the grade four line, faking confidence and giving off almost an air of defiance in case anyone dared to pick on the new kid.

Am I a terrible mom for doing this to them? For taking them away from their friends and teachers whom they adore? It would be so easy to surrender to this guilt. After all, if we were in Toronto this day would be an easy, happy day—aside from the fact that summer vacation was over. There would be hugging and laughing and a lively game of tag or one-touch would break out. No transition, no fear, no vulnerability but a sense of control over their world. I've heard that a mom is only as happy as her most unhappy child. My tears return.

Throughout the day I write, I wander around the house by myself, and I masochistically drive by the school a few times, knowing that the boys will not be joyously running in a pack as they would have back in the city. At least they have each other.

At the end of school, Peter has returned from a meeting in Toronto and joins me in the playground to await the news of the day. As anxious as I am at these times, Peter is usually worse. He prefers that I man the front line, then he jumps in with backup or clean up as the case may be.

Reviews are reserved. Cole talks about socializing with some kids in his class, but Tanner remains quiet. Satchel is less enamoured with his first day, and his excitement has subsided significantly. He was ignored the entire day. Satchel is so confident that we totally forgot about the social challenges that high school brings. Would he end up being that guy in those after-school specials who doesn't quite fit in with the different cliques of kids? Is he the Karate Kid? Where do we find our own Mr. Miyagi?

In the evening, I lay with Tanner in his bed for an hour, absorbing his tears on my shirt and feeling my own guilt return. "Be patient with them," I say. "They need time to discover what a great guy you are." He eventually falls asleep, exhausted from the stress of the day. Meanwhile I lay awake, second-guessing every decision we've made in the last few months.

Nostrils up, Bedard. Nostrils up.

73.

I'm Just Waiting for a Friend

One week later, Satchel tells me he has been sitting with the guys at school and that some of the girls have asked him if he would like a tour of the town.

"That's so great, but ... what do you think a 'tour of the town' means in Small-Townian language?" I ask suspiciously.

"Mom. Really?"

"Never mind. Way to go. I'm so happy for you."

Cole and Tanner have joined the cross-country team and have both been chosen for the school soccer team. They meet up with friends in the yard when we arrive in the morning, and they seem more relaxed and happy. We have leaped the first hurdle. I stand watching them for a few minutes, relieved at their successful transition so far. Then I look around at the yard emptying out and think, They're okay. Now, what about me? And my eyes well up again. I have no friends. My phone doesn't ring. There are no texts or emails. The kids have an immediate peer group in their classmates, and Peter has his work relationships and tacks on visits with his friends on his occasional business trips to Toronto. I think about my friends in the Beaches, chatting it up, preparing for a jog on the boardwalk together,

299

making plans for after school, and sharing summer holiday news. I promised I would not feel sorry for myself because I chose this. But I still do.

I think about the M.E. adventures and how much fun we all had, and I wonder if another group, here in Fonthill, is in my future. I look at the many moms in the schoolyard, some hurrying off to work, others trailing smaller kids and meandering back to their cars, and some watching and waving at their kids in their class lines at the school entrance just like me. Will I be able to forge friendships with any of them?

Then, as I'm leaving the yard, I spot a mom standing alone. Ah-ha! Someone has strayed from the pack, and my opportunity for a surprise attack is nigh. I straighten myself up, wipe away the tears, and approach, stealthily slinking through the tall grass so as not to alert her of my presence. As I get nearer, I notice that she has an urban-esque look to her: subtle make-up, hip clothing, nice highlights ... the perfect prey. I close in and pounce.

"Hi, you dropping off a few?"

"No, just one. You?"

"Two today. We're new to the school so just figuring this all out."

"Oh, we're new as well, and I don't know any moms at the school. Perhaps we should exchange emails and get together for a coffee. I'm Michelle."

"Sure, that sounds great," I say, casually, holding back my desperate elation and stopping myself from physically grabbing her in case she is a figment of my imagination, a blonde oasis in my vast, friendless desert. But wait a minute... that was a little too easy. Maybe she's a serial killer? Maybe she's a porn star dressed down like an everyday mom on a Tuesday morning? Maybe she's an Avon Lady? Maybe I should avoid her? Then again, I've never been friends with a porn star, and it might be super interesting, so I will continue to subtly seduce her into my empty friendship web and regale her with star-studded accounts of life in the Big City. No, be humble. Don't condescend or intimidate. That's what people expect from city-dwellers. Nobody who lives outside the city cares about what's going on in the city. And I have discovered that many people have moved here from towns even smaller than this and to them, this is the city. So, low-key is the plan. Let her take the lead. If we get together for coffee or tea, wear something stylish but not ostentatious. Minimal bling. Look put together but not like you're trying too hard. Keep the conversation light and local. And last of all, don't over-think this and ruin it all!

74.

Bloody Hell!

While I'm waiting to connect with Michelle for the first time, the bright side of not having lots of friends around here is that I have time to work out again. I am losing my vacation weight, and I have time to write. The other day I put my headphones on and bounced myself silly on our trampoline for half an hour until my legs were rubbery. Now that's a good workout. I don't have a fancy gym membership because there are no fancy gyms close by with no fancy fees to pay, but I goof around in the basement and piece together years of accumulated gym and yoga activities while watching recorded romantic comedies so that I can get my estrogen fix at the same time. Sounds kind of pathetic, but it does meet two of my needs simultaneously.

Feeling a little lonely on the drive back from Satchel's school one morning, I see something that piques my interest. It is a sign. Literally, it is a sign, outside of the community centre, which reads, Give Blood, along with dates for donating. I think of the M.E. group and of the near miss at creating a blood-donor event, which fell through because Samantha was afraid that the personal questions might make some people uncomfortable. At

302

the time I didn't understand her trepidation, but I would soon discover what she meant. In honour of the M.E. group, I make a pact with myself that I will come back the following day and open up my veins in the name of charity.

I try, unsuccessfully, to appear nonchalant about the whole thing when I tell my family about the bloodletting, but Cole senses my worry. "Don't worry, Mom. It will be okay. They give you a juice box at the end." As if that will quell any of my obvious angst.

I show up the next day at the community centre, palms sweaty, and make my way inside where I am directed to a seat and wait to be ushered through a series of stations on my way to giving up precious platelets for the greater good. There are around twenty donors at that particular time in various stages of giving, all of them looking quite at ease. I stand out like a sore thumb.

The first station is easy: I.D. check and sign in. I am not shy about letting people know I am a first-time donor. Losing impulse control is what sometimes happens to me when I'm nervous, and I often say the first thing that comes into my head. So, if nervous, meaningless chatter doesn't alert my blood brothers and sisters of my inexperience, the shiny sticker on my shirt, which reads First Time Donor, is a giveaway.

The second station is where my anxiety level increases significantly: a finger prick (ouch!) to draw enough blood to test my iron level. I find myself thinking, Please have low iron. Please have low iron. Alas, my iron level is fine, and I move into the next chair.

In a civilized fashion, each time we change to a different station we move along the chair line, and when the music stops we all sit down. Throughout this process I can see donors sitting back in recliners, hooked up to blood bags, positioned in a circle in the center of the room. I am getting closer and closer to that circle and my apprehension increases. Next, however, is the blood-pressure and personal-question station. As the nurse fastens the band around my arm, I find myself thinking, Please have low blood pressure. Please have low pressure.

I know already that I have low blood pressure, but is it low enough?

The nurse checks her instruments and says, "You have low blood pressure."

"Yes!"

"But within a normal range."

"Awww!"

This nurse then proceeds to ask me a series of questions, the likes of which make me blush. I quickly understand Samantha's concern about making this a group event. For instance, "In the last twelve months have you given money or drugs to anyone in exchange for sex?" Or "In the past twelve months have you had sex with a male who has had sex, even once since 1977, with another male?"

That's pretty specific, intimate knowledge. I was eleven in 1977. WTF? Apparently, my lifestyle choices gave me a passing grade, and I move into the final chair line—the one that directly precedes the recliners.

Just before my turn, a woman standing next to me, who had just finished donating, starts squirting blood from her arm. I sharply elbow the woman on my other side, "Look! Look!" I stammer.

The drops on the floor turn into a puddle as a nurse hurries to find a sterile pad to cover the steady stream. I feel a little queasy from the drama and from the smell of bleach used to clean up the floor. The woman sitting next to me says, "Wow, I've never seen that happen before."

Of course not.

Finally, I am in my own uneasy chair. A nurse is checking the veins in my arm when a woman across from me gets up from her chair, having finished the process. All of a sudden, blood starts squirting from her arm and all over the floor. "She's bleeding!" I exclaim, trying to avert my eyes.

Out come the nurse, the pad, and the bleach.

A man beside me tries to reassure me by saying, "This is my forty-sixth time donating, and I've never seen that happen before."

Of course not.

"This is the time when you might want to look away if you're so inclined," says my nurse, as she is about to insert the needle into my arm. I am absolutely so inclined. While the needle does its thing, I chat, unfiltered, with the nurse, asking her all kinds of questions.

"How many people are you expecting to see here today, and how does that compare to other locations?" Because I like to be on a winning team.

"We'll see about a hundred and twenty here today, judging from past attendance. Probably the best turn-out is in Elmira. It's a small town, but the Amish population come out in droves," she replies.

I picture a parade of horses and buggies parked outside of the town hall and the families who exit them in their dark clothes and hats. This compels me to ask, "How old do you have to be to donate?"

"Seventeen."

"You gotta think that those 17-year-old Amish kids must be pretty embarrassed answering those personal questions. That must be the closest they've ever gotten to porn," I say. Out loud. Unfortunately. This time it is the nurse's turn to blush.

Things go swimmingly for the next few minutes until a woman in our circle gets up from her chair, and, you guessed it, starts bleeding out of her arm. "Another bleeder!" I declare, as if making this announcement has become my designated role on behalf of the group. My blood sisters and brothers look briefly at the woman in distress and then back at me, concerned, as the blood drains from my face, and they expect me to finally bolt or pass out.

"Wow," says my nurse. "I've never seen that happen twice in one day."

"Three times. In twenty minutes," I correct.

Of course.

"It usually happens to men," she continues. "They don't think it's necessary to put three-fingered pressure on the opening after they're finished."

Eventually my tube is removed, and you can bet I put three-fingered pressure on my arm until my three fingers turn blue. Then I belly up to the bar with my fellow donors, all of whom are repeat customers. "You did great. See you in fifty-six days?" says one fellow.

Fifty-six days seems a little near, and I am feeling weak, not from my blood loss but from thinking about all that unexpected hemorrhaging going on around me. Not surprisingly, I've never sat through a horror film in my entire life.

But sitting there with all of those benevolent folks, post bleed, also gives me a feeling of satisfaction, and I begin to see this whole experience as an encapsulation of the M.E. vision: It's local, it's something I'd never done before, it's charitable, and it didn't cost me a thing. Looking at the bandage on my arm, I feel invigorated and hopeful of things to come. Out here I have a whole new pallet of adventures to embrace. And using this experience as a metaphor for accepting change, I know that I will recover and that I will do this again.

Cole, who relishes being right, nailed it. It was okay, and I got a juice box at the end.

75.

We Are All Works in Progress

It is not lost on me that one of my goals for the year was to reconnect with my community. So how did I end up here, far away from the people and the place that I once held so dear? I still appreciate all that the city has to offer. It's a vibrant, eclectic, mecca of culture which I will enjoy visiting. But given the time to explore and examine our lives within it, I realized that the city has outgrown us in some ways, and that we have outgrown the city in others. I, in particular, don't need it the way I used to think I did. Sometimes I am completely overwhelmed with assimilating into small town living and other times I am completely underwhelmed, and I search for potential around every corner. I've already found it at the quaint café around the corner, which makes a decent version of a non-fat, no-foam, Earl Grey tea latte. There is a good pizza joint and even a new yoga shop in town that offers Athletic Yoga. And I look forward to getting to know my new friend Michelle better. She is as sweet as she is warm and welcoming and actually works with her husband in their insurance-adjuster business.

Have I met some of my other goals? Have I reacquainted myself with me? Have I found myself? My friend Glenn says that perhaps you can't ever really misplace yourself because you are constantly evolving, so you will never find the person you once were. Spending a year observing and reflecting has shown me that that's likely true and that we are all works in progress. I am secure with my current purpose in life, and I know that my family appreciates the work that I do to manage Bedard Inc. Their success is my success.

And the concurrent path of writing all of this down over the year has proven to be therapeutic and given me a healthier perspective on life and family. Seeing my sister frequently has been a bonus to this move as we live closer and get together often. Come Thanksgiving, we'll be hosting a family get-together for twenty-seven, but we'll have the space to spread out, instead of crowding into one room and having everyone shift positions, like a sliding puzzle, each time someone needs to use the washroom.

And lastly ... am I a writer now? Well, I write things (actually quite a lot of things this year), and thankfully, without one obituary in the mix. And while I still forget my words constantly, having the benefit of time to write down what I want to say, and revise it seven times before anyone else has access to it, is comforting.

As I look at the piles of writing I've completed so far, Mr. Self-doubt creeps in and hovers close. "You're kidding," he says. "Is this really what you've been spending your time on all year?" Yikes! Okay. Breathe. What's the worst that could happen? I could fail miserably, and these pages could offend, bore, or nauseate the folks (if any) who might read them. In which case, my husband and I are modelling to our kids that sometimes you have to take a risk, put yourself out there, be brave, and be ready to deal with (or ignore) any judgment that's passed unto you. At the very least, I have a journal to look back on from the year of living thoughtfully, engaged in the lives of my family. And ultimately, anyone who messes with my ego too much will have to deal with Cole, who will protectively puff out his boney chest and challenge them with his most intimidating, "What the beep!"

The End.
And the Beginning.

Acknowledgements

I am so thankful to my friends, old and new, who took me in and who so readily shared their enthusiasm for, and frustrations about, their choice to dedicate themselves fully to their families. Over the summer some of them have gone back to work part-time and some are now full-time and have called in a nanny or daycare for support. Others are questioning their role as a SAHM as their children grow older and are more self-sufficient, and some others are committed to hanging in there for the long term, to stay available until the chicks have flown the nest.

Ironically, I know that their instinctive nurturing and supportive natures helped me to grow and gave me the confidence and courage to leave them, not unlike the way they are preparing their children for adulthood. As a parent, the measure that you've done your job well is that your children are happy, healthy, and gone. By those standards, my friends have raised me well. Now, as a representative of small-town living, it is my responsibility to lure them out here because they are what I miss most in my new life.

I am also thankful to my former employer for helping me to tip the first domino in the line of decisions. I miss my students and my peers at school, but I will stay in touch and keep connected to education through volunteering and tutoring until I return to teaching in some form in the future.

A big shout out to Rachelle and Carol at Beyond the Book, who put this manuscript onto their chopping block and saved readers the torture of interpreting thousands of unnecessary words. Cheers, also, to Friesenpress for helping to shape this into the finished product.

I am always and forever thankful to my children for forgetting that anything they say can and will be held against them in anything I write. They are my muses for most everything I do, way beyond the writing of this book, and they show me daily what it means to love, laugh, cry, hope, think, and feel. I am so insanely in love with them and so proud that they chose me to be their mother (because the wands choose the wizard).

Most of all, I am thankful to my husband for green-lighting this experiment from the beginning (although he doesn't remember agreeing to any of it) and for helping to edit this book and remove all of my Mrs. Malapropisms. Having me stay home means he is working a little harder at his job, but because I am home, he has the flexibility now to make it less daunting than it could have been.

I am amazed at Peter's patience and understanding every time I have a "great idea", once even adding, "If you weren't so insane, you'd be out of my league." He is a family man through and through, who would do anything to keep his flock safe and happy. He is an inspiration and a role model for all of us, providing a calm during our stormy days and showing a self-lessness that allows us, even pushes us, to feel empowered and to live out our dreams. He is happiest when we are happy (and when the Blue Jays make the playoffs). I couldn't ask for a better husband/father to our children/friend. So, while a great deal of this book is about family, it is also very much a love story (without any gratuitous sex scenes—sorry, this still isn't that kind of book). Thanks, Pete, you will always be my leading man.

About the Author

Jane Bedard is a freelance writer whose humorous and moving articles on parenting and family have appeared in The Globe and Mail, Canadian Living, Reader's Digest, Mamalode.com, and Parent.Co. She is a regular contributor to The Voice of Pelham newspaper and continues to take steps to hone her craft. Jane earned a B.A. in English and enjoyed careers as a copywriter, then as an English and French teacher, despite feeling less mature than her students.

Residing outside Toronto, Canada in the thick of the testosterone of three sons, a husband, and two male cats, Jane dodges balls (tennis, soccer, golf, basket, fur) and seeks the funny in every situation, no matter how challenging. When she's not writing or driving her kids to sporting events, she is also not cleaning her house; however, she is always on the lookout for new friends and adventures.

Printed in Canada